ACTIVISTS IN CITY HALL

ACTIVISTS IN CITY HALL

THE PROGRESSIVE RESPONSE TO THE REAGAN ERA IN BOSTON AND CHICAGO

PIERRE CLAVEL

CORNELL UNIVERSITY PRESS
Ithaca and London

Publication of this book was made possible, in part, by a grant from the Clarence S. Stein Institute for Urban and Landscape Studies, Cornell University. The publisher also gratefully acknowledges the support of the institute's director, Michael A. Tomlan.

First published 2010 by Cornell University Press

First printing, Cornell Paperbacks, 2010

Printed in the United States of America

Library of Congress Cataloging-in-Publication Data

Clavel, Pierre.
    Activists in City Hall : the progressive response to the Reagan era in Boston and Chicago / Pierre Clavel.
        p. cm.
    Includes bibliographical references and index.
    ISBN 978-0-8014-4929-1 (cloth : alk. paper) —
    ISBN 978-0-8014-7655-6 (pbk. : alk. paper)
    1. Boston (Mass.)—Politics and government.
    2. Chicago (Ill.)—Politics and government.
    3. Community activists—Massachusetts—
    Boston.   4. Community activists—Illinois—
    Chicago.   5. Urban policy—Massachusetts—
    Boston.   6. Urban policy—Illinois—Chicago.
    7. Flynn, Raymond L.   8. Washington, Harold, 1922–
    1987.   9. Progressivism (United States politics)   I. Title.
    JS614.A1C53   2010
    320.9744'6109048—dc22   2010017637

Cornell University Press strives to use environmentally responsible suppliers and materials to the fullest extent possible in the publishing of its books. Such materials include vegetable-based, low-VOC inks and acid-free papers that are recycled, totally chlorine-free, or partly composed of nonwood fibers. For further information, visit our website at www.cornellpress.cornell.edu.

Cloth printing   10 9 8 7 6 5 4 3 2 1
Paperback printing 10 9 8 7 6 5 4 3 2 1

For Caroline, Pierre, and Tom

❧ Contents

❧ PREFACE

Neighborhood activists went into city halls in Boston and Chicago in the 1980s and, in doing so, changed the way these cities were governed. They did not do this by themselves, nor in one stroke. They allied with mayors and adapted to continuing neighborhood pressure. They learned from significant government initiatives that had focused on urban issues since the 1960s. And they drew upon a social movement background that had been building since the 1950s, long before Chicago elected Harold Washington its first black mayor in April 1983 and Boston elected the populist Raymond Flynn the following November.

The 1960s had been a decade of raised hopes and disappointment. President John F. Kennedy had issued a call to service on behalf of the federal government and inspired the nation until his assassination in 1963. Civil rights activists marched in the South, attracted white volunteers, and were beaten and murdered. They inspired younger blacks, who mobilized one thousand white volunteers in Mississippi in 1964 who were themselves sometimes beaten and murdered. At the end of that summer, civil rights activists found themselves rebuffed at the Democratic National Convention. The white volunteers went back to their campuses and energized a student movement that protested college policies and subsequently the Vietnam War, a movement that later shifted its focus to other objectives—women's and environmental movements, among others.

The Great Society programs initiated by Lyndon Johnson after Kennedy's assassination raised the hopes and energies of many citizens and government workers at all levels. New programs reached out to citizen and neighborhood groups with provisions like "maximum feasible participation." Some, like the early childhood–education program Head Start, were generally successful and popular, but others, including programs that provided urban-renewal subsidies to private developers, were destructive of neighborhood fabric and proved to be the focus of a new social movement rooted in the neighborhoods.

Through all these ups and downs—and despite their differences—there was a growing number of people whose aim was largely the same: they sought a more "just and equal" society. There were thousands of such persons. Some were government officials and bureaucrats; many were neighborhood activists—some with connections to the civil rights movement itself; still others were students or faculty in local colleges and universities. Over the period of a decade or more, they were building skills and capacities.

Eventually, whether seeking a transition from a movement lifestyle or for other reasons, many of them created or connected with institutions they thought could change the society over the long run. Many groups used government, church, or foundation support to start housing, health, education, and other programs in their neighborhoods. Many of these initiatives survived and took root in the neighborhoods or other venues, like regional nonprofits or special-purpose city or state agencies.

In some cities, beginning about 1970, such groups gained a place on city councils. There were a few cases in which activists achieved majority control and mayoralties, and dozens more where at least some city council representation and associated administrative change occurred.

This book tells the story of those who won city hall. Its focus is on mayors Ray Flynn in Boston and Harold Washington in Chicago in the 1980s, and the community activists who played major roles in their administrations. This segment of U.S. urban and political history is significant at more than one level. In Boston and Chicago in the 1980s, it was significant for advocates of community development even to win—even on the surface they presented a great contrast to the normal city government controlled by business interests. Flynn and Washington nurtured such contrasts. Both had been outspoken advocates of the poor and of neighborhood interests; and in Washington's case, he was also Chicago's first black mayor.

The largely untold story is that these new mayors, once in office, brought significant representation of a community development constituency by appointing members of this constituency to positions as department heads and on staff as well as creating roles for hundreds of organizers, activists, and volunteers. The ranks of these activists had been growing for a decade or more and they had been meeting neighborhood needs while traditional forms of city-service delivery—political machines and city bureaucracies—were shriveling because of funding cuts and mass perceptions of their own inadequacies.

But also, the community activists comprised a new organizational force that engaged those already established in the campaigns and the permanent city bureaucracies. How the activists managed that—and that a productive interaction was even possible—is a big part of the story. They needed to engage. The community development groups' ideas could be implemented more effectively when backed by the legitimate authority of city government—a mayor and political leadership with the will to incorporate good ideas. My conclusion, developed in the chapters that follow, focuses on significant innovations, essentially administrative devices that give weight to the claim that a new form of city administration emerged in Boston and Chicago: "planned manufacturing districts" and other efforts at manufacturing retention in Chicago, and "linkage" in Boston, were the most prominent. But equally important were the many small changes that betokened a new political culture that lasted after Washington's death in 1987 and Flynn's departure in 1993.

This book is mainly about Boston and Chicago, but I also review earlier developments in smaller cities such as Hartford, Berkeley, Madison, Santa Cruz, Santa Monica, and Burlington, Vermont, and the contemporary but not quite comparable case of San Francisco. These complement and, I think, add weight to the Boston and Chicago stories. Burlington pioneered in municipal support for community land trusts, protecting the affordability of housing and contributing to that city's claim that 20 percent of its housing was publicly owned or regulated as "social housing." Santa Monica established rent control governed by an elected board, keeping significant dollars in the pockets of that city's largely renter population. San Francisco pioneered controls on downtown development, particularly through the passage of Proposition M establishing linkage fees in 1986. Notable in all of these cities was the social-movement force behind the more institutionalized politics and administration. Few or no other cities combined movement with administration with as much effect.

How I Came to Write This Book

These social movements were very strong, but I came to the subject of the progressive city through a somewhat different route. I was a city planner before I became an academic. In school for the Master of Regional Planning degree at the University of North Carolina, I had written a thesis that immersed me in the works of Patrick Geddes, a Scottish biologist and promoter of "civics" and town planning at the end of the nineteenth century. I was sold on Geddes' idea that the city was an organism that had to be nurtured by encouraging the cooperative enterprises of its people, and that planning was a way to do that, by creating institutions that would help people see the city as a whole.

City planning, as practiced at the time, seldom did this. Even then the field was dominated by architects and the occasional social-science trained person who saw planning as an opportunity to sell a vision of the city. Sometimes they thought of themselves as "teachers," but they were teaching a vision they themselves had created rather than one the city's people came to themselves. Later, as I worked as a professor in the field, even these visionary planners retreated to smaller and more-modest ideas: what they could get support for were "projects." Attempts to see the whole city were denigrated. Planners were cautioned, "The planner proposes, the politician disposes." Incrementalism was in vogue.

This was tiring. When at the end of the 1970s I began to hear of cities electing populist or "leftist" leadership, I thought a different approach to managing and planning cities might develop, and began to investigate. I had been in graduate school with Norman Krumholz, later planning director in Cleveland, Ohio. In 1975 Krumholz and his staff had produced the Cleveland Policy Plan, which advocated a redistributive vision for that city. In 1979 John Forester and I went to the last national meeting of the Conference on Alternative State and Local Policies in Pittsburgh. I met Florence MacDonald and Veronika Fukson of Berkeley Citizen Action. That inspired me to organize a conference panel discussion on "The Progressive City" the next year, featuring Berkeley's Eve Bach and Hartford city council leader Nicholas Carbone, that later turned into an article coauthored with them. In 1981 I began intensive research in Hartford, Berkeley, and Cleveland; Derek Shearer, a main organizer of the Conference on Alternative State and Local Policies, invited me to Santa Monica; and it was impossible to ignore Burlington, Vermont. I interviewed and tape-recorded dozens of people in each of these places. The result was *The Progressive City,* published in 1986.[1]

I knew that I had not told the whole story of the "progressive city," because important things—particularly about race—were happening in much larger cities. San Francisco was too far away at the time, but Boston and Chicago were within reach. Big cities would be more complex, and where I did not have personal connections, research would be logistically difficult. The combination of obstacles proved almost insurmountable. I did manage a year's sabbatical traveling back and forth to Chicago in 1988–89, and a semester in Boston in 1992.

Bob Giloth, who had once been a graduate student at Cornell, suggested Chicago, where Wim Wiewel was director of the Center for Urban Economic Development (CUED) at the University of Illinois–Chicago. Wiewel arranged office space, and that university provided me with a part-time teaching appointment in 1988–89. I spent a sabbatical year there working with Wiewel, doing interviews, collecting information, and editing *Harold Washington and the Neighborhoods,* for which we got ten community activists, academics, and city officials to write chapters describing their experiences working for Washington, who had died the year before. It was most rewarding to help others tell their stories, as opposed to being the main voice myself.[2]

There were two other significant outcomes of that year. One was the creation of the Harold Washington Neighborhood Papers collection at the Chicago Historical Society, with the help of a grant from the Chicago Community Trust engineered by Wiewel and executed by the society's enterprising archivist, the late Archie Motley. Motley made it his goal to create a record of the efforts of the activists who had worked in Washington's city hall. He understood how, once Washington's allies in the interim mayoralty of Eugene Sawyer left office, their memory would be at risk; he let them know that, when they were ready, he would have a truck at the city hall loading dock to accept boxes of files for posterity. Several administrators took advantage of the opportunity, and important records were preserved.

The other product of my collaboration with Wiewel was a small conference and video, directed by Denis Mueller and Elizabeth Montgomery of Community Television Network. The conference was in 1991, and the video was produced the following year. Both resulted from a grant by the Chicago Community Trust. Some of the main characters in the Chicago chapter appear in it. We made DVDs and distributed them to the participants we had addresses for.

In Boston, Rolf Engler helped with an office and visiting-scholar appointment at MIT for the spring semester of 1992. I got a great deal of help from Peter Dreier, then a key staff member in city hall, and from Marie Kennedy and Chris Tilly, scholars who often wrote critically of city hall.

These people and institutions—in both cities—helped me enormously. The stories themselves proved quite challenging. I think I was wise to focus on the planners and activists, since they relate to the background and profession I know personally. But the politics and history of Boston and Chicago are fraught with complexities that I do not pretend to have mastered, an order of magnitude much larger than the smaller cities I had studied earlier.

I often asked myself why it took another seventeen years after that semester in Boston to submit this manuscript for publication. The best reason is that Boston and Chicago were too complicated, and too hard to spend extensive time in, for me to write a responsible account at the time. I liked the stories my informants told, however, and finally decided they ought to see the light of day. I hope the reader will indulge the many gaps in this presentation.

Archives

By 2005 I had accumulated a number of documents and images from Boston and Chicago, as well as from other cities I and others had studied or worked in. Through the generosity of the Clarence Stein Institute at Cornell and with the enthusiastic cooperation of staff members in Cornell University Library's Division of Rare and Manuscript Collections, my colleague Kenneth Reardon and I were able to create a cooperative archiving effort called the "Progressive Cities and Neighborhood Planning Project" to generate and support collections in the cities described here. The project includes the production of theses, dissertations, and publications and has resulted in early steps toward the creation of local archive management committees in two cities in addition to contributions to the Cornell library collections. These activities are described on the project website, http://www.progressivecities.org. The collection, separately managed at Cornell University Library, is described and indexed, and accessible in the library's online catalogue as "The Guide to the Progressive Cities and Neighborhood Planning Collection, 1969–2005," http://rmc.library.cornell.edu/EAD/htmldocs/RMA03414.html.

The Plan of This Book

Chapter 1 presents a historical and conceptual introduction to the idea of the "progressive city," first as it appeared in Boston and Chicago, then as it emerged in the nation after about 1970, and then in the context of economic shifts and demographics for these cities and for U.S. cities generally.

To answer the question of what was "different" about progressive cites, chapter 2 presents a review of progressive governments initiated in the 1970s in Berkeley, Hartford, Cleveland, and Madison; and in the 1980s in San Francisco and smaller cities such as Burlington, Santa Monica, and Santa Cruz. I use this review in order to frame and lead up to the more-detailed studies of Boston in chapters 3 and 4, and Chicago in chapters 5, 6, and 7.

Boston and Chicago were different from these other cities in several ways. Progressive government came later in Boston and Chicago—in April 1983 and November 1983, respectively. But events in Boston and Chicago added important weight and detail. Like Cleveland and Hartford but unlike the rest, these were "heartland" cities: certainly Chicago, but even Boston was closer to the traditional center of the nation than the others. The comparisons are presented in detail in chapter 1, but in summary, Boston and Chicago were bigger and more complex. Race was a larger factor, as indicated by the smaller and decreasing percentages of whites, and especially of non-Hispanic whites, in the populations of the larger cities.

Each city dealt with the central racial cleavages in society, though they handled them differently. And more than any other places, they evolved alternative solutions not only to city problems but national problems as well. Chicago—almost alone—took at least a stab at an industrial policy as it attempted to reduce the exodus of manufacturing jobs. Boston largely left manufacturing to the private sector; but more than other places, Boston attempted to harness a real estate boom to service redistributive aims.

Examples from cities of Boston's and Chicago's stature are more plausible harbingers of change than those from the other places described in chapter 2. This is not so much that Flynn and Washington, and their administrators, had immediate impact on other mayors—though both were active in such forums as the U.S. Conference of Mayors. Longer term, more would be written because there is more history, more general interest. This happened for Chicago in the work of Joel Rast, whose remarkable account of that city's industrial policy rounds out and extends the story I lay out in this book. Peter Dreier does something similar in his accounts of Boston's housing policies and the establishment of linkage.[3]

Chapter 8 puts the events in these cities further in context, addressing issues not presented earlier. I do not aim at a theoretical effort, but rather to present the contrast between what the activists and political leaders in Boston and Chicago achieved and experienced and the intellectual and political context in which they operated. This may suggest changes in or modifications of that context—for example, the rather deep-seated presumptions that radical changes are possible only at the national level, or that political organization inherently tends toward top-down decisions and structural bias. That the progressive cities achieved a measure of difference from this presumed norm should add to our stock of ideas and their diversity.

Acknowledgments

My first debt is to Anne Solomon Clavel. She encouraged and gave critical review for this project from the time of its first presentation at a Planners Network conference in Washington, DC, in 1980. That was crucial. Along the way I had lots of other help, including from people I learned from or was inspired by. Laurence Wylie, my undergraduate adviser at Haverford College in the 1950s, urged me to talk to people in commonsense ways not burdened by interview schedules. Alan Altshuler gave similar advice at Cornell, and the late Barclay Jones, a different kind of scholar, was more of a mentor than he thought. Jack Parker, head of the Department of City and Regional Planning at the University of North Carolina, suggested the inspiring works of early planners Patrick Geddes and Lewis Mumford. I did a thesis on Geddes, and Andrew Scott, another teacher and mentor, said that sometimes, if one studied a person whose thinking was well centered, it might focus one's own work.

In the "progressive cities" themselves, I found that among the people I interviewed, there was, collectively, a sense of a city as a "just and equal society," along with an idea about how to get there. I began to see my role as simply to record their ideas, perhaps putting them in a little better order, into coherent prose. It was not to my mind a problem of "objectivity"—I might try to get that later—and I tried to get the "other side" of the story from critics and antagonists of the new activist governments.

I took favors from many of my informants. George Hemmens and Rob Mier helped with lodging in Chicago. Rafaella Nannetti had me to dinner, as did, on other occasions, David Moberg, Larry Bennett, David Ranney, and Pat Wright. Chuck Orlebecke took me to the gym to play basketball. CUED was and is a terrific institution, where I had conversations with many of the people who appear in and helped with this book: Ranney, Wright, Doug Gills, and Rob Mier from UIC and CUED all showed me how an urban university can support community development in the neighborhoods.

I had help from many others in the years after these initial stays, including Bob Giloth, Thom Clark, Doug Gills, and many people cited in interviews throughout the text. Bennett read and commented on the manuscript in its entirety, and Giloth on the Chicago chapters—all at an earlier stage, and I know I have failed to correct all of the faults they pointed out. In Boston I have a large debt to Peter Dreier, whom I interviewed at great length—some of these interviews appeared in the book I coedited with Norman Krumholz, *Reinventing Cities: Equity Planners Tell Their Stories* (1994). Equally I leaned on Marie Kennedy and Chris Tilly, whose critical work inspired me. Kennedy and Dreier each read earlier versions of the Boston chapters. Later I came across Michael Liu's dissertation on Boston's Chinatown as it encountered the city's redevelopment efforts. I should also mention the assistance of two Cornell alumnae in Boston: Kate Carpenter, who did a set of interviews in 1999, and Martha O'Connell, who provided assistance with several essential aspects of the project in 2009.

My academic colleagues at Cornell were a constant source of encouragement: Bill Goldsmith as colleague, sometime coauthor, and always my authoritative source on questions of history and theory; John Forester organized a whole new branch of "planning theory," eventually helping me see what I was doing more clearly; John Reps is a giant of professionalism and scholarship. One of my special debts is to Stuart Stein, who was my first boss in professional work in Providence, Rhode Island, where he produced one of the great plans, that for College Hill, in 1959. He gave critique as I wrote a dozen plans and reports, and he later eased my way into academic life at Cornell.

Cornell also helped me financially and administratively. Richard Booth, Department of City and Regional Planning chair in 1992, helped with a leave of absence when I was in Boston in 1992, and sabbatical leaves made possible residence in Chicago in 1988–89 and time for research in subsequent years. Ken Reardon, department chair in 2004-2007, was supportive in the establishment of the "Progressive Cities and Neighborhood Planning" project and archives, and partnered in the first of several applications for support from the Stein Fund. That fund, made possible by a bequest from Aileen Stein and conceived by Kermit C. Parsons in the 1990s, was administered by Michael A. Tomlan and provided important support to this project.

Many students helped me. Renee Jakobs, Catherine Hill, Maile Takahashi, and Crystal Lackey did MRP theses on Burlington. Ken Reardon and Xolela Mangcu did dissertations on Chicago. Reardon did a set of interviews in Boston, some of which I have quoted, before he decided to concentrate on Chicago. Earlier, Robert Giloth managed a summer project that produced an "Annotated Bibliography on Progressive Cities" authored by himself and assistants Jakobs, Francie Viggiani, and Carol Chock. Sharon Gaber then managed a continuation of that, including putting out volumes of interview transcripts including those done by herself, and Jordan Yin was a continuing source of assistance and inspiration. Jonathan Thompson's articles on Madison, Crystal City, Detroit, and the Conference on Alternative State and Local Policies were sources for me. Sara O'Neill Kohl's original work on Chicago's "early warning" initiatives made its way into parts of chapter 6. Others managed the mountains of records from Chicago, Boston, and other places that went into the final years of this effort: Janine Cuneo indexed the first boxes sent to the Cornell library collections; Crystal Lackey, Sarah McKinley, Anisa Mendizabal, Karen Westmont, and Sean Bennett also played important roles.

I also acknowledge Peter Wissoker, acquisitions editor at Cornell University Press, who made the initial gesture resulting in this book being published and nursed it for several years before passing responsibility to Michael McGandy, whose attention to detail and sense of its basic purpose have been remarkable. Others at the Press have been a joy to work with: Marie Flaherty-Jones, Susan Specter, Emily Zoss, and Mahinder Kingra. Jane Dieckmann prepared an excellent index.

There were other scholarly or published works on some of these cities that made it much easier for an outsider like me to make sense of my topic. I cite these in the relevant places but want to mention some in particular. David Mundstock's "Berkeley in the 1970s" is an extensive manuscript, ostensibly unfinished but running to hundreds of pages, available on the website http://berkeleyinthe70s.homestead.com/. Richard Gendron and G. William Domhoff's *The Leftmost City* provided almost all I needed for my brief and completely secondary account of Santa Cruz. Norman Krumholz's work on Cleveland is in many articles, papers, and, in particular, his coauthored work with John Forester, *Making Equity Planning Work*. Krumholz took the lead, doing the lion's share of the work producing *Reinventing Cities: Equity Planners Tell Their Stories,* which includes interviews of several Chicago and Boston people, and others in other places.[4] Larry Bennett's several works on Chicago also helped me. In the text I mention Peter Dreier's many articles on Boston, as well as Marie Kennedy's work there, often with Chris Tilly and the late Mauricio Gaston. And I must make the usual disclaimer: none of these people have any responsibility for the defects in what I am presenting here.

❧ ACRONYMS

BCA	Berkeley Citizen Action
BRA	Boston Redevelopment Authority
CBL	Contract Buyers League
CBOs	community-based organizations
CCCD	Coalition for Community Control of Development
CCED	Center for Community Economic Development
CDBG	community development block grant
CDCs	community development corporations
CDFC	Community Development Finance Corporation
CED	community economic development
CEDO	Community and Economic Development Office
CRA	Community Reinvestment Act
CUED	Center for Urban Economic Development
CWED	Community (later Chicago) Workshop on Economic Development
CWT	Chicago Works Together
DED	department of economic development
DSNI	Dudley Street Neighborhood Initiative
EDIC	Economic Development and Industrial Corporation
EZ	enterprise zone
GRNA	Greater Roxbury Neighborhood Authority
IPS	Institute for Policy Studies
LCDC	North Lawndale Christian Development Corporation
LEED Council	Local Economics and Employment Development Council
LIRI	Local Industrial Retention Initiative
LISC	Local Initiatives Support Corporation
MACDC	Massachusetts Association of Community Development Corporations
MET	Mayor's Office of Employment and Training
MRP	Master of Regional Planning degree
NDEA	Neighborhood Development and Employment Agency

NLEDC	North Lawndale Economic Development Corporation
PFC	People for Change
PFD	public facilities department (later public facilities and development)
PMDs	planned manufacturing districts
PRAG	Policy Research Action Group
PZACs	Planning and Zoning Advisory Committees
R&D	research and development division
RFP	request for proposal
SMRR	Santa Monicans for Renters' Rights
SON/SOC	Save Our Neighborhoods/Save Our City Coalition
TWO	The Woodlawn Organization
UIC	University of Illinois–Chicago or University of Illinois at Chicago
UIC-CUED	UIC, Center for Urban Economic Development
WCDC	Woodlawn Community Development Corporation
WECAN	Woodlawn East Community and Neighbors
WJN	Westside Jobs Network
WSF	West Side Federation

The Progressive City: Concept and Context

Raymond Flynn, a white populist from South Boston, began as the "neighborhood mayor," distinguished by his effort to treat major issues of racial division as economic problems held in common with his white populist base. Harold Washington, Chicago's first black mayor, survived two years of "council wars" with the remnants of that city's political machine and was on his way to a new kind of government regime when he died at his desk early in a second term. Both mayors achieved important policy breakthroughs that outlasted them: Flynn moderated an office-development boom, while siphoning millions of dollars for affordable housing. Washington implemented measures to save manufacturing jobs, against the tide of national policy and trends. Both Flynn and Washington took office as the Reagan era of retreat from government aid to local governments was in full swing, and their main achievements were adaptive: rather than depend on spending, they used the full force of government to shift private sector priorities. They were "liberal," but in a new way.

Not Just City Hall

On the surface, these were significant policy victories implemented by city hall administrators. Beneath the surface, both sets of policies—and much else in these mayoralties and afterward—came from the neighborhoods, representing thousands of citizens and hundreds of activist leaders. It was not simply a neighborhood social movement, just as it was not simply city hall. It was the way elements of both made fruitful contact, struggled with their differences, and eventually prevailed in the face of resistance.

These changes in government priorities came from the neighborhoods and were debated and even tested there, by neighborhood activists, before they came into the electoral campaigns or to city hall. In Boston, new affordable-housing ideas surfaced as early as the 1970s among activists. These included Flynn, who was close to some of them. A native of South Boston, Flynn had returned from Providence College in 1963 as a basketball star, tried out for the Boston Celtics, then circulated around the city, where he met some of the new generation of neighborhood leaders. One of these was Mel King, an African American who was coming to prominence in association with neighborhood causes. King and Flynn both found themselves elected to seats in the statehouse in the 1970s. King had assembled a group of the city's activists and academics at a regular "Wednesday Morning Group" where they aired out ideas about how to improve the city. Flynn knew about these, and may have attended at times. Dozens of community development ideas got aired, and some of them were later made state law. One idea was "linkage"—a proposal to tap real estate development in the downtown for housing subsidies that benefited the neighborhoods. Developers seeking permission for a major project would be required to pay a fee to a trust fund for affordable housing, in order to offset the escalation of housing prices brought by the development. Linkage was later put on the ballot in Boston by a statewide organizing group, Mass Fair Share, and the outgoing mayor, Kevin White, proposed and the city council enacted a weak version at the end of his term in 1983. Flynn and King, battling to be mayor in the 1983 preliminary election, both endorsed a strengthening of the measure, and it would be the new mayor's challenge to accomplish that over the strenuous opposition of the city's real estate interests. The effort would be a central theme in Flynn's mayoralty, and he drew on populist activists in Mass Fair Share and others who had come into his administration in city hall. They—people like Raymond Dooley, Neil Sullivan, and Peter Dreier—were quickly named "Sandinistas" as the leftist voice balancing Flynn's more-conservative appointments to head departments and join the city-hall staff "inner circle."

Chicago's manufacturing retention policies also had neighborhood roots. There were many players, and the key ideas had gestated in the neighborhoods long before Washington adopted and adapted them during his campaign in 1983 and 1984. One key figure was Robert Mier, who had come to teach at the University of Illinois–Chicago (UIC) in 1976. He was a

Vietnam veteran with a PhD from Cornell. At UIC he started the Center for Urban Economic Development (CUED), which linked students to jobs with neighborhood organizations. In 1982 Mier was facilitating a meeting on economic development, where the activists present sought an alternative to "Enterprise Zones," a Reagan economic-policy idea that had been put forward in the gubernatorial campaign for that fall. They (the activists) wanted "jobs, not real estate." They wanted economic-development subsidies to be distributed directly by their neighborhood organizations rather than by city hall, and "balanced development" rather than "trickle down" policies that emphasized projects in the downtown. The meeting led to the establishment of the Community Workshop on Economic Development (CWED) to support these aims.

Later, Mier found the CWED ideas resonating with Harold Washington, who by the end of the year had declared his candidacy for mayor. Kari Moe, an activist who helped set up CWED, was in Washington's campaign as issues coordinator, riding with him in the campaign car. She fed policy ideas to Washington in the car, and he then translated them into terms immediately understood by the crowds at each stop. Mier found Washington's performance on the campaign trail "remarkable—he could put these ideas in concrete terms better than any of us ever could." He later became Washington's commissioner of economic development, supporting efforts to retain manufacturing jobs in the face of pressure to eliminate them in favor of real estate development.

Main Features of the Progressive City

The elections of Harold Washington in Chicago and Ray Flynn in Boston were quite unexpected. There had been some exceptions—to be described in the following chapter—but the norm then and later was that cities, whatever the inequities, would be run by political machines working with business elites, typically in service to real estate development interests seen as the "engines of growth." There had been theories of "growth coalitions" and "growth machines" that seemed to capture the reality. "Growth" took precedence over "equity" and "social justice."

In contrast, and against the expectations of urban theorists, by the 1970s and 1980s some city governments were promoting markedly different policies and approaches to the balance between economy and equity. Boston and Chicago were the most prominent, but there were others. Rather than answering to a business base, these city administrations were generally elected with large popular mobilization. Rather than subordinating all to growth, they proposed redistributive policies toward a balance with the needs of poor families and neighborhoods. And rather than elite government, they sought to open up to greater public participation. In the process, there was a period of remarkable experimentation with job creation, affordable housing, new forms of business ownership, and new participatory styles in government administration. In these cities, the balance between popular demand and business efficiency was a matter of experimentation and popular discourse.

Many activists won office or acquired appointive positions this way in the 1970s, gaining minority seats on city councils and positions in state legislatures. Progressive control of city councils and mayoralties deserve notice. There were perhaps a dozen serious examples, the best known being Hartford; Cleveland; Madison; Berkeley, Santa Monica, and Santa Cruz, all in California; Burlington, Vermont; and later Chicago, Boston, and San Francisco; but one can make a case for others.[1] These cities were characterized by the following:

1. A *social base* in antiwar, labor, civil rights, neighborhood- and tenant-organizing, and other movements—usually rooted in poor and marginalized groups—that found a focus on city administration. There were high hopes, including some to simply "take over" city halls, many of which were<OK?> quickly dashed.[2] But campaigns could be exhilarating. Doug Gills wrote of Harold Washington's election as mayor of Chicago in 1983 that it was "a magic moment...there was something beautiful about it, and something that brought the dead to life. People who had been dead since the 1960s, not in a physical sense but emotionally, spiritually dead, came alive! I saw and worked with winos who put on ties and picked up their pens and clipboards and walked precincts during the Harold Washington campaign."[3]

2. An *alternative vision* of the city. The post-1960s progressives took office with ambitious goals that separated them dramatically from the governments they replaced. Simply stated, these groups sought to redistribute public resources from rich to poor, and to open up government to wider participation. This contrasts with the more-modest aims of most city governments. In some cases they had formal statements or plans. Cleveland planners produced the *Cleveland Policy Planning Report* in 1975.[4] Berkeley activists produced a book, *The Cities' Wealth* (1976), referred to as "an economic plan" for the city.[5] Santa Monicans for Renters' Rights created a short set of "principles of unity" prior to winning majority control in 1981. In Chicago, a meeting of community organizations produced a "platform" that became central to

Harold Washington's mayoral campaign in 1982 and reappeared in subsequent documents, including *Chicago Works Together* (1984), the city's economic plan.[6]

3. *Administrative innovation.* The social movement, once in office, precipitated governance—a professionalism that took the movement to a new level, stimulated by *redistributive measures* that served the base: rent control in Santa Monica and Berkeley, linked development agreements in Hartford and Santa Monica, legislated "linkage" rules in Boston and San Francisco, and support for community development corporations (CDCs) in Chicago and Boston. Burlington's support for the Burlington Community Land Trust eventually placed as much as 20 percent of that city's housing supply under public subsidy or protection from price inflation. Chicago's signal achievement was the implementation of a serious industrial policy favoring the retention of manufacturing jobs.

4. *Participatory reforms* that were made possible by the supply of activists from the base. Berkeley and Santa Monica broadcast city council meetings on the radio, in part because a large population was mobilized to listen. Berkeley expanded representation on city boards and commissions to reflect the scores of willing citizens who were interested in serving. Similarly, a national labor market developed for activists, persons who had made contact with one another in social-movement activities.

5. *Longevity.* Most of these progressive governments and coalitions established themselves long-term. There was a kind of administrative and political hegemony, as critical policy victories led to others, that observers saw as cascade effects. By 2009, Burlington progressives had held the mayoralty for all but two years since 1981. Berkeley Citizens Action and Santa Monicans for Renters Rights retained control for most years after the early 1980s. Paul Soglin was mayor of Madison twice from the 1970s into the 1990s. Flynn won reelection handily in 1987 and 1991, then resigned in 1993. In Chicago, Harold Washington died at his desk after four and a half years in which he became a dominant figure. His coalition then splintered, but elements of his policies had enough support that his successors maintained critical parts of it for several years.

Two Sequences, Not One

How should we see these developments? First, was the progressive city a radical takeover in city hall? In the smaller places, the cities were "taken over" by a progressive regime, or seemed to be. Some movement activists, having worked hard for the election of these mayors, may have thought so as well, giving force to hopes that things would now be easier and to concerns that they should still not relax their effort, though inevitably they often did.

But each of these cities also presents at least *two stories, not one*. First, there was the effort to win office, govern, and administer in an intense, public, naturally conflict-ridden, and what some called "revolutionary" way. Second, there was the social movement that had been in existence before and would continue after the mayors themselves were in office. Each of these went through a sequence of development. In the chapters that follow, I describe each separately, prior to an assessment of the whole.

At first I did not see the two sequences, particularly in writing about smaller cities like Santa Monica, Berkeley, and Burlington. In those places the city-government takeover by "radicals" based in social movements took center stage. Later, I began to see a more separate role for social movements, most immediately as a neighborhood movement but one also connected to civil rights and other groups. These movements had a life before and after any government initiatives, and had their own trajectories, including the creation of other institutions outside the government. This was not the same as what occurred in city hall.

The two-stories approach provides a useful framework for looking at the progressive city and the Flynn and Washington mayoralties in Boston and Chicago, particularly if one looks not just at what happened in the 1980s but what resulted later. Rather than put a period at the end of the "progressive mayoralty" (or city council majority), it is better to see it as part of a longer process, a trajectory of social movement and institutionalization, and we can better see the hegemony each challenged by taking a longer view.

It is possible to diagram the way cities find their way toward neighborhood organizing or progressive administration, or both. I did this in *The Progressive City,* an earlier work based on research in five smaller cities and from the standpoint of electoral coalitions and leadership that had captured control of council majorities or mayoralties: Hartford, Cleveland, Santa Monica, Berkeley, and Burlington.[7] I defined a "progressive city" as the intersect of two dimensions, redistributive and participatory reforms initiated by the city government (see figure 1.1). For those places, one could see a progression traceable across the diagram. These "progressive city" cases seemed to exist toward the outer frontier in the diagram compared to the "normal city," which was closer to the origin. However they also varied along the curve. Some of these cities seemed to have more success with a series of administrative reforms carried out against a background of civic ferment but not

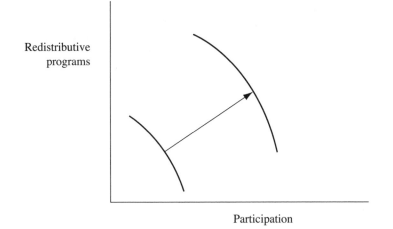

Redistributive
programs

Participation

FIGURE 1.1. The progressive city: defined

necessarily involving a well-developed pattern of neighborhood participation. This could be a problem, as they stalled with significant redistributive efforts not balanced by participation: Dennis Kucinich in Cleveland and Nicholas Carbone in Hartford were each defeated in 1979 in part because of the opposition or apathy of the neighborhood organizations. Others started in a more participatory manner. Perhaps these deviated further from the "normal" on both dimensions, eventually. Burlington was the clearest example, but there were significant efforts in Berkeley and Santa Monica as well.

Even in Cleveland, where progressive government ended dramatically with Kucinich's defeat in 1979, there was a comeback over a twenty-year period as neighborhood-based housing organizations strengthened and city hall operated more as a complement to coordinated neighborhood leadership. In that sense Cleveland was now more thoroughly a progressive city.[8]

Thus a more nuanced conception of the "progressive city" would include the observation that all or most of the innovations characterizing these places had roots in a social movement that found a common cause in neighborhood issues. This shifted the focus. Not only was there a dual problem from the standpoint of the progressive city administrator and political leadership, but there were also two standpoints from which to see the history of these cities: that of the city government on the one hand, and that of the movement and its successor institutions outside the city government on the other.

Conceptually, the revised approach is only partly different from the earlier one. Redistribution and participation remain the salient dimensions of variation among cities. But the institutions—and our view of them—become

City administration

	Undeveloped	Developed
Highly developed, redistributive capacity	Administrative capacity develops ahead of base.	City administration builds on, then builds support base (the progressive city).
Undeveloped	Neither city administration nor social base is well developed (the normal city).	Social base (neighborhoods) develops prior to city administrative response.

Social base

FIGURE 1.2.   The progressive city: elaborated

more deeply layered. Instead of the city government being the main focus, we now look at the government along with the neighborhood organizations that support or oppose it. Instead of "redistribution," we might expand that dimension to include "administratively developed" to recognize that success in redistributive policy is partly a matter of having the administrative wherewithal to implement a redistributive concept. Instead of the government-focused term "participation," we will signify the less fragile institutions represented by CDCs and the like by referring to a developed versus undeveloped "social base." The new diagram, converted to a set of boxes, appears as figure 1.2.

This diagram suggests a starting point for a review of the succeeding chapters. As in the earlier diagram, the "normal city" is toward the lower left while the "progressive city" is to the upper right. In the course of time it would seem that a city could move through the boxes. But how did cities move toward the progressive corner?

A first set of observations would refer to the engine of change: What is the social base for movement along either dimension? Or rather, what did the progressive-city activist think was the social base?[9] Next, how did places move—i.e., from one part of the diagram to another? If there was a movement base, how did either sort of institution—neighborhood group or city administration—develop, and what were the trajectories, taken separately?

Then there is the question of the relationship between the two dimensions. Here the story becomes harder to disentangle, and many things are only partly known at best. In part, the problem is that the development is uneven and incomplete. Few of the "progressive" city governments in the United States were still in power at the end of the 1990s, though they remained a powerful metaphor for future developments and might yet return to prominence in some cyclical fashion. For example, elements of the Washington and Flynn programs continued under their successors, Richard M. Daley in Chicago and Thomas M. Menino in Boston. Progressive governments remained in control in Berkeley and Santa Monica, though their programs had moderated; and something similar happened in Santa Cruz and Madison. In Burlington, the Progressive Coalition had developed further. Hartford and Cleveland, having defeated their radical leadership in 1979, witnessed revivals in lesser respects.

Political and Economic Context

The "progressive cities" emerged in the shadow of Lyndon Johnson's Great Society program and the reaction to it that found its voice with Ronald Reagan's campaign theme that "government is not the answer to our problems. Government is the problem." Reagan gave support to reactionary impulses that had been permanent features of U.S. society. But New Deal liberalism had nearly run its course in any case. The Great Society social programs that Johnson had initiated so conflicted with other priorities—the Vietnam War most visibly—that even viable programs were underfunded and less successful than they might have been. Underlying this, the nation's economy was undergoing a structural shift. Most important, manufacturing sectors that had been the mainstay of the New Deal and the postwar recovery began to decline. This meant the loss of well-paid jobs, a decrease in the power of labor unions, and the exacerbation of racial conflict within the major cities.

Demography and Economics

The bare bones of this story are told in economic indicators and in certain well-rehearsed statistics of national and urban population changes. Cities grew in absolute terms and as a proportion of the nation's population until about the 1960s; after that much of the growth went to the suburbs while the central cities leveled out or declined. Meanwhile the composition of cities changed from largely white to increasingly other than white and increasingly poor. Suburban areas remained less ethnically diverse, with some variation and change over time. Table 1.1 tells the story.

The changes represented here have been rich fodder for urban planners and other advocates of attention to "urban problems." The overall race and ethnicity numbers—from 13 percent to 20 percent "nonwhite"—and much

Table 1.1   Population, Race, Income, and Poverty for the United States,
by Type of Place, 1970–90

	1970	1980	1990
U.S. totals			
Population	203,211,936	226,545,805	248,709,873
Nonwhite (%)	13.0	17.0	20.0
Median family income ($)	9,590	19,917	34,225
Poverty (% of households)	10.7	9.6	10.0
Central cities			
Population	63,796,943	67,854,344	77,843,533
Nonwhite (%)	23.0	31.0	34.0
Median family income ($)	9,507	18,398	32,076
Poverty (% of households)	11.0	12.9	14.1
Suburbs (rest of metro)			
Population	75,621,868	101,576,279	114,882,208
Nonwhite (%)	6.0	10.0	13.0
Median family income ($)	NA	23,303	41,407
Poverty (% of households)	NA	5.8	6.0
Non-metropolitan places			
Population	63,793,115	57,115,182	55,984,132
Nonwhite (%)	10.0	12.0	13.0
Median family income ($)	7,832	16,592	27,591
Poverty (% of households)	15.4	12.0	13.0

Sources: For 1970: U.S. Bureau of the Census, *1970 Census of Population*, vol. 1, Characteristics of the Population, Chapter B, General Population Characteristics, table 48; Chapter C, General Social and Economic Characteristics, table 116. For 1980: U.S. Bureau of the Census, *1980 Census of Population*, vol. 1, Characteristics of the Population, Chapter B, General Population Characteristics, table 39; Chapter C, General Social and Economic Characteristics, table 73. For 1990: U.S. Bureau of the Census, *1990 Census of Population*, Metropolitan Areas 1990, CP 1–1B, General Population Characteristics, table 3; CP-2, General Social and Economic Characteristics, table 3.

higher, at 34 percent in central cities—suggest a challenge to those who prefer a homogenous population. The median-income and poverty numbers reflect the overall shift toward inequality, and the changes were precipitous in many central cities. Hartford, Cleveland, and Chicago reached 25.7, 25.2, and 18.3 percent respectively on the poverty indicator in 1990. William Goldsmith and Edward Blakely, in *Separate Societies* (1992), provide spectacular evidence of this shift—a steady increase in one standard indicator from 1968 to 1989, while the ratio of white to African American median incomes increased as well.[10] But these indications only begin to show the full picture. For that one must look to the changes in economic structure, the shifts in federal budgets as they affect the cities, and the financial constraints under which the cities themselves had to operate.

Table 1.2 Manufacturing as Percent of Total Nonfarm Employment, 1970–90

YEAR	TOTAL NONFARM (THOUSANDS)	MANUFACTURING (%)	ALL OTHER (%)
1970	71,006	25.0	75.0
1980	90,528	21.0	79.0
1990	109,487	16.0	84.0

Source: U.S. Department of Labor, Bureau of Labor Statistics, Databases and Tables, Establishment Data, table B-1, http://www.bls.gov/data/#historical-tables.

Manufacturing Declines

The shifts in the economy are most simply described in terms of the shifting magnitude of job gains and losses by sector, as these can mirror changes in productivity and demand. The most dramatic was in manufacturing. The U.S. Bureau of Labor Statistics gives these numbers and percentages (see table 1.2).

Federal Budget Shifts

In response to increases in needs indicated by the demographic picture, and constrained by the shifts in the economy, federal-government response took the form of changes in expenditure patterns, both in social programs to lessen the impacts of changes and in transfers of funds to localities as they—local governments—set out their own implementation and tried their own solutions. One feature was the increasing proportion of the gross domestic product (GDP) devoted to social entitlements like Medicare and the social programs of the Great Society, initiated in the 1960s but increasing at least through the 1970s. (See table 1.3.)

Table 1.3 Federal Transactions as Percent of Gross Domestic Product, 1960–90

	1960	1970	1980	1990
Defense expenditures	7.8	7.7	5.1	5.3
Nondefense expenditures	1.8	2.1	2.3	1.9
Government social benefits transfers	3.7	5.0	7.7	7.6
Grants to state and local governments	0.8	1.7	2.6	1.9
Transfers to rest of world	0.7	0.4	0.2	0.2
Interest	1.5	1.7	2.4	4.0
Subsidies and net wages	0.2	0.4	0.3	0.5
Total current expenditures	16.4	19.0	20.6	21.5

Sources: Historical Tables, Budget of the United States Government; *Fiscal Year 2009*, table 14.2, 309–16, http://www.gpoaccess.gov/usbudget/index.html.

In summary, the defense-expenditures share of GDP decreased after 1970, offset by increased domestic spending, especially on "social benefits" like social security and Medicare. The raw numbers may be misleading because of the need to account for inflation and the general expansion of the national economy, but historical trends showing federal expenditures as percentages of GDP are revealing: between 1960 and 1990 the total rose from 16.4 percent to 21.5 percent of GDP. But of more immediate importance to city officials was the cutback in intergovernmental grants that, after taking an increasing share of GDP, peaked and then declined. The actual high point was 1978.[11]

Strain on Municipal Budgets

Cities were at the point of impact of these demographic and economic changes. Manufacturing job losses, poverty, breadlines, homelessness, and friction among ethnic groups and races were felt intensely in the mayor's office and city council meetings. It was all costing a lot of money, and their revenue sources were under pressure. Roughly, there were two sources of revenue: intergovernmental grants from states and the federal government, and their "own source" revenues—primarily the property tax. These had grown overall as a share of the national economy, but they peaked near the end of the 1970s.

These numbers only hint at the impact of the federal-program cuts and shifts at the end of the 1970s and in the early 1980s. Again, the raw numbers may be misleading: the GDP shares in the right hand columns of table 1.4 show the declines after 1980 (really 1978). The impact on the composition of municipal revenues was marked: from the *1972 Census of Governments* to that of 1992, intergovernmental revenues dropped from 33 to 28 percent, leaving the rest to be made up by "own sources."

Table 1.4   General Revenues by Source, U.S. Municipalities (Census of Governments 1992, 1972, 1982)

	DOLLARS (IN MILLIONS)			PERCENT OF GDP		
	1972	1982	1992	1972	1982	1992
General revenues, total for municipalities	35.0	91.3	175.1	2.9	2.9	2.8
Intergovernmental	11.5	31.6	49.5	1.0	1.0	0.7
Own sources	23.5	59.6	125.6	1.9	1.9	2.0

Sources: For federal outlays for grants to state and local governments: U.S. Bureau of the Budget, *Budget of the United States Government,* Fiscal Year 2009, Historical Tables, table 12.1, 232, http://www.gpoaccess.gov/usbudget/index.html. For municipal revenues: U.S. Bureau of the Census, *1972 Census of Governments,* vol. 4, Government Finances, in addition to *1982 Census of Governments* and *1992 Census of Governments.* For percent of GDP (Gross Domestic Product: numbers are derived from Council of Economic Advisors, *Economic Report of the President, 2006,* table B-12; total GDP for 1972, 1982, and 1992 are, in billions of dollars, 1,207, 3,146.6, and 6,337.7, respectively.

Implications for Progressive Cities

The "progressive cities"—those described in this book—varied like others in the United States. Their populations varied. Chicago, with a population of 3,369,359 in 1970, was the second largest in the nation, while Santa Cruz and Burlington were in the thirty- to forty-thousand range. Santa Monica, Burlington, and San Francisco gained or lost less than 2 percent from 1970 to 1990. Santa Cruz gained 53 percent; Berkeley, Hartford, and Boston lost 10 to 12 percent; Chicago lost 17 percent and Cleveland 33 percent. Their more specific demography and economic conditions are shown in table 1.5.

For the progressive city, as for most other cities, there would be challenges due to population change and poverty, the cutbacks in intergovernmental grants, and the strains on taxpayers faced with new limitations in their own economic status. For a time in the 1970s and 1980s, in the city halls, these overall trends would not be so clear. Nixon had defeated Hubert Humphrey by mobilizing a "silent majority" of voters who thought change was coming too fast. But federal funding for urban programs was still rising, and new directions were not obvious. For progressive activists, one alternative was to hope for a continued revenue stream and simply change priorities locally. There was brief new hope for this approach when Jimmy Carter became president and supported a new "urban policy" effort and appointed a National Commission on Neighborhoods. But Carter reversed course after two years in the face of budget shortfalls, and after Reagan had defeated him

Table 1.5 Population, Race, Income, and Poverty, Progressive Cities, 1970–90

	TOTAL POPULATION		NON-WHITE (%)		MEDIAN FAMILY INCOME ($)		HOUSEHOLDS IN POVERTY (%)	
	1970	1990	1970	1990	1970	1990	1970	1990
Boston	641,071	574,283	20.5	40.9	9,133	37,726	11.7	12.3
Chicago	3,369,359	2,783,726	41.0	61.8	10,242	30,707	10.6	18.3
Berkeley	116,716	102,724	35.4	41.7	9,987	44,671	10.6	9.4
Burlington	38,633	38,889	1.0	4.7	9,908	35,943	7.7	11.2
Cleveland	750,869	505,616	40.6	52.0	9,107	22,448	13.4	25.2
Hartford	158,017	139,739	36.1	69.3	9,108	24,774	12.6	25.7
San Francisco	715,674	723,959	39.6	53.2	10,503	40,561	9.9	9.7
Santa Cruz	32,076	49,040	4.0	20.7	8,516	40,157	10.7	7.2
Santa Monica	88,289	86,905	7.0	24.8	10,793	51,085	7.3	5.7
United States	203,211,936	248,709,873	13.0	20.0	9,590	35,225	10.7	10.0

Source: U.S. Bureau of the Census, *1990 Census of Population,* Social and Economic Characteristics, table 3, section 1, [CP-2-1C] Urbanized Areas; and [CP-2-6] California. U. S. Bureau of the Census, *1970 Census of Population,* General Social and Economic Characteristics, California, table 89; table 90; and Chapter B, General Population Characteristics, table 23.

in the election of 1980, a final straw in the wind was the McGill Report suggesting that severe cutbacks be made in urban spending and that there should be "no attempt to preserve cities in their historic roles."[12]

These developments had their effect on cities. By the 1980s, the idea of the "progressive city"—full of promise in the 1970s—was in a new phase. The novelty and expectations of the 1970s had settled. This is how Berkeley activist Eve Bach described the progressive takeover of Berkeley's city hall in 1979: "The newly elected leadership, which had earlier seen the city as a source of capital formulation—a vehicle that could carry cooperative housing, economic development, tax reform, community-based energy, and social services programs—had moved into the driver's seat just as the needle on the gas gauge moved toward empty."[13]

There were two meanings of "gas on empty" affecting the actions of cities' progressive leadership. One was the strain on city budgets. Nationally, city budgets, increasingly dependent on state and federal aid, were barely keeping pace with the growth of the economy.

If one looks at the available numbers for specific cities, the picture is generally consistent. According to the Census of Governments reports on cities with a population of ten thousand or more, population figures in Berkeley, Santa Monica, Hartford, Cleveland, Boston, and San Francisco all peaked in 1977; in Chicago and Burlington they reached their highest point in 1982, after which they, and all the others, declined.[14]

Changes in Attitudes toward Cities

These numbers are meaningful, but fiscal constraints need not have been decisive handicaps for city policy. Cities might have been able to enact redistributive policies despite federal budget cuts.[15] But there also was a negative attitude toward cities, the second meaning of "gas on empty." When New York came close to default in the mid-1970s, there were headlines like "Ford to City: Drop Dead." State referenda capped property taxes in California and Massachusetts. Samuel Beer noted an ominous shift in conservative tactics toward the welfare state. Great Society social programs had engendered an interest-group mobilization that forced up spending: federal grants, which had reached a level of 15.6 percent of state and local outlays under the Kennedy and Johnson administrations and 21.4 percent under Nixon and Ford, rose to 25.9 percent under Carter in the late 1970s—a cause of the conservative reaction that followed in the 1980s.[16]

Many events portended difficult times for cities. The Reagan election in 1980 brought class warfare boldly to the surface. Breaking the air traffic controllers' strike in 1981 sent a signal of labor's weakness in the new decade. Reagan's budget director targeted the interest groups of professionals behind Great Society programs for budget cutting—his famous goal to "defund the Left."

These federal initiatives mirrored state-level shifts. Most discussed may have been state tax policies, particularly Proposition 13, the Jarvis-Gann initiative in California, which was passed in 1978; and the similar if less draconian Proposition 2½ in Massachusetts. They were passed by voter initiative, suggesting mass sentiment against government spending. Two other examples of constraints imposed at higher levels made a difference. One was state legislation to abolish or weaken rent control. Another was state- and federal-level passivity and occasional hostility to labor and community efforts to retain manufacturing jobs. Plant closings in the late 1970s and early 1980s shocked rust-belt cities and precipitated various responses: advance notification was one proposal, so that workers and communities could plan an orderly transition. Another was legislation to facilitate employee buyouts, including with the use of pension funds and government subsidies. But these faced corporate intransigence, even in cases where profitability made it plausible to keep plants open. Some state legislatures passed helpful legislation; others did not. But corporations—national and international in scope—could relocate, and ultimately local efforts were unable to counter this. National legislation might have exerted some regulatory constraints, but no effective legislation was forthcoming. In the end the Chicago effort to keep some steelmaking operations alive failed, owing in part to the lack of outside reinforcement.

✿ CHAPTER 2

What the Progressive City Was

During the "progressive" period in American history, mayors like Hazen Pingree in Detroit (1889–96) and Tom Johnson in Cleveland (1901–09) fought for public transportation and public power. One could search further for antecedents.[1] But these are not the topic of this book, and their memory was not a major factor in, say, the postwar period.

The "progressive city" of the 1970s and succeeding decades went through phases. There was an early period of hope and experimentation. In the 1980s one sees a consolidation in a few cities, including Boston and Chicago. A third period, one of denouement, followed at the end of the 1980s, modified to some degree, and in a few places unabated, through 2010.

The Progressive City Emerges: Early Success, 1970s

A first wave of "progressive city" victories and accomplishments occurred in the 1970s, catching the imagination of activists and showing the potential for winning office. Activists who identified as progressives captured city council seats, city council majorities, and mayoralties in dozens of places. Starting in 1975, hundreds attended the annual conferences and regional meetings of an umbrella organization, the Conference on Alternative State and Local Policies.

Berkeley, California

Berkeley radicals captured the nation's attention in 1964 when the free speech movement on the University of California campus mobilized thousands of students against the university administration. Eventually movement activists pressed on the city government. "Radicals" gained city council seats in 1970, and by 1974 a stable coalition of residents and university students formed as Berkeley Citizen Action.[2]

Until 1979, BCA never had more than three seats on the nine-member city council, but it used voter initiatives to make inroads on city policy. Its initiatives, even when unsuccessful, mobilized a voter base of student activists, minorities, and middle- and working-class constituencies resident in the city. Rent control, a successful initiative in 1972, remained a focus of contention—the more conservative council majority refused to support it with appropriations, it was constantly under court challenge, and was invalidated in 1975. But BCA, while losing initiatives on police reform and other issues, won on proposals for a Neighborhood Preservation Ordinance (1973) and a Fair Representation Ordinance (1975).

Though BCA was in the minority and its achievements may seem overshadowed by the climate of conflict, the group was significant in creating organizational commitment and establishing models and even a theory of city governance. A large part of this was due to the remarkable group of volunteer activists and thinkers who organized around Loni Hancock, one of the first coalition members elected to office in 1970. Eve Bach, Ed Kirshner, and Neil Mayer were enrolled or former graduate students in Berkeley's city and regional planning program. Bach and Kirshner cowrote (with others) *The Cities' Wealth,* a short book that described a set of reforms and proposals for Berkeley that could potentially be adopted in other places: police reform, municipal takeover of the privately held electric utility (Pacific Gas and Electric), rent control, and cooperative low-cost housing were among these.[3] BCA activists unveiled *The Cities' Wealth* as an "economic plan" for Berkeley, and Veronika Fukson, looking back later, mentioned that it functioned that way: besieged by landlords when defending a rent-control measure on the city council in 1980, she said the book was "a comfort from loneliness."

The Neighborhood Preservation Ordinance, passed by initiative in 1973, included restrictions on speculative construction and occasioned debate that had a long-term effect on the city's planning and development policy: the ordinance called for restrictions on demolition, mandatory revisions of plans and zoning, and proposals for inclusionary zoning requiring build-ings of four or more units to reserve 25 percent of the units for low- or moderate-income persons. The Fair Representation Ordinance of 1975 had wide effects on government operations, opening participation on boards and commissions, and providing a flow of information and informed advice to city council.

BCA moved into council leadership in 1979, when black activist Gus Newport won as mayor, three other BCA candidates won council seats, and a nonaligned holdover signified her willingness to work in coalition to make a 5–4 majority. BCA then implemented parts of its program. The council passed a milder version of the rent-control ordinance that had been struck down in court in 1976, and pursued cooperative housing developments. In November 1984 BCA swept four additional seats for an 8–1 majority. With this, the BCA moved aggressively. Newport hired economic-development activist Neil Mayer in 1985, and the city subsequently expanded its redistrib-utive initiatives to include support for minority businesses in south Berkeley, a voter initiative for commercial rent control, exactions, first-source hiring, and inclusionary zoning.

They appeared to overreach. A crucial move had been the city's program for scattered-site public-housing projects in 1985. Middle-class neighbor-hoods resisted, and the now-minority "liberals" succeeded in scaling back the BCA council majority in the 1986 election. Most important, the opposition forces also succeeded in a voter initiative creating a district council repre-sentation scheme, which undermined BCA by turning voter interest from citywide to neighborhood issues.

Thus began a third Berkley phase: BCA had moved from a period as minority "radicals" generating ideas backed by often massive participation, to the period of governing coalition under Newport from 1979 to 1986, then after 1986 to a long period of less intense and less radical progressivism. In 1986 Newport resigned, and early BCA council member Loni Hancock returned to take the mayoralty as a more conciliatory figure in 1986–1994, attempting to consolidate the "progressive" position in the city and eventu-ally distancing herself from BCA. There followed a period of stalemate.[4] Longtime BCA state legislator and ally Tom Bates moved into the mayoralty in 2002 but governed as a "progressive" rather than a BCA leader.

One could ask whether BCA could have done things differently in 1985 so as to maintain the leftist initiatives begun under Newport. Eve Bach con-cluded the problem was demographics, not strategy. Certainly Newport took risks. If so, if the BCA initiatives were unsustainable, at least the 1979–86 BCA council leadership had projected a sense of the city that people could remember well, and it had stood on principle. In Bach's terms, "there is something clean" about that.[5]

Hartford, Connecticut

In Hartford, Nicholas Carbone became majority leader of the city council in 1969 and initiated such innovations as a city real estate program, a neighborhood-police experiment, and various new, client-oriented services such as a city energy policy for low-income tenants and support for the nationally known Hartford Food System.[6]

Throughout the 1970s, the city was a magnet for activists wishing to experiment with policies oriented to the poor populations in cities.

It was an administration-based effort, with Carbone as the center of power. For some time until the middle 1960s, government had been "managerial," and it ran smoothly, city council working hand in hand with a city manager and business leadership. But by 1969 the city was experiencing the fourth of a series of "hot summers," with riots and arson in the city's black North End. There was a power vacuum. In the face of these disorders, three council members resigned, and Carbone, aged thirty-two and seen as up-and-coming and smart, with neighborhood roots, was tapped by the state Democratic Party to help fill the vacuum.

The business leadership, dominated by the national headquarters of insurance companies like Aetna, Travelers, and Connecticut General, wanted to shape the city as a regional center to accommodate its expanding office space needs as well as retail stores and cultural institutions, but the neighborhoods were a problem. Neither they nor the city government as it was then organized seemed to have the key. Carbone was energized by the challenge and learned fast. He was made deputy mayor by the council in 1971 and soon was seeking ways to put the corporate agenda into some kind of shape that would also address the burgeoning neighborhood needs.

The real estate program may have been the most important innovation. As Carbone explained later, Hartford's policies were based on the realization that the city had few resources beyond some land and tax abatement authority; and that it could in principle trade land and tax abatements for control over the operation of downtown projects, such as requiring guarantees of city-resident, minority, and low-income hiring during construction and later operation. His first major project was the Hartford Civic Center, a hotel, sports arena, and shops complex that had been proposed earlier with the backing of the business leadership. Carbone went to the state legislature and got the tax abatement authority, and he successfully negotiated the project with the new policies. With the tax abatements as incentives, there proved to be sufficient demand to put in place other downtown projects, and Carbone was able to claim a similar set of benefits for the public. Eventually he concluded a series of eleven major downtown projects.[7]

By the mid-1970s, Carbone saw that the real estate strategy, by itself, would not solve the city's problems. The poverty was simply too overwhelming. But he distinguished his approach from that of other cities with poor populations. Aides John Alschuler and David Smith cited the

> contrast to most decaying center cities changing the population mix. "We've got to attract more middle class people," is the standard slogan for the battered-city mayor. Nick Carbone, the Hartford Democratic Party leader, and his people see the constituency of the city as an appropriate political constituent and do not spend a lot of time worrying about having another one.[8]

The effort to raise incomes and cut costs for low-income residents became the central theme for much of city policy under Carbone. The city sought to cut energy costs to residents by using public funds to create a winterization retrofit corporation. There was also the creation of a development finance institution, an investigation into creating a city bank, and efforts to use city purchasing to stimulate new enterprises. Carbone described a shift from a mainly bricks-and-mortar approach to one that balanced the downtown projects with an emphasis on services to the neighborhoods.[9] This shift coincided with shifts in federal policies during the period, as the Nixon administration ended the "bricks-and-mortar" urban renewal program in 1974, replacing it with the more flexible community development block grants (CDBG) program.

Hartford's progressive government had a ten-year life span but was defeated by middle-class reaction and the increasing dissatisfaction of the city's growing neighborhood organizations. Carbone, frustrated by the limits of his council position and advocating a charter reform to a strong mayor system, challenged the popular mayor George Athanson and lost in the election of 1979. The city council majority fell into a period of reaction and stalemate. It was a seismic shift in the city, and for years afterward participants and commentators grappled with what had happened.

But there was a progressive aftermath: soon a coalition of activists rallied around a campaign for "linkage," and in 1987 there emerged a neighborhood- and labor-based coalition called People for Change (PFC) that, allied with Mayor Carrie Saxon Perry, elected key city council representatives in that year and 1989. In 1991 PFC won three seats and formed a coalition with a newly elected insurgent slate of Democrats. Governance, in the face of severe budget constraints, proved problematic, and PFC lost all its seats in 1993 and did not contest elections thereafter. One outcome was that Puerto Rican and African American representation, largely symbolic in the 1970s when Carbone led the council, became dominant in the 1990s.[10] But open government—one feature of many progressive governments of the period— remained elusive in Hartford.

Cleveland, Ohio

Cleveland's best-known experience in post-1960s progressive government followed the election of Dennis Kucinich as mayor in 1977. Kucinich had a conflicted two-year term characterized by city hall opposition to corporate control of the city; but Kucinich's policies had been the result of groundwork by city planner Norman Krumholz, his staff, and a set of neighborhood organizers.

Krumholz went to Cleveland to work as planning director for African American mayor Carl Stokes in 1969. He soon collected a staff of young planners who began to think through redistributive schemes that would benefit the city's minority and working-class neighborhoods. They produced the landmark *Cleveland Policy Planning Report* in 1974 that identified its overarching goal as "creating opportunities for those who have few." The report set the tone for city policy in a series of controversies, with Krumholz and the planning department playing an advocate role; these included a battle to save the city's municipal power company, MUNY Light, as a yardstick rate setter that constrained the larger private utility's rate increases; and hard negotiations involving the sale of the city's transit system to the regional entity, requiring it to maintain transit rates and route spacing advantageous to the city's transit-dependent poor and elderly.[11]

The plan was the work of a group of new staff people led by Ernest Bonner, who had been teaching economics at the University of Wisconsin.[12] Krumholz and his staff found allies in the city's growing neighborhood movement and its organizers, who brought people into meetings in support of initiatives they saw in their interest. That movement was strong. The city had been the site of one of the first of the Economic Research and Action Projects (ERAP) of the Students for a Democratic Society in the early 1960s; the Ohio Public Interest Campaign (OPIC) was a significant force in the 1970s; and the Commission on Catholic Community Action (CCCA) funded neighborhood organizing throughout the city. Krumholz and the CCCA director, Harry Fagan, were close, and his new staff planners and Fagan's organizers interacted socially. Information flowed freely between the community organizations and the planning department. The planners could gauge levels of support or opposition for city policies under discussion. Neighborhood activists could figure out when to mobilize.

Kucinich's mayoralty was fraught with conflict. He sought to be an "economic populist" and to avoid the issues of race in the divided city by emphasizing common interests of class. In this he was unsuccessful. But he took on the city's corporate leadership, which, in its annoyance, supported a recall election (Kucinich won), and a referendum to eliminate MUNY Light (Kucinich won). Finally, when in the scheduled election in 1979, Kucinich lost to Republican George Voinovich, one press account concluded, "Cleveland Voters Want a Rest."

Krumholz found a new role, however. In 1979 he founded the Cleveland Center for Neighborhood Development at Cleveland State University, continued to do research supporting the city's neighborhood organizations, and in his role as professor in the university's College of Urban Affairs, became a tireless advocate for what he now named "equity planning" in national forums. In 1990 he coauthored *Making Equity Planning Work* with John Forester—which was to become the centerpiece of national—and worldwide—advocacy of its approach.[13] Meanwhile the community organizations evolved, both as an organizing force and in new roles as developers of affordable housing. The organizing was important. In the 1980s and 1990s foundations and "intermediaries" sought to use the neighborhood organizations as developers, and at times pressured them to put less emphasis on involvement of neighborhood people and their interest in services of various sorts. When some organizations refused, the foundations had to go along.

By the 1990s the city administration, which had turned away from social concerns toward a bricks-and-mortar approach after Kucinich's defeat in 1979, began to accommodate neighborhood interests, in response to neighborhood-based pressure. In 1981 the CDCs had created the Cleveland Housing Network (CHN) that supported individual CDCs. Eventually the city's private foundations, which had been pressing CDCs to build more market-rate and fewer subsidized, affordable units, changed course. The dimensions of support for progressive initiatives had broadened.[14] Chris Warren, a veteran of the 1970s organizing campaigns and CHN director, became the city's community development director, and neighborhood interests had a place at the table formulating city policy.

Madison, Wisconsin

In 1973 Paul Soglin defeated the incumbent mayor William Dyke in Madison. Soglin had been a student at the University of Wisconsin in Madison in the 1960s and was a leader in the anti–Vietnam War movement. After being beaten by Madison police at a campus protest in 1967, he was "radicalized" into entering local politics, hoping to bridge the divide between students and residents of the city. He was elected alderman for a student-heavy district in 1968. He served six years as mayor, stepping down in 1979. He served three more terms as mayor, beginning in 1989, resigning a year early in 1997.

Soglin's mayoralty was marked by radical values and "good government" reforms. He won notoriety among conservative critics by visits to Cuba and support for the Left on social issues but eventually won general approval for good administration and reforms such as reorganization of the city police department, renovation of the city bus system, and support for affordable housing. In 1975 the city hosted the first national conference for the Conference on Alternative State and Local Policies that was being set up by Lee Webb and Derek Shearer, who both remembered Soglin assistant Jim Rowen as a key figure in that.[15]

In his second period in office in the 1990s, Soglin governed as a centrist Democrat but was able to look back on his 1970s mayoralty for a number of reforms that later formed the center of Madison politics, noting responsibility for downtown improvements, a city day-care program, public transit improvements, housing programs, and the significant gender diversity in the city's fire and police departments.

In 2003 Soglin ran for another term in office but was defeated in a close race by a next-generation "progressive," Dave Cieslewicz. But even in the 1990s, the city was gearing up for a progressive "second act" as a third-party force called Progressive Dane elected nine of twenty city council members, creating a progressive-centrist balance. So the 1970s could be thought of as a transitional period in Madison. Soglin came in as a radical, governed toward the center, and helped move the council to the left.[16]

Conference on Alternative State and Local Policies

While Cleveland, Hartford, Berkeley, and Madison were exemplary of the emergence of progressive local governments in the 1970s, there were many other places where activists ran for office and tried to work for a variety of redistributive and participatory policies. The best evidence of this more general trend was in the early meetings and publications of the Conference on Alternative State and Local Policies. The conference came about when Lee Webb obtained funds from a set of foundations to nurture activists seeking to influence local and state policy. In the 1960s Webb had been active in Students for a Democratic Society; later he became a journalist.

By 1970 he was teaching at Goddard College in Vermont, and he began lobbying the state legislature to pass bills—a capital gains tax on speculative land purchases, a "lifeline" electric rate bill, and a bill that would give dental care to small children on a sliding scale based on income, the poorest receiving a full subsidy. These initiatives got coverage in national papers. Webb had a network of people interested in similar issues, and soon they began exchanging ideas.

Webb saw the potential of these exchanges, and he wrote fund-raising letters to liberal foundations. He quickly had commitments of $110,000. Webb lodged the grants at the Institute for Policy Studies in Washington, and by 1975 he was commuting from Vermont. He worked with staffers at IPS, Barbara Bick and, later, Ann Beaudry. He allied with other colleagues, traveling around the country to test the waters for ideas and for people who might be interested in the new organization. Notably, he worked with Derek Shearer, then a freelance journalist. Both Shearer and Webb wanted to generate change at the local and state levels, and saw that there was a significant mass of innovations and ideas being promoted there. Their main effort was a set of conferences to bring people together and give the ideas a larger airing. The first conference was set for Madison, Wisconsin, in June 1975. It was hosted by the city—Soglin had recently been elected mayor. Nearly three hundred people attended. There were twenty topical workshops, and Colorado state treasurer Sam Brown gave the opening plenary speech. The outcome of the meeting was the formal creation of the Conference on Alternative State and Local Policies, with the recommendation to encourage regional conferences around the nation and to meet again at a national conference the following summer.[17]

At the outset there was a major emphasis on conferences and publications. Shearer and Webb had found an outpouring of articles, memos from city and legislative staffers, and copies of legislation that they included in bound "Readers" made available to conference attendees in Madison as well as at the several regional and national conferences that followed.[18] There were regional conferences held in Madison, Austin, Hartford, Oakland, all during 1975–77. After the national conference in Madison, there were annual conferences in Austin, Denver, St. Paul, Bryn Mawr, and Pittsburgh. By the time of the Pittsburgh conference in 1980, attendance was up to six hundred.

From 1975 until the beginning of 1978, Barbara Bick edited a newsletter that had a regular feature called "What's Going On," alerting readers to election victories and defeats, new proposals, agendas of upcoming conferences, and reports of conferences just finished.

After the Austin conference in 1976, some of the participants began to react to the Sunbelt and university-town flavor of the conferences, noting the absence of black activists and officials. One comment was:

> At our first annual conference in Madison there were no elected officials from major urban areas. One year later in Austin a caucus of elected officials from little cities with big universities would have overwhelmed one called by elected officials from big cities with lots of poor people. If it comes as no surprise that people of color and those who represent constituencies of working class ethnics have not found the Conference a comfortable political environment, it should, nonetheless, be a cause of substantial concern.[19]

Some of the answer would come, the next year, from northeastern cities, Hartford and Cleveland especially, with their emphasis on economic issues. But these were not racially integrated administrations, much as they tried to build bridges across race lines. Nor was there a black activist and professional contingent in significant numbers. There weren't many in the nation, and those few tended not to be attracted to the populism and socialism of the ex-radicals among the white membership. Washington, D.C.'s Marion Barry and Boston's Mel King were the exceptions, not the rule.

After 1980 the conference turned more to state than local themes. It held no more national, general-membership conferences. Its publications became focused on particular topics. Producer oriented, the publications had the look of efforts organized by entrepreneurs or organizers who saw a theme and were looking for an audience rather than—as in the first years—an organization facilitating a diversity of interests wanting a place to convene. There was not a base of mayors and city council majorities. There was certainly hope in the beginning, a sense of the possibility that the trend would go toward capturing control of city governments. But this hope faded. There was solid majority control in a few places, but defeats in Cleveland, Hartford, and Madison in 1979 gave pause to any hopes for a general advance.

At some point Webb perceived the constituency for the conferences was diverging from what he saw as more-productive work crafting and supporting legislation and policy. The national conferences ended. Webb focused on promoting specific legislative initiatives, more at the state than local levels. By the mid-1980s he moved on, and the conference never regained its earlier focus. Its legacy was scores of local legislative and administrative initiatives pursued successfully, hundreds of people who won elective or appointive office, and dozens of conference proceedings and briefing books gathered from locally generated sources—particularly the early efforts of Shearer and Webb.[20]

Consolidation: 1980s

By the 1980s the idea of the progressive city had evolved and changed. Progressives gained control in the smaller cities of Santa Monica, Santa Cruz, and Burlington, and continued their long run in Berkeley. They followed the pattern of earlier cases, but with more stability.[21] And there was a strong electoral movement in San Francisco.

Santa Monica, California

Santa Monica passed the nation's strongest rent-control ordinance in 1979 and broadened its program to enact a wider set of redistributive measures. Key leadership came from Ruth Goldway, elected mayor in 1981, and administrative help came from John Alschuler, who had been an assistant city manager working with Carbone in Hartford—thus some of Hartford's expertise helped in developing a set of real estate development agreements, while local activists built on the mobilization around rent control to initiate a series of reforms and innovative policies.[22]

In Santa Monica in the 1970s, development pressure collided with the interests of middle-class families and individuals who had moved to the city to take advantage of its relaxed bungalow neighborhoods and seaside location. Political organization followed: when rents continued to rise, Santa Monicans were receptive to rent control. Populist Republican lawyer Robert Myers wrote a strong ordinance that passed by initiative in 1979, in a year that also brought three members of what would become Santa Monicans for Renters' Rights (SMRR) onto the seven-member city council. One strength of the ordinance was the provision that the rent board would be elected popularly rather than appointed by the city council. This meant that periodically candidates would run for election on an issue that was in the immediate self-interest of a massive majority of voters—the city was 80 percent renters—and this had a spillover effect on city council elections. SMRR netted two additional seats in 1981 for a 5–2 majority and elected one of the 1979 winners, Ruth Goldway, as mayor.

The rent-control ordinance triggered a set of additional reforms that SMRR was able to implement in the ensuing decade:

1. In response to the sentiment that supported rent control, the city council majority fashioned a general program to shift its alliances from property developers and landlords to the interests of the renter and small homeowner majority of the population. It dramatized this

position by declaring a moratorium on development immediately after its election in April 1981 and establishing a set of citizen task forces to formulate development policies. During intensive negotiations in the summer of 1981, a series of major developments came under scrutiny as task forces noted social costs and developers negotiated compensatory steps.

2. The city manager retired soon after the SMRR victory, opening the position for the council to hire Alschuler. With Alschuler as city manager and Robert Myers as city attorney, not only could the city hammer out the details implementing development agreements, they could also put in place budgeting and other "good government" improvements. Myers, for example, made great improvements in handling some of the legal issues arising in police administration.

3. During the period between the rent-control victory in 1979 and winning council majority in 1981, SMRR had engaged in a study group with UCLA faculty that looked for ways the city could capture the costs associated with intensified development. With property-tax increments obviated by California's passage of Proposition 13 in 1978, the group focused on exactions from developers. In consequence, the planning commission, now led by Derek Shearer, sought to use the "housing element" mandated by state law, to generate a proposal for "inclusionary zoning," requiring developers of large projects to set aside units for affordable housing according to standards set by the city. Under Shearer's leadership on the planning commission, the city went beyond rent control and housing issues to matters of progressive urban development, becoming a national model for creating urban farmers' markets, bike ways, neighborhood-scale economic development, city curbside recycling, pedestrian shopping streets, and the use of nonprofit city corporations to manage and reanimate public assets such as the historic Santa Monica Pier. Shearer thought Santa Monica became a model for "balanced economic growth" and animation of urban space.

4. One of the reforms proposed by SMRR had been police reform, to include citizen groups in neighborhoods and to support police activities. SMRR, once in majority control, supported police in several ways. One of these was the appointment of Robert Myers as city attorney. Myers, while best known as the author of the city's strong rent-control ordinance, was also a conscientious advocate of city staff. One way to support the police had been to settle the constant stream of citizen complaints and suits that all police forces encounter. Myers began turning these around much more quickly than before.

5. The city council began to support community organizations, providing grants to allow them to hire staff and to support volunteers better. This practice began to generate a corps of citizens with organizational experience outside city hall, contributing to SMRR's—and the city's—capacity to work effectively on public problems and field candidates for office.

6. There was a reaction to SMRR from landlords and "moderates," including some on the city council who had been endorsed by SMRR. Mayor Ruth Goldway lost reelection in 1983, reducing the SMRR majority to 4–3, and the group lost its majority in 1984. But SMRR regrouped and new people ran for the city council, with the result that SMRR regained the majority in 1988 and began a new set of initiatives in that year, with Denny Zane, one of the 1981 SMRR council majority, now as mayor. By 1999 SMRR had won two consecutive city council elections with 5–2 majorities. A headline in the *Los Angeles Business Journal* announced "People's Republic is Back—Door Shuts on Growth," noting an alliance with unions pushing for a $10.69/hour minimum wage, and a moratorium on new apartment and condominium construction.[23]

SMRR's latter-day electoral stability may have come at a cost. SMRR, co-opting homeowners and others interested in issues other than rent control, may have moved away from its earlier commitments. But the rent-control law, so obviously in the interest of the city's majority renter population, was the key device allowing SMRR to enact its larger constellation of reforms. As late as 2000 SMRR was claiming that no one had won a seat on the rent board without its endorsement since its inception in 1979 (the string was broken in 2008), and even opponents of SMRR ran on the premise they would better manage rent control than SMRR, rather than against rent control per se.

Burlington, Vermont

Burlington elected socialist Bernie Sanders mayor in 1981; he and his successor, Peter Clavelle, developed a progressive regime that was still in control of city hall in 2010.[24] Sanders defeated the incumbent, conservative Democrat Gordon Paquette, winning by ten votes after a grassroots campaign knocking on doors, and after a period of neighborhood organizing by the populist Vermont Alliance and a group of volunteers assigned by the state VISTA office.

Sanders, who was committed to opening up the city's government and to economic development initiatives that would favor the city's poor and working-class residents initially faced fierce resistance from the aldermen and city departments and commissions. He responded by appointing advisory commissions, getting media coverage, and in effect taking his program to the people. When the planning department and aldermen resisted his economic and community development initiatives, he created a Mayor's Committee on Economic Development, including business representation that recommended a more active encouragement of community development and the establishment of a new Community and Economic Development Office (CEDO), which was finally approved by the board of aldermen, with three Republican votes, in 1983.

The new office proved to be the leading edge projecting ideas that soon captured the confidence of a majority of voters. Initiatives were each delegated to a different assistant director: CEDO supported neighborhood planning assemblies, set up in each of the city's six wards, now serviced by an assistant director for community development and each with a budget of $15,000 for projects to be determined by the residents. There was a community media and TV project designed to foster communication among citizenry and community groups and the city, while also providing training to make young people in the city more employable. There was the city's waterfront development project, given much advantage when it went to court to get title to waterfront land owned by the Central Vermont Railway, thus making possible general public access and the creation of low-income housing units there. Eventually there was an eco-industrial park in a seven-hundred-acre tract of land that combined crop production, electricity generation from wood chips, and composting.

Sanders, from the outset, sought to stimulate economic growth and job expansion. The creation of CEDO, in fact, became possible when at least a segment of the business community concluded they could get more growth from Sanders than from Paquette and the reactionary Democrats and Republicans on the board of aldermen. And Sanders certainly entertained the prospects of "development" in a series of projects, notably the waterfront proposals, encountering criticism from the Left as he did so. He seemed to be trying for a balance—encouraging developers with subsidies and tolerating high-end residential components, while extracting as much public space and access and low-end housing as he could.

The challenge was to get job growth that would be distributed across the income spectrum. CEDO did some relatively minor programs that targeted specific constituencies. One was the "Boom Pie" Ordinance that sought to place women workers in the construction trades, providing training and requiring specific portions on city-funded jobs. A more comprehensive strategy seemed on the agenda when, in 1986, CEDO commissioned *Jobs and People: A Strategic Analysis of the Greater Burlington Economy,* which recommended a focus on locally owned and worker-owned and managed firms.[25]

Most noteworthy of CEDO's projects was the Burlington Community Land Trust (BCLT), a community organization that was the linchpin of a city policy to produce and rehabilitate units that would be permanently affordable for low-income families. Sanders, despite reservations about denying fee simple ownership to the persons housed (they kept title to the dwelling, but the land trust kept the land), supported BCLT with a $200,000 initial grant for administration. A large number of initiatives for affordable housing then happened. Between the establishment of BCLT in 1984 and the end of Clavelle's mayoralty in 2006, the city increased the numbers of nonprofit housing providers from one to six. Remarkably, they got voter support in a referendum for a one-cent increase in the property-tax levy, to be assigned to a housing trust fund supporting the housing organizations. In 1994 John Davis, the city's first housing director, wrote that the city now had 1,600 units of "nonmarket housing," 10 percent of the city's total. In 2009 the city put the figure at 2,700 units, 17 percent of the city total.[26]

The city's housing policy delegated significant authority to nonprofits like the BCLT. The reason, according to Davis, was pragmatic: "There was an ever-present apprehension among Sanders' supporters and staff that each year might be their last." Therefore they sought initiatives that would outlive their hold on city hall, believing that "a nonprofit infrastructure should be established *outside* City Hall—*independent* of City Hall."[27] In 1993, when Sanders's Progressive Coalition successor as mayor, Peter Clavelle, lost reelection after two terms, the progressives' idea about institutionalizing programs in the nonprofits was put to the test. Key staff, including Davis, left the government and formed a consulting business, Burlington Associates. Davis and some others also formed a breakfast group among the housing-oriented nonprofits, whose purpose was to keep the housing policies and city support alive. They were aided by the election, at the same time as Clavelle's defeat, of a majority on the board of aldermen, and the Republican mayor was unable to do much damage. In 1995 Clavelle won election again and continued in office until stepping down voluntarily in 2006, having served longer than any mayor in the city's history.

Through these sorts of steps, the city seemed to be continuing on its progressive path. Clavelle seemed a more moderate leftist than Sanders—he smiled if people called him a "Social Democrat" or a "left-of-center

Democrat." The sequence of Sanders and Clavelle seemed to have been a good one, their complementary styles accomplishing more than either would have done alone.

Santa Cruz, California

Progressive majorities first occurred in this small (58,000) California city in 1981, the same year that SMRR first had control in Santa Monica and Sanders won in Burlington. As in these places, there had been earlier developments. Richard Gendron and G. William Domhoff in *The Leftmost City* (2009) provide a detailed account of the rise of a progressive coalition in Santa Cruz and its domination of local politics through 2009.[28] In Santa Cruz the most important development seemed to be the establishment of the University of California, Santa Cruz. It matriculated its first class in 1965, and in 1969 established a Community Studies Department. It was a liberal arts college, open to new ideas, including that of getting students engaged in community work. The Community Studies program had put over one thousand students to work on community projects in the city by 1990. The over five thousand students in the college became a voting bloc. Neighborhood organizations also developed and ran candidates, often led by UC Santa Cruz faculty and staff members or their spouses, so that progressives had a minority foothold on the city council through the 1970s.

There was resistance from the business community and others to some of the progressives' most important goals, and in the late 1970s they began to join in a more coordinated fashion. The progressive breakthrough in 1981 came when campus-based activists found common cause with neighborhood concerns. The campus-based chapter of the New American Movement supported Michael Rotkin, an instructor in the Community Studies Department, and Bruce Van Allen, who had been a leader in the Downtown Neighbors Association and a rent-control advocate. They won endorsement at a forum organized by the Westside Neighbors in 1979, and soon a number of other groups—previously unwilling to get into politics—added endorsements, and an informal "progressive coalition" emerged. This led to further gains, securing a 4–3 majority when the Downtown Neighbors Association candidates Mardi Wormholdt and John Laird won election in 1981.

With the new majority, the progressives moved ahead boldly through the 1980s. They doubled social spending in 1981 by postponing infrastructure spending for a year, creating a revolving fund. Over the decade, spending went from $150,000 to $1,500,000 annually. They created new revenue streams from amusement and room taxes, and fees on phone and cable-TV hookups. They instituted affirmative-action hiring and installed a new city manager, one result being the replacement of one-third of the city's police force. Activists had also entered politics on the Santa Cruz County Board, and won a 3–2 majority in 1974. The leading figure was Gary Patten, who held office until retiring in 1993. During this period he was a key figure coordinating city and county policy initiatives, working with his aide and fellow activist, Andy Schiffrin, who was trained as a city planner at the Massachusetts Institute of Technology and then worked for the Boston Model Cities program as a planner and director of housing development before moving to Santa Cruz. Control of the five-member county board swung back and forth until 1981, when progressives regained the majority and held it at least into the 1990s.

The shift to majority control after 1981 was not easy sledding for the Santa Cruz progressives. There was resistance and a need to shift priorities. Gendron and Domhoff sum it up in the phrase "progressive success but socialist decline." The progressives pulled back from steps that might have seemed to go too far, or that would likely result in defeat. They would not touch homelessness. They never succeeded with rent control, which had been the central cause for some in their number. The electoral formula seemed to be: service the neighborhoods, and support at least some issues that were important on campus.

The progressive coalition that held power through the 1980s was put to the test by the 1989 earthquake, which destroyed the center of the city's downtown. Business leaders saw this as a chance to regain control of the city, since they would naturally be in a key position during any rebuilding process. But remarkably, progressive forces maintained electoral control by buying into a downtown agenda, while simultaneously listening to the neighborhoods by reducing the potential boundaries of the reconstruction area. Progressives were still in control in 2009.

San Francisco, California

San Francisco is notable for the success of its thirty years of grassroots organizing, nominally around "growth control" applied to downtown office construction, tied to a set of related policies and proposals. But mayors and downtown "growth coalition" lobbies had resisted, and when a populist mayor, Art Agnos, was defeated for reelection in the early 1990s, critics saw the antigrowth movement as negativistic and incapable of forming the coalitions necessary for governing. It is arguable that, in less obvious ways, grassroots pressure transformed San Francisco's political culture. But the administrative and political capacity to realize the potential of that culture remained elusive.[29]

On the surface the story followed the pattern of many other U.S. cities. Growth-coalition interests and city officials used federal redevelopment programs to "Manhattanize" the city's downtown through the 1970s. Protest came from residents, environmentalists, and working-class interests wishing to maintain factory and commercial jobs. A liberal mayor, George Moscone, dealt activists into his coalition. The city planning commission instituted linkage fees, Moscone funded community organizations with CDBG funds, and supervisors voted a forty-foot limit on construction in residential districts. Activists put growth-control initiatives on the ballot several times starting in the 1970s. But Moscone was assassinated in 1978, and through 1983, mayors, with the support of local media and business interests, defeated all of them, though with decreasing margins.

In the early 1970s the antigrowth movement came from middle- and upper-class homeowners who saw downtown office high-rises were hurting the quality of life in residential neighborhoods. Potential allies saw the movement as top-down and narrow. One African American leader criticized the movement as "more interested in buildings than people," adding that "they never talk about poor people and there's a self-righteousness in these groups that really bugs me."[30] Later, activists with a different vision joined the antigrowth forces and succeeded in getting enactment of measures tying restrictions on growth to "linked development"—payments from developers to compensate residents for costs attributed to the concentration of land uses in the downtown such as subsidies for affordable housing, for the municipal transit system, and for employment programs. And over time, as more groups got involved and discussion continued, support broadened. Finally, in 1986 Proposition M passed, establishing a cap on office construction and mandating policies for environmental protection, neighborhood preservation, and the support of jobs and affordable housing. Support for restrictions on development as well as for the redistributive linkage programs had become general.

Mayors and city agencies eventually supported the grassroots efforts. After the antigrowth forces prevailed in 1986, liberal mayor Diane Feinstein allowed her administrators to take a series of steps implementing their ideas. She supported nonprofits, agreed to reallocations of CDBG funds, and mobilized city agencies toward affordable housing production. According to Stephen McGovern, she "recognized the primary role... of community-based nonprofit housing development corporations as the producers of affordable housing. She gave up the notion of trickle down."[31]

With Feinstein prevented from running again by term limits, populist state senator Art Agnos ran for and won San Francisco's mayoralty in 1987 and continued to implement progressive policies. He appointed antigrowth and affordable-housing advocates to city government positions. The planning commission began opening its meetings to public participation. The city administration supported new growth limitations in the downtown and advocated new redistributive policies: it raised the "mitigation fee" on new development, leveraged linkage revenues with private sector contributions toward affordable housing subsidies, further entrenched the transit linkage program, adopted inclusionary housing provisions, and moved toward implementation of an employment linkage program.[32]

While Agnos had run as a populist and was elected by a voter base that had been mobilized around Proposition M, he found it more difficult to govern. Like Feinstein, he found it necessary to try to balance the potential benefits of growth—linkage payments, after all, depended on the flow of development dollars—with the programs of the antigrowth and redistributive constituency. But he proved less adept at it than Feinstein, encountered opposition from left as well as right, and lost reelection in 1991.[33]

This was sobering to anyone with thoughts of progressive hegemony. Richard DeLeon took the lesson that, while the progressive movement remained alive, there were long fault lines: "Middle class preservationists and environmentalists became less sensitive to the plight of the poor.... The progressives were firm and clear in telling Agnos what he could not do, but they offered little more than sophisticated variants of 'soak the rich' and 'support small business' in telling him what he should do to solve these real problems."[34]

After the early 1990s progressives and the "growth coalition" coexisted. Stephen McGovern saw an established progressive political culture in San Francisco that succeeding mayors now accommodated: the planning commission gave unprecedented scrutiny to developer proposals, thus implementing the spirit of Proposition M in a new way. The developer-oriented mayor Willie Brown (1995–2003) appointed growth-control advocates to high government posts. He also secured passage of a $100 million bond issue to fund affordable housing, and then used the funds to "leverage an additional $300 million from Wells Fargo Bank and $50 million from the AFL-CIO Housing Trust Fund for affordable housing."[35] Domhoff, in an article on the Internet, asserts that "the growth machine moved forward without any problems from almost the day on which DeLeon ends his book."[36] Both views seem true, perhaps a pattern for other cities as well.

CHAPTER 3

The Movement Becomes
Politics in Boston

Like some other cities, Boston had nurtured elements of U.S. populism and socialism in the 1970s. What was different was how these worked their way into the electoral campaign when, after a tie in the preliminary election, Ray Flynn defeated Mel King for mayor of Boston in 1983.

Flynn was from an Irish family in South Boston. He was a basketball star at Providence College, and later, when he returned to Boston, he was elected to the state legislature and city council. He experienced South Boston's reaction to the school busing conflicts of the 1970s as not the big deal it was for politicians who made a career of it. He was a populist, a social conservative, intrigued by the majoritarian socialism of Michael Harrington of the Democratic Socialists of America. He found his political voice as a champion of neighborhood causes. He would reminisce about coming back from college and a tryout with the Boston Celtics, and playing ball in neighborhoods like the West End that were being decimated by urban renewal. He got to know Mel King that way. In 1971 he found himself elected to the legislature from South Boston and served there with King. Then in 1978 he was on city council through the mayoral race in 1983. As mayor he led a series of administrative and political initiatives that established an essentially populist way of governing. He drew national attention as a voice for popular interests during a period when national politics went toward cold-war triumphalism and domestic social reaction. In 1993 Flynn left the mayoralty when the Clinton administration offered him the post of ambassador to the Vatican, and he faded from the scene.

Mel King was an African American, a political leader for Boston's blacks, and also an organizing force for the progressive left. He appealed to and united people across lines of race, gender, and sexual orientation. He had established a leadership position among community organizations in his own neighborhood, the South End, running unsuccessfully for the Boston School Committee three times in the 1960s. He then won election to the state legislature in 1973 and held that office for a decade. He ran a campaign for mayor in 1979, and in 1983 articulated for the first time in the country the idea of a "rainbow coalition" that was later used by Jesse Jackson at the national level in 1984 and 1988.

Following his victory over King, Flynn faced many neighborhood-based initiatives and challenges. A racially diverse Coalition for Community Control of Development held two conventions later in Flynn's mayoralty, demanding a share of control over development projects, and reflected even deeper, racially charged dissent, such as had been symbolized by referenda to establish Roxbury as a separate municipality in 1986 and 1988.[1] What made Flynn's mayoralty historically important, however, was the way in which his campaign and later his governing formula adapted—or failed to adapt—ideas drawn both from the U.S. black civil rights tradition and from a different populism, a neighborhood movement that had begun in the 1970s.

Flynn in the end capitalized on many but not all of the potentials and initiatives conceived by Boston's progressive activists, and after he left office in 1993 the city missed his populist edge. What remained was a milder version of urban populism, complemented by the increasing role of nonprofits and a vigorous new diversity in the population of the city.

Mel King and Community Development in Boston

The 1983 election campaign, the eleven-year Flynn administration (1983–1993), and its aftermath have to be seen in the context of at least two decades of history. King was at least as central to this as Flynn, but the history of protest and organizing was part of both men and included neighborhood protests, elite and academic controversies, the history of development initiatives around the health of downtown, and above all, the trauma of busing, which, in the 1970s, focused the long frustrations around race and class that had, until then, been in the background for the majority of the population. But we should start with King.

In 1981 King published a book, *Chain of Change,* that chronicled the evolution of African American politics in Boston and, by implication, in the nation generally.[2] In it he distinguished a "services" orientation, where blacks' political aims were simply to get better treatment from whites, as a first stage, one that characterized Boston's blacks until the 1960s. A second stage was devoted to organizing, and a third to building the community's own institutions. The book was both theoretical—it was as good an idea of what "community development" meant as had appeared—and autobiographical, for King himself had been involved in most of the examples he cited for Boston.

Chain of Change tackled the key dilemmas that confronted organizers of groups that were out of power: (1) whether to appeal to pragmatic, pocketbook issues alone or to speak to underlying structural questions; and (2) whether to operate separately or in coalition with others. For King, a black man, there is no doubt that there was a structural question. That was racism, the subject of dozens of small struggles chronicled in the book. And the solution, for the African Americans who were the main reference in the book, was structural: to overcome not just the objective reality of the hurdles put down by the larger economy and politics, but also the subjective sense of inferiority. For this blacks needed to control their institutions, such as schools and businesses, and ultimately gain political power.

Did this mean blacks should push on separately? Not necessarily, but to deal with the structural question it was essential to get control of institutions, and one way to get control was to go ahead separately when feasible. Going ahead successfully, coalition would be possible. Closer inspection of the book, which evolved out of an effort to chronicle the black movement as it emerged in the 1960s and 1970s, yields a set of propositions:

1. The personal development of black people, long deferred in the effort to adapt to conditions of racist organization rooted in earlier slavery, pervades the book. King encountered the problem at every turn: black people sometimes failed to mobilize because of the deep-rooted belief that they could not.[3]
2. Personal development was connected to organizational development. King thus found it useful to adopt a participatory style as director (they changed the title to "Executive Servant") of the New Urban League; and he cited the emergence of new schools and other institutions organized in a participatory way.[4]
3. Organizational development required the control of whole institutions, including land and capital, in a concept captured by the term

"community control." This might mean schools, or businesses. King
seems to have developed his ideas through his work as director of the
New Urban League in 1967–71.[5]

4. Control of institutions might entail getting a share of political power.
Thus King helped organize a series of campaigns to put blacks in political office, including his own campaigns for the Boston School Committee in the 1960s; the creation of the Black Political Task Force that
helped organize support for a number of candidates, including his own
successful runs for state representative in 1971, 1973, 1975, and 1977;
and his candidacies for mayor in 1979 and 1983.[6]

This set of ideas, and King's elaboration of them later, made him distinctive among organizers and leaders. Perhaps the central idea was that of
"community control," which provided a path between simple separatism
on the one hand, and dependency on the other. This idea was articulated
in *Chain of Change,* and seems to have been a part of King's many efforts
as organizer and community leader. The reason we know it is distinctive is
the number of community leaders and movements across the nation that
have fallen into either the dependency or separatist categories. On the one
hand minority candidates won city council seats and mayoralties at the cost
of excessive compromise. But neither was there a viable separatist extreme,
and there were examples of leaders of ethnic minority movements who
were destroyed after taking a separatist course. King's ideas of community
control, on the other hand, offered a way to get some of the benefits of
autonomy, without the crushing opprobrium of the majority that defeated
the separatists. In *Chain of Change,* King argued that blacks should "confront the racism that makes us desire to keep our distance from the system. . . . Why do we often choose not to engage other people—particularly
white people—when there is no way that we can exist on this earth without
some rapport and some contact?"[7] King was not reluctant to get into politics. In this he departed from the organizing principles followed for years by
many populist organizers, who thought ties to political institutions would
sap the energies of poor neighborhoods. There were many reverberations of
this notion in the 1970s and 1980s. When he succeeded, holding a seat in
the state legislature in the 1970s, he initiated or cosponsored several pieces
of legislation that had lasting usefulness for neighborhood and populist
causes.

He had also, in 1971, taken a position at MIT where he established the
Community Fellows Program. This brought in community activists to the
Department of Urban Studies and Planning for periods of up to one year.

It was, at the very least, a way for activists to take a perspective on their work by interacting in a different environment. Some went on to the two-year master's degree in planning. MIT also gave King a base from which to connect community and political work to a larger arena of intellectuals. Some of this came together in the Wednesday Morning Breakfast Group that King organized. From his position in the legislature, he had met with many activists and groups, many organized around opposition to a proposed interstate-highway connector that would have destroyed parts of the city. Later, once organized, they saw other development issues affecting neighborhoods, particularly around plans to relocate the Orange Line, an elevated transit line through Roxbury. As a way to keep these groups meeting, King said, "If you meet with me, I'll cook your breakfast." And so they met at MIT "for six or seven years." Out of this came a set of new institutions, proposed and passed in the legislature, including the South West Neighborhood Authority and the Community Development Finance Corporation (CDFC), "with $10 million to help finance CDC-generated businesses in 1974 or 1975. Then," King added, "we created the Community Economic Development Assistance Corporation (CEDAC) to do technical assistance."[8]

King also helped nurture the Boston Jobs Policy, stipulating resident hiring on projects paid for by city funds. It had been promoted by Chuck Turner, a Roxbury activist who became one of the first community fellows at MIT. The Wednesday-morning group also discussed "linkage," later adopted by then-mayor Kevin White (in 1983) in the face of increasing community pressure. Linkage required developers to contribute toward affordable housing—an idea that had been tried informally in Hartford in the 1970s and was later adopted in San Francisco and some smaller places. King also used his position to speak out on a set of distinctively leftist positions: he spoke against militarism and discrimination, took leadership of an effort to pass a bill to divest state funds invested in South Africa, visited Cuba, and worked to create a black caucus of state legislators.[9]

Policy specifics emerged when King ran for mayor the first time in 1979. In *Chain of Change* King emphasized that "process is what we were about," and he saw the campaign as a chance to bring together various constituencies that had been left out of the mainstream of policy and were striving for their goals "on a one-by-one basis and they were being played off against one another." King characterized the campaign as a place where these interest groups began to come together—"groups like the Alliance for Rent Control, the Gay Caucus, women's groups, the Third World Jobs Clearinghouse, the Boston Jobs Coalition, and the elderly."[10]

Neighborhood Organizations

Decentralization was an abiding theme for King, and he had developed ideas from a trip to Cuba in 1979, where he saw the Committees for the Defense of the Revolution that "inspired in me the idea of ward and precinct organizations mentioned at the end of *Chain of Change*. I realized that this was our base. We never could quite make it happen in Boston."[11] He elaborated on this in the concluding chapter of *Chain of Change* and in a 1987 paper that took as a point of departure the sentiment that had supported a (defeated) referendum to establish Roxbury and neighboring areas as a separate municipality called Mandela:[12] (1) "Each precinct would elect—or somehow choose—a team of people who would organize the precinct around various issues: housing, health and environment, education, employment, finance, economics, politics, recreation/culture, and so on.... Each team member would also assess the precinct's resources and skills as well as its issues, needs, and demographics in his or her area of expertise."[13] (2) There would also be a coordinating group that would "serve as an organizing body and resource unit to the precinct units," and there would be a process of creating a "community scoreboard." (3) King had outlined the community scoreboard in *Chain of Change* as a kind of survey procedure that could be both a process for general involvement of the residents and a research tool with which to build policy ideas. (4) In *Chain of Change* the proposal was aimed at the black community of Boston, but it had more-general ramifications. King wrote: "Each Ward Council will in turn send representatives to a Black Community Council,... and eventually to a Boston City Council, made up of representatives from all the wards in the city."[14]

Alternative Economics

King's colleagues at the Wednesday-morning group included a broad array of interests, but his legislative initiatives in the 1970s were mainly oriented to community business development. One person King particularly mentions from the start of the Wednesday-morning group reflected this: David Smith was an economist who had produced a widely circulated report called *The Public Balance Sheet,* and who signified a connection with the liberal-to-radical edge of that profession.[15] Another was Elbert Bishop, a board member of the Center for Community Economic Development (CCED), a federally funded unit oriented to the promotion of community-based business development. Others at the Wednesday sessions remembered names like Gar Alperovitz and Carl Sussman. CCED featured a combination of organizational and economic analysis that supported the notion of community control and was a support organization for the national community-development movement.

King, moving into the legislature in 1971, and leading the legislature to the creation of the Community Development Finance Corporation (CDFC) and, later, the Community Economic Development Assistance Corporation (CEDAC), provided a series of institutional bases for the community economic-development advocates.[16] An earlier part of the support system for community development was the Community Enterprise Economic Development Program (CEED), established in 1976 as a small pilot program for "production oriented as opposed to social service—or 'advocacy oriented'—community development projects."[17]

Community control would not have sat well with mainstream economists, but there were others emerging in the 1970s whose ideas were more supportive. There were a number in the Boston area, and many others with the Union of Radical Political Economics (URPE). URPE, based in New York, had outposts at various universities including the University of Massachusetts at Amherst, where David Gordon and Samuel Bowles taught. These academics were on the whole oriented to national issues and to economics as an academic discipline, but some who had urban and regional interests, like Markusen, made signal contributions to local groups. Another important member of this group, who settled at MIT in 1971, was Bennett Harrison. Harrison was an influential person whose first major work, *The Economic Development of Harlem*—coauthored with New School economist Thomas Vietorisz—took issue with black militant leaders who, though politically progressive, supported traditional economic-development strategies focused on subsidies to individual firms. Instead, Harrison and Vietorisz argued that economic development needed to be planned as an ensemble of firms and cooperatives where social objectives took a place alongside private profit. These new initiatives, they said, would then be a political force as much as an economic presence, and the community would therefore advance, providing a measure of local ownership and control to its residents.[18] With this view the authors entered the debate that had begun in the 1960s over inner-city development policy. The mainstream view from liberal commentators was that inner-city, African American neighborhood development projects were self-defeating, a kind of "gilding the ghetto"; they would reduce the pressure for integration as opposed to dispersing the same populations into the larger metropolitan area, where schools and other facilities were more advantaged; and they would further increase the migration of southern blacks into northern cities, putting an intolerable strain on the cities' already-overburdened capacities to assimilate them.[19] Vietorisz and Harrison said the data disputed this argument, and provided support for those advocating community control.

Harrison, in a 1974 monograph, summarized and extended his argument, and gave a rationale for the newly emerging and still apparently promising initiatives from the many community development corporations that had begun operations in central cities, including Boston.[20] The attack on the inner-city development idea was strongly argued, but Harrison countered it: "Instead of thinking almost exclusively about reversing the rural-to-urban migration of nonwhite Americans, we should perhaps be giving more attention to the development of policies for helping the cities and their constituent communities to absorb their new immigrants." He followed up with an impressive review of the possibilities: cases of CDCs that were apparently developing manufacturing operations, and a review of investment possibilities that reflected the unsettled but still hopeful politics as the Nixon administration attempted to navigate the pockets of activism it faced from black militants, newly organizing white working-class areas, and the recently disenfranchised but still formidable liberal establishment. It was still possible, in a work that appeared in 1974, for Harrison to give overt consideration to the black claims for "reparation" and the debates for and against alternative ways to accomplish them.[21]

Eventually, after 1983, the community economic development (CED) infrastructure provided much of the model for an affordable-housing emphasis, which eventually overtook the job-creation enterprises that they—and King—had advocated. Tufts University professors Rachel Bratt and Kenneth Geiser, recounting the way this happened, listed a set of reasons: (1) Many of the early CDFC projects had ended in failure, with sixteen of twenty-five ventures liquidated or reorganized. (2) Job creation was also disappointing, with only 474 jobs created or retained through 1983. (3) There was frustration over finding the right kinds of business deals to finance. The community-economics advocates had begun with the idea that there were many deserving ideas, the problem being to find them financing (the role of CDFC) or technical assistance (CEDAC). What they learned was that "it is primarily the quality of the entrepreneur, not the business plan, that makes for a good investment. CEDAC staff discovered the lessons bankers learned years ago: management experience and expertise is indispensable and very hard to find. Community zeal can achieve great things but the delicate navigation of and single-minded attention to a business's health, like the expertise acquired by surgeons or highly trained workers, cannot be found or developed easily in most communities."[22]

In any event, efforts to create jobs within neighborhoods would have had a difficult time getting much political attention in the 1980s, when the Massachusetts economy was booming—the "Massachusetts miracle." A 1987 report to the Boston Redevelopment Authority (BRA) by Ann Greiner pointed out that the main economic problem in Boston at that time had become a shortage of highly skilled labor. This justified housing subsidies, according to the report.[23] This is indicative of the general atmosphere. Housing subsidies moved ahead in Boston. Job development was less important.

The Neighborhood Movement Grows

While King undertook the series of struggles chronicled in *Chain of Change,* a distinct if overlapping and complementary series of protests and organizing steps was occurring in Boston's neighborhoods. It had been growing since the 1960s, and it was broader than the communities of color. Dozens or hundreds of activists had poured into the city and settled in various neighborhoods, bringing with them their own ideas of community control. There was, by the time of the 1983 election, a more or less defined sense of confrontation between rich and poor, conservative and populist forces—the result of years of effort and intense discussion among many persons and groups. While a real estate development agenda had been sharply defined by the alliances between a business power structure and a series of mayors starting in the 1950s, symbolized in a series of urban-renewal and highway projects that had displaced hundreds or thousands of homes, it was now beginning to be seen as a problem, not progress. There developed an effective resistance.

In the background were a generally powerful student movement and an antiwar movement in the 1960s. A rent-control movement had culminated in the passage of legislation in Cambridge, Somerville, Lynn, and Boston in 1969–72, and this led to extensive tenant organizing. There was a series of protests against highway construction. An important early development was the creation of Urban Planning Aid (UPA) by a group of city planners and activists.[24] Its best-known effort was its successful organization of communities to stop construction of an "inner belt" highway through Cambridge, later leading to abandonment of more-extensive plans for an Interstate 95 connection through parts of Jamaica Plain, Roxbury, the South End, and Chinatown, finally convincing the state that the additional highway was not needed, and paving the way for relocation of the Washington Street rapid transit line to the corridor two decades later.[25] Arguably the more fundamental victory here was for the principle that neighborhoods could exert a measure of control over their own development futures. UPA continued operating in support of community groups through the 1970s, not just on the subject of highways, but other issues as well.[26]

Massachusetts Fair Share and Majoritarian Organizing

In varying degrees all of these initiatives related to a community-organizing history and tradition that had developed throughout the nation. Each group had to deal with the question of how rooted they could be with the mass of the population; and how to develop a productive interchange between popular sentiment and their own analysis of the society. The approach that had the most popular success in Boston was that adopted by Massachusetts Fair Share. Fair Share had its origins in Chelsea, a working-class city next to Boston, when Lee Staples joined with Mark Splain and Barbara Bowen to begin organizing in 1973.[27] After leaving the National Welfare Rights Organization in 1970, Staples had been in graduate school at UCLA, where he studied with Warren Haggstrom in the School of Social Welfare in an attempt to learn a more effective approach and methodology for community organizing. He remained in Los Angeles for an additional year doing community organizing that brought together both low- and moderate-income people across class lines. Staples and others had worked in welfare-rights organizing in Boston at the end of the 1960s. But the welfare-rights approach was not working, Staples said. "We were being isolated. The biggest backlash was really from white working-class people, and we decided to move to a majoritarian strategy." In Chelsea, the organizers determined to preserve all the good things about Welfare Rights—they wanted "something statewide," Staples said, "something militant and into direct action, to keep to the door-knocking, direct membership, local chapters, do the basically street-work kind of thing." They also wanted it to "be more democratic at all levels," he said, "more power vested with the leaders and less with the staff, and . . . some kind of self-funding mechanism." They became the first project of George Wiley's Movement for Economic Justice, which he spun off from Welfare Rights. Wiley, once a professor of chemistry at Syracuse University, founded the Syracuse Chapter of the Congress for Racial Equality (CORE) in the mid-1960s and later founded the National Welfare Rights Organization (1967). The Movement for Economic Justice (MEJ) was established in 1972 as a national support center to develop the majoritarian strategy.

It took two years, but they slowly developed credibility in Chelsea. They did "direct organizing," meaning bringing the population into meetings and knocking on doors to see what issues residents were concerned with. They won a fight to remove the tolls on the Mystic River Bridge that connected

Chelsea to Boston. They had successes on local issues and kept going, cutting across race and class lines and neighborhood lines. They had small grants from the Movement for Economic Justice and other foundations, but operated hand to mouth on a very small budget, and as Staples put it, "[we] put ourselves on and off unemployment" in order to survive.

But this was not enough. Wiley had been raising money through the Movement for Economic Justice, but he drowned in a boating accident in August of 1973. Despite successes like the Mystic Bridge victory, membership dues were inadequate to support the group in Chelsea. So they expanded. Staples moved out of Chelsea and went to Waltham, Barbara Bowen took the lead in East Boston, and Mark Splain stayed with Chelsea. Now they had three chapters. In 1974 they heard of an approach that raised funds through door-to-door canvassing for contributions in middle-class areas in Chicago. They adapted this model by canvassing for both donations and membership dues based on new organizing issue campaigns, such as fighting utility rate increases, that went beyond neighborhood concerns and cut across class lines. In the spring of 1974 canvassing "just took off like a shot," said Staples. "We went from a budget of $40,000 for our collective of five people to a staff of over a hundred and a budget of over a million in less than a year." New chapters were quickly established in blue collar cities in the Greater Boston area as the organization began to move toward its goal of becoming statewide." At about the same time, in August of 1974, Fair Share began a merger process with two other groups. The result brought in significant new leadership—Michael Ansara from the Boston Community School was one—but also shifted Fair Share to more of a hierarchical structure with foundation money coming in and a "huge staff." The organization "grew real fast, particularly around utilities stuff and property tax issues."[28]

But now Massachusetts Fair Share, established in a number of places, and with a strong financial base from canvassing and foundation and government grants that came with the canvassing success, experienced a series of contradictory developments. While Fair Share chapters were only established in working class areas, "at large" members who joined by virtue of money collected by door-to-door canvassers often came from wealthier suburban communities. Some of the organizers felt that the canvassing approach began to drive the selection of organizational issue campaigns, compromising their commitment to the poor, largely African American constituencies they had originally sought to organize going back to Wiley's Movement for Economic Justice. Staples put this point well:

Those issues which played well for canvassing purposes in the suburbs and were not unprogressive or whatever; but they weren't necessarily

low-income people's issues....It's complex, but essentially the organization moved to become almost a white, lower middle-class, upper
strata of the working class, homeowners' organization. That's an over-
statement, but it was certainly not a low-income, poor peoples' organization; although still rhetorically committed to a majoritarian strategy.
It just so happened that the "majority" was leaving out the concerns of
low income people of color in the inner city....So it wasn't like there
was ever a majoritarian strategy played out there.[29]

Meanwhile there was no question the organization was effective. It continued to grow, and it seemed to be an important instrument for "progressive" and leftist causes. But by 1977, there began to be some turnover. Staples
decided to retire, and began to work on an abandoned house he bought in
Hopkinton, where his wife was a teacher. Mark Splain stepped down as staff
director and asked Michael Ansara to take over, then moved into Staples's
position as director of Metro, the unit that oversaw organizing in the towns
around Boston. Staples came back after a few months to start a citywide
Fair Share chapter in Worcester. Splain and Barbara Bowen began to align
themselves with ACORN—more of a poor people's group—and brought
Staples into a new initiative called WAGE—Workers Association to Gain
Employment—which eventually spun off of Fair Share.

But there was also a level of solidarity. Staples's recollection was of dis-
agreement among solid friends ("a lot of debate, like these guys are friends,
right?"). And Fair Share's momentum continued. Michael Ansara recalled
that it avoided an open split.[30] Throughout the late 1970s and into the 1980s,
canvassing brought in members and funding, and made Fair Share a credible
voice for a part of the public that politicians and interest groups needed to
listen to. Partly for this reason, other sources of funding appeared. In the
years 1977–80, the Carter administration was in Washington, and Carter
had created an Office of Neighborhoods in HUD and appointed former
activist Sam Brown to head VISTA. At the time of the merger that created
Fair Share as a statewide organization in 1975, the Catholic Campaign for
Human Development provided funding. The figures are not necessarily reli-
able, but Fair Share's budget went from its $1 million claim in 1975, to $2.3
and then $2.8 million in the early 1980s.

Starting at the end of 1981 the organization began to suffer financial
problems as it failed to control expenditures and suffered actions from creditors and the Internal Revenue Service. Fair Share stopped paying withhold-
ing to the IRS, and in 1982 paychecks were late. Ansara was unable to get
accurate accounting from his staff, and a 1983 external audit found that

Fair Share had not kept books for six months. No one knew how much the organization owed, or to what creditors. Ansara took the blame and resigned in August 1983.[31] But the organization retained assets and had political momentum well into the 1980s.

Other Groups

Fair Share was the most prominent of the activist groups of the late 1970s and early 1980s, and perhaps exemplified the class and race issues that affected many of them. In carrying the "movement" into middle-class and white neighborhoods and cities, they represented interests that varied from those—like ACORN—that focused more on the inner-city blacks.

Certainly, some of the other groups in Boston's neighborhoods took a more systemic look at their problems than most in Fair Share or other populists did: they looked at the underlying structure of inequality and power and found it difficult to work with Fair Share. Fair Share and many other groups, hoping to meet the middle and working class on their own ground, restricted themselves to issues they could get majority assent to in the neighborhood. As Alinsky had argued, these tended to be mundane pocketbook issues—utility rates, toxic pollution, tenants' issues—with not much common denominator other than a kind of general class anger at the powerful. Some of the other groups had a more extensive analysis.[32]

CDCs: Movement as Institution

By the 1980s, many neighborhood-level groups had already been providing services of various kinds and had begun to move into real estate development: housing rehabilitation, sometimes new development on vacant land, occasionally commercial development. They varied in how they approached politics, and in the extent to which they maintained a participatory approach to their clienteles. Some were born in the 1960s and 1970s in the struggles King recounted in *Chain of Change*. Others were spin-offs of the student and antiwar organizing at the end of the 1960s. Illustrative of the different trajectories of these organizations are three prominent ones: City Life, Dudley Street Neighborhood Initiative (DSNI), and Urban Edge.

City Life

City Life, which never quite evolved into a production-oriented CDC, began with a core of four women activists in Charlestown, who sought to tie their own theoretical analyses of economic crisis to a multiracial working-class constituency, and who engaged people with skills in demography to help them select the community that would be most promising for their work.

In 1971 they settled on Jamaica Plain. They started a bookstore from which they put out the *Jamaica Plain Weekly War Bulletin,* which they leafleted on streets on the weekends, and they tried to get people involved in tenant organizing. Like Staples and the Chelsea organizers, they lived on temporary jobs and on unemployment. They formed the Tenant Action Group in 1973 and operated in parallel with other such organizations as the Somerville Tenant Union and the Coalition for Rent Control. It was part of a rich environment of activism. Steve Fahrer, one of the group's organizers, recalled there were "groups that had a tenants' organization, that had a newspaper—some of them were related to food co-ops, some of them did other things, in almost every neighborhood.... Almost all of the groups really believed in people before profit."[33]

The Tenant Action Group soon became City Life. Kathy McAfee, one of the original founders, said, "We soon had a labor committee, a workplace committee.... We had a women's committee.... We were working some on welfare issues and some on education issues."[34]

In the early 1980s, after ten years as an informal group held together by their beliefs more than material accomplishments, they became a more formal entity, creating a steering committee, which they thought of as their core group, plus a set of committees oriented to particular topics. But they never became a formal community development corporation. They found ways to operate together with other, more formally organized CDCs to do housing development for poor people in the area. The issues had changed. McAfee, in an appendix to an article she had written ten years earlier, said the "1980s [was] a decade of economic resurgence, [while] the 1970s [was] a decade of disinvestment."[35] Now the problem was increasing prices, and the changes were coming too fast to adjust to. Steve Fahrer said, "There were times that you didn't go downtown for two months, [then] you'd go [and] look and there'd be like buildings missing. Or there would be new ones.... It was incredible.[36]

Meanwhile there were homeless people on the streets in Jamaica Plain. City Life participated in efforts to provide affordable housing. They helped rehab a former school building, taking advantage—with great difficulty—when the Flynn administration decided to make surplus facilities available for nonprofits to do housing. When the Flynn administration set up neighborhood councils, City Life was able to draw on its relationships and organizing skills to win seats on the new body. Fahrer thought efforts like this gave them credibility with the Flynn administration. In the 1990s they were still publishing a neighborhood newspaper in English and Spanish, and were still vigorous in an advocacy role at the end of the decade.

DSNI

Boston's most famous community development organization was the Dudley Street Neighborhood Initiative (DSNI) in Roxbury.[37] Roxbury had other community organizations, including the mainly Latino Nuestra Comunidad and La Alianza Hispana, and the mainly African American Roxbury Multi-Service Center, but all of these had been operating in relatively narrow service-delivery roles into the early 1980s, while the disinvestment and decline of the larger Roxbury area accelerated. Other Roxbury organizations like the Greater Roxbury Neighborhood Authority (GRNA) took on more of an advocacy role, and some of their leaders were prominent in the Rainbow Coalition that supported King's mayoral campaign in 1983.

DSNI had its origins in 1984 when La Alianza Hispana and Nuestra Comunidad CDC put on a community-search conference to do a strategic plan, with MIT's help. In 1981 Roxbury Community College had done a community survey, and La Alianza had sponsored an MIT class plan for the area. The La Alianza director at the time, Nelson Merced, seeking funding to rehab La Alianza's building, contacted the Riley Foundation, which was looking for a project; Riley trustees toured La Alianza and met with Melvyn Colon, director of Nuestra Comunidad. La Alianza and Nuestra Comunidad met with Riley, which had decided to commit major funds ($2 million), and constituted the Dudley Advisory Group. In October they defined boundaries, and in November set up a governance structure representing mainly organizations, with four community members out of a twenty-three-member board, which they planned to bring to a general community meeting early in 1985.

Early 1985 became a time of great consternation in the Dudley area when the BRA leaked its own plan there.[38] One result was that when in February the Dudley Advisory Group convened its large meeting to get community support for the Riley-backed DSNI, there was an unexpected response: grassroots leadership emerged and pressured successfully for a different governance structure, with a majority of board members elected from the community. Through a sequence of events, resident control strengthened. A resident, Che Madyun, became board president the following November, indicating the shift from social-agency to community-resident control. That winter DSNI used Riley Foundation funds to hire Peter Medoff, an organizer who had worked in Hartford, as leader of a professional staff, and he began work in March 1986.

Medoff's approach was more that of an organizer than a technical planner. DSNI hired Andrea Nagel as organizer, and Medoff and Nagel knocked on hundreds of doors. They found the key issue residents cared about was trash dumping on dozens of vacant lots in the area. In response, Medoff and Nagel created a campaign they named "Don't Dump on Us," and through a great deal of organizing they eventually got the city to pitch in with tools to help residents do cleanups, prosecute lot owners who did illegal dumping, and tow away abandoned cars.[39]

Later, DSNI undertook physical reconstruction of the neighborhood. They did a plan for an "urban village" center using extensive resident input and blocking city efforts at faster but less sensitive development. In a major development that got national publicity, DSNI received a precedent-setting delegation of city eminent-domain power to acquire vacant lots in the plan area, created a land trust that could keep housing permanently affordable and capture the increment in value for the community, and eventually developed hundreds of units of new housing.

DSNI became famous, though, less for the quantity of development than for the quality of participation. Its governance, in particular, had unique features. First, there was essential resident control rather than the staff-led form that was common in organizations. Second, DSNI was formally multiethnic. The population of its area was roughly 40 percent black, 30 percent Latino, 20 percent Cape Verdean, and 10 percent white. But the DSNI bylaws gave each group equal representation on the board. They also got translation equipment with headsets so that public meetings could be conducted in the three represented languages: English, Spanish, and Cape Verdean Creole, and the DSNI newsletter was also published in the three languages.[40]

DSNI was fortunate in its leadership, which was sophisticated in the nuances of participatory management and resident control. Medoff resigned in 1988, to be followed by Gus Newport, former mayor of Berkeley, California. Newport led DSNI through the tortuous tangle of financing and delays that characterize many CDC initiatives. Eminent domain was a tool that gave DSNI a starting advantage, but it needed funding to acquire the land. Soon the Ford Foundation approved a $2 million loan, impressed by the city's innovative grant of eminent-domain power, the comprehensiveness of the urban-village plan, and the citizen input. The funding was to bring the plan to fruition, particularly five hundred units of affordable housing. Newport resisted pressure to omit community elements, which extended the time beyond the 1991 target that had been set by Lisa Chapnick, director of the Boston Department of Public Facilities and Development (PFD)—another partner—responsible for zoning approvals. There was tension with Ford over DSNI's lack of developer experience, and with PFD over missing the deadline. All of these organizations had their own credibility invested in the DSNI scheme, and there were a large number of elements that had to be coordinated for the deal to go ahead. Ford finally delivered the check on June 24, 1992. Housing units and the urban-village center were built at various points through the 1990s.

Later, DSNI was still taking a comprehensive view.[41] By the mid-1990s its third director, Greg Watson, who had been commissioner of agriculture for the state, pursued other aspects of the DSNI vision in addition to housing. In one account, its economic-development side would include "a block-large bioshelter, up to three acres, where residents could grow produce and perhaps even fish for neighborhood restaurants and a permanent farmer's market."[42]

Urban Edge

Other CDCs lacked the sort of ideological commitment evidenced by City Life, or the elaborate participatory commitment of DSNI, but rather mastered the technical and real estate know-how to produce ever-larger numbers of housing units. Urban Edge, in Jamaica Plain, was one of the most visible of these. It was begun by Ron Hafer in 1974, and started out constructing new units for sale. In 1986 it moved its headquarters several blocks south to Eggleston Square, a heavily impacted neighborhood on Washington Street, where the elevated Orange Line was about to be dismantled, and began investing in rental housing. By the mid-1990s it was managing over nine hundred rental units and had been through two iterations of related community organizing and services provision.[43]

Urban Edge wasn't just doing housing. It was organizing its own tenants, and even creating tensions between the central staff and its organizing unit, which was finding demands not only for social services, like day care and health facilities—which it then promoted—but also for better landlord services, like fixing up their own units. Urban Edge then became associated with a general economic revival of the Eggleston Square area. They became known as nonideological, and were recognized in the press for filling in the gap between activists and city hall, and for getting things done: "Activists had to give up their disdain for capitalism.... City Hall had to give up some of its control over neighborhood improvement workers; many wound up on the payroll of Urban Edge."[44]

This was a different approach than that of City Life or DSNI, a kind of humanized capitalism, but Urban Edge's way became more the rule than the exception in the 1980s.

Busing

But all of this was confounded—probably coarsened is the right word—by the busing controversy, centered in South Boston, in the middle of the 1970s. Boston schools had been de facto racially segregated, and in 1972 civil rights lawyers brought a class-action suit against the Boston School Committee in federal court, seeking redress. Judge Arthur Garrity's ruling in 1974 required that blacks and other minorities be bused to previously mainly white schools. In South Boston, violence erupted as the population resisted. Once resistance occurred, it became a matter of principle to either defeat or uphold the judicial ruling. Mel King was quoted as having doubts about the wisdom of busing but threw his support to black schoolchildren when it was clear that they saw the problem as one of principle:

> It was hard not to wonder if we were doing the right thing. There were times when students had something to teach us. I will never forget a conversation I had with a 15-year-old student assigned to South Boston High. "We have to go," she declared with passion. "If they run us out of that school, they can run us out of the city. They will be able to stop access whenever they want."[45]

The busing controversy consumed Boston. Resistance to the threat of busing became an issue that candidates for the school committee ran on, starting most famously with Louise Day Hicks in the early 1960s. Hicks and others fanned the flames of white populist sentiment, and the school committee steadfastly resisted pressures to integrate schools that were racially imbalanced. There was a buildup of pressure on the school committee, from blacks within the city who began to organize protests, petitions, and occasional school boycotts, and from liberals both inside and outside the city. Some noted parallels to the struggle for school desegregation in Selma, Alabama, a decade earlier. As in the South, there were elites in Boston with a stake in the status quo; there was political and institutional leadership that sought to avoid the issue; there were working-class whites who saw little point in accommodating black demands for equal rights and services; and there was, among outsiders, the slow buildup of outrage at continued segregation. All of these were precipitating forces.

Starting long before Garrity's ruling, school committee politics had been a magnet for a kind of populist anger, with civil rights protest interpreted, in white working-class neighborhoods, as elitist and externally imposed. In Boston, with bastions of white privilege located across the Charles River at MIT and Harvard, this was easy to do. Hicks ran for a spot on the school committee on an "us against them" platform starting in the 1960s, and on occasion she outpolled candidates for mayor. Civil rights demonstrations brought out her voters. "The more they march," she said, "the more I win."[46]

This populist ascendance came in the context of polarization: white—often liberal—elite power, and the slow development of minority voices. As for the first, working-class people in Boston had only to look at the rise of office development in the downtown and the increases in congestion and new professional employment that was driving up housing prices. Or they could look toward the growing university and medical presence, or the prominent university growth at Harvard and MIT across the Charles River.

Meanwhile, the 1950s and 1960s saw the painfully slow development of minority voices. Ronald Formisano observed how the "young professional blacks moving into Boston in the 1950s waged an uphill battle to politicize the apathetic rank and file. Ruth Batson...Paul Parks, Melvin King, Rev. James Breedon, Thomas Simmons, Thomas Atkins, and Ellen Jackson."

But, Formisano added,

> In Massachusetts and Boston, as in the nation, two different currents flowed through the middle 1960s. One was liberal, optimistic, cosmopolitan, universalist and pro-integration, while the other was reactive, fearful, localist, in part anti-integration and anti-black, and in part opposed to change, any change, of which there seemed to be a great deal in the mid-1960s.[47]

By the 1980s, when King and Flynn tapped neighborhood protest to finish tied for first and second in the September 1983 preliminary election, many were exhausted from the conflicts over schools and ready for constructive programs attacking other neighborhood problems. But destructive legacies of the school issue remained.

One of these was the diminished hope that "black and white together" could solve urban problems. Writing of a radio talk-show exchange between civil rights lawyer and NAACP leader Thomas Atkins and a suburban caller after Martin Luther King's assassination in 1968, Anthony Lukas found dramatic words to describe the situation:

> The next caller was a woman from Lexington, the suburban community.... Hers was a smooth, cultivated voice with that waft of extra breath characteristic of Yankee Massachusetts. But this afternoon it was an agonized voice as well: "Everyone out here feels terrible about

this," she said. "Please tell us, Mr. Atkins, what can we do to help you? What can we do for the Negro community?"

For a moment there was silence. Then, his voice rumbling in the lower registers, choosing his words carefully, Atkins began: "Right now, there's nothing you can do for us. Right now, it isn't even safe for you to come in here. Right now, the best thing you can do is leave us alone and let us try to get our act together. If I may say so, what you ought to do is to go back to your own community and try to get your people together. Try to get them to start caring, to start responding, to start looking at themselves, at their own motivations and attitudes on the matter of race. Before you can do anything for us, you have to look into your own souls."[48]

Lukas was setting the scene here, describing the perceptions of his chief white liberal (and elite) protagonist, Colin Diver, six years before Garrity's 1974 ruling and the peak years of the busing crisis. But Atkins's advice was a general theme in race relations over the decade before and after. Such advice had become common usage among black and white activists after the frustrations of the Student Nonviolent Coordinating Committee (SNCC) "Freedom Summer" project in 1964. Whites, having been invited to participate in that heroic campaign and having bought into the "beloved community" ideals where black and white together would work, nonviolently, for a "just and equal society," came to understand the frustrations of blacks at the failures of white society to protect their legitimate activities in Mississippi, and most centrally the failure of the Democratic Party to seat the Mississippi Freedom Democratic Party delegates at the presidential nominating convention in Atlantic City that year.[49]

One of the ways white activists and other liberals resolved the conflict between their own desire to move toward the "just and equal society" together, as integrated communities, and what they saw as the legitimate need for blacks to move ahead separately was to see what seemed a race problem as really one of "class." Lukas found the words for it, characterizing Diver at the end of the 1970s:

As the decade wore on, Colin came to perceive the "American dilemma" less in purely racial and legal terms, more in class and economic terms. Wherever he looked, he saw legal remedies undercut by social and economic realities, Eventually, he believed, the fundamental solution to the problems of a city like Boston lay in economic development. Only by providing jobs and other economic opportunities for the deprived—black and white alike—could the city reduce the deep sense of grievance harbored by both communities, alleviate some of the antisocial behavior grounded in such resentments and begin to close the terrible gap between the rich and the poor, the suburb and the city, the hopeful and the hopeless.[50]

These conclusions would not have satisfied all of the Boston activists. But they probably fit the consciousness of the majority.[51]

The 1983 Campaign

Thus a key movement background in Boston was the schisms between blacks and whites. This was significant for organizers. Since organizers and activists had to generate support from grassroots constituencies, issues that divided constituencies had the potential to divide the organizers. Many were committed to the ideal of a multiracial approach to their goals. But race would at best be divisive, and the peculiar history of school integration in the 1970s was a big challenge. The role of the organizers, politicians, and voters on the left in Boston politics in the 1980s has to be seen as shaped by this background.

Thus the 1983 mayoral election had a double twist that made it different from earlier ones. There was a newly vigorous element of neighborhood protest, and it was potentially divided along race lines. The early front-runner was David I. Finnegan, who had served as school committee president and was well known as radio talk-show host. He was a fiscal conservative, had financial backing from business, and had been in the race since March. In May the incumbent, Kevin White, unpopular after four terms in office, announced he would not run for reelection, and by the summer there was a nine-person slate of candidates in the mid-October preliminary election, from which the top two vote getters (failing an absolute majority for any one) would face off in November. Finnegan was the consensus leader through mid-September, when a poll showed him slipping into a tie with Flynn and King.

The poll results jarred the contest and began to mobilize "moderate" opinion. *Boston Globe* reporters and columnists reported dismay, then a lack of consensus among "business" spokespersons. The dismay was directed at Flynn, seen as not competent by some, though most preferred to report a lack of consensus in the face of a populist surge, represented not only by the Flynn support but by support for King, seen as even further to the left.[52] In the preliminary election on September 11, both populists, King and Flynn, had the plurality, within 270 votes of one another, each with 29 percent of the vote, with Finnegan third at 25 percent, and thus eliminated.

Next came a new focus on King, reflecting an upsurge in notice of his conciliatory role in the state legislature, his consistency of positions, and his discard of radical dress styles (dashikis) in favor of business suits. There was also discussion of whether King could win, which translated to the question of whether the city was "ready" for a black mayor. Most thought not, but at least some in the press threw their support to King. It seemed the city was hopeful that the election, if not a King victory, could help the city put the ordeal of the busing crisis of the previous decade behind it.

The candidates reinforced, even led this mind-set. It was a far cry from the previous decade's school committee elections, when some South Boston candidates won elections attacking busing and defending neighborhood schools, coded race cards that attracted White House support.[53] King, reaching out to white voters, made the argument that "race discrimination hurts everyone." Flynn was attacked by Finnegan in the final run-up to the preliminary election for passing out different flyers in black neighborhoods, but it served only to dramatize Finnegan's slippage in the polls, and Flynn's message on race—"Let us focus on the issues (housing, class inequality) that unite us, not those that divide us"—resonated with the larger city population.

The debates and shifting fortunes of the preliminary election engaged the electorate. King mobilized the black neighborhoods, and the turnout in those neighborhoods was over 60 percent, the highest in decades. And between King and Flynn, the two distinct approaches to race were aired. King argued the city ought to confront racism openly and forthrightly: "It's important that we begin with the term 'racism' because if we don't, we are not going to come to the kinds of solutions to the problem that Boston requires." And King said, "I think we needed [busing] because people were being denied access to housing... because of the color of their skins."[54]

In addition to race, and elaborating on the argument in *Chain of Change,* King also adopted the "rainbow" approach, one that expanded from his earlier focus on blacks to embrace other excluded constituencies, so that his coalition was, according to a *Globe* column, a "collection of blacks, whites, Hispanics, homosexuals and women."[55] King's message balanced respect for the separateness of each element with a hope for transcending the gulfs between them. Later he described how he came to think about the "rainbow" idea. After working with these groups, he "noticed there was a kind of common issue, namely, how do you overcome the effects of a political process and its structures that deny access to these groups?"[56]

Another main feature of the campaign was the neighborhood focus. King had built a reputation around concerns for more global issues. In the 1983 campaign he was to bring these down to earth: "Most of my work had been around issues, yet obviously the people with the issues lived in those neighborhoods."[57]

Flynn, whose initial base was the white working-class South Boston neighborhood, asked that people put "social issues" aside. He did not suggest that questions of race, sexual preference, or abortion were unimportant, simply that people in the city unite around those which they had in common, which he thought were class issues: Could the city focus on the distribution of wealth, he asked, by supporting tenants, building affordable housing, and channeling funds into neighborhood facilities?[58] A *Boston Globe* article encapsulated the contrast: while King wanted to talk about racism, "Flynn refused to accept the racist label on Boston. . . . 'The real problem is economic discrimination,' [Flynn said,]. . . . 'We have to share some of the [downtown] economic wealth into the neighborhoods.'"[59]

Boston organizers and activists had a chance to choose what approach to take on the issue of racial justice during the 1983 mayoral campaign. Flynn, who had been identified with the South Boston antibusing activists a decade earlier, took the view that economic oppression affected both blacks and whites, and all should focus on those issues. Housing and jobs would be the central pieces of his campaign. Pragmatically, Flynn had a base in the South Boston Irish constituency and needed to reach out to liberals and activists beyond that base. The result was awkward for many people.

But King did not resonate with many who might otherwise have supported either. One (black) who supported Flynn said: "[King] was arrogant. He wanted to hang on to the dashiki. But that era had passed. In the 1960s you could get by with Black is Beautiful. But this was the 1980s."[60]

There were many who thought it would be pragmatically necessary to support Flynn, on the premise that a black would never win. It did not generally get put that way in print. Instead, the sentiment of (white) Flynn supporters was that he could better "reach out"—presumably to white reactionaries—and pull the city together racially. This ended up as the *Globe*'s main argument when it endorsed Flynn: "We see in Flynn's campaign a greater willingness to reach out, to include diverse elements in the decision-making process, to compromise with others on the difficult problems facing Boston."[61] Judy Meredith, at Flynn's victory celebration, said she believed he could best bridge the gap between the races in Boston because of his own background in conservative South Boston. Racism is more of a white problem than a black one, she said.[62]

King's supporters saw "reaching out" differently. University of Massachusetts–Boston historian James Green dismissed the focus on economic issues alone with a succinct statement: "People of color couldn't choose whether or not to make racism an issue, like the white organizers did. If you were black in Boston you couldn't escape the issue."[63] In a *Boston Globe* op-ed, Green summarized the case for electing King: "Mel King has already taken his campaign beyond populism...not by ignoring racism and bigotry, but by insisting that everyone is hurt by discrimination."[64]

It was in vain. Flynn took 66 percent of the vote. The campaign, however, remained a treasure in the city's memory. Michael Kane, a neighborhood activist who had supported King, was nevertheless most charitable toward Flynn: "They elected the two most pro-neighborhood people as finalists and then what followed was...probably unique in American history, where you had two from a major city who were basically out-lefting each other. You know, where the DSA position was the right-wing position." In the neighborhood forums, he said, "You were hearing different theories of community empowerment and organizing....It was really an education for the whole populace."[65]

When the results came in, the two campaigns said the right things. King, conceding defeat, said, "Sounds like there are two winners tonight." And Flynn put on a King button, "in full view of the television cameras."[66]

✒ CHAPTER 4

Flynn's City Hall and the Neighborhoods

Flynn now had the challenge of governing the city. Later, Neil Sullivan wrote that "many presumed that Ray Flynn would be a one-term mayor." Despite the surge of neighborhood activism that had propelled Flynn and King to prominence in 1983, the city was divided between downtown and the neighborhoods: real estate and developer interests, a deficit in liberal votes on the city council, and a more generally conservative ideology on the part of much of Boston's population were always in the background as Flynn began his administration and considered his policy options. Finances were in crisis, with limits imposed by the recently passed Proposition 2½ property tax cap, and city services and infrastructure had suffered the effects of years of budget cutting.[1]

One can ask the effect of the scars of racial conflict, which had so involved the city's attention in the 1970s busing conflict and its aftermath. Good feelings and the relative civility of the campaign might have been cause for optimism. Some Flynn supporters thought of the possibility of enlisting King, hoping for a rapprochement between the two leaders since there was much in common. There were reports of an offer of a position in the city administration to King, and another to King ally Ken Wade.[2]

But issues of race would have to be confronted amid the reality of administration and governing, which Flynn, not King or the Rainbow Coalition, would now confront. Nothing came of any overtures to King or Wade. As

Flynn administrators recalled years later, race issues were in the background rather than the foreground of their immediate concerns moving into City Hall. Still thinking, perhaps, in the "majoritarian" frame Staples and others had elaborated on when speaking of Fair Share, they would tell the story of the Flynn administration—a remarkable one—in a race-neutral way. Issues would arise, and they would deal with them as best they could, pragmatically.

Initial Steps: 1984–85

Flynn pushed ahead. Regardless of any hopes for rapprochement, the new administration also faced the juxtaposition of political forces in a more traditional sense: the relatively organized developers with substantial profits in sight on the one hand, and the relatively diverse and unorganized but powerfully felt neighborhood interests on the other. The real estate industry, anxious to capitalize on increased office and housing demand, was well organized in the Greater Boston Real Estate Board and waited anxiously as Flynn delayed deciding whether to approve eleven "pipeline projects" (major downtown office projects that had been awaiting city action) for construction, and the city's business constituency watched to see whether Flynn would be "antigrowth."

Transcending the administrative and finance questions and the developer interests was Flynn's own sense of the neighborhood constituency, and the two nonbinding referenda that had been put on the ballot by Mass Fair Share and passed with great majorities in the November 1983 election—one for "linkage" and the other for "neighborhood councils" (NCs). Linkage was an idea that had surfaced at about this time in a few other places—San Francisco most notably—that cities, facing costs imposed by major real estate development, could require developers to compensate by paying a per-square-foot fee into a city-controlled trust fund, usually for affordable housing.[3] The Boston ballot proposal would "require developers to rehabilitate, develop, or partially fund one unit of low- to medium-cost housing for each unit or luxury housing created, or for every 1,000 square feet of office or hotel space that is placed on the market." The neighborhood councils' proposal was for "democratically selected neighborhood councils, . . . which could 'approve, initiate, or veto new development in their neighborhoods.'"[4] Both King and Flynn had supported linkage but opposed the neighborhood councils referendum because of the veto-power provision.

But Flynn's first moves were on neither the neighborhood-oriented referenda nor the developer questions. First was the need to act on a campaign promise to "clean house" after the sixteen years of the White administration and simply to deliver services, and finance them. There were serious problems in the schools and with the police; and the city budget was in deficit—there would have to be cutbacks in city jobs. There was little to be done immediately about some of these, and Flynn would delegate others. But finances loomed large. He had to create some financial room to maneuver before the policy challenges he was elected to confront could even begin to get serious attention.

He did clean house: Neil Sullivan "got the interesting assignment of telling 36 people that they were no longer needed. . . . We released all but three department heads. . . . We were elected to change the government at the top and that included department heads."[5] At the same time, Flynn needed to confront the policy questions. He would not present a purely populist government, concerned only with the needs of the neighborhoods and the city's working class. He conceived his task as a larger one: he needed to convince bankers and developers that he supported development, while not betraying his populist neighborhood roots.[6] This would be a tightrope act. Boston history and that of cities generally is replete with mayors who began with populist rhetoric, only to find themselves in the hands of local real estate interests for whom the neighborhoods came second. The outgoing mayor, Kevin White, was an example.

Thus, Flynn might easily have moved to the right as time went on. Instead, he and his top aides saw the problem as *both* to nurture the real estate boom (the golden goose) and extract from it sufficient resources to help the neighborhoods. How this played out would dominate policy through Flynn's first two terms.

Staffing

One could see these double aims in Flynn's first round of appointments in 1984. In this—encouraging both the neighborhoods and the developers—Flynn gave central roles to the white populist Left: he hired key personnel from Mass Fair Share and other "movement" organizations, like Ray Dooley and Neil Sullivan, but not from the Rainbow Coalition.

Thus, people from the neighborhood movement and allied organizations were to take key positions, not only in an Office of Neighborhoods but also in staff positions within his inner circle in city hall. In one retrospective account there were "only four top aides—two on the right and two on the left—who consult with Flynn most frequently. . . . Dooley and Sullivan are considered liberals, while executive assistant Joseph Fisher and operations director Robert Consalvo are viewed as conservatives." Those on the left were quickly labeled the "Sandinistas." The "conservatives"—and the press—were not always comfortable with the leftists. The conservatives called themselves the "real Americans," said Sullivan, who nevertheless looked back on them with affection and respect, and with a measure of pride at the way these disparate elements had found a way to mesh.[7]

At the top, in addition, Flynn made appointments from outside or from other backgrounds. One—to the Department of Traffic and Parking in March—was Lisa Chapnick, who later rose to prominence as head of the Department of Public Facilities and Development (PFD). Flynn recruited her at age thirty-five from the state department of economic affairs. For the head of the Boston Redevelopment Authority (BRA), the key planning and development agency, he chose Stephen Coyle, thirty-eight, who was working in San Francisco for an architecture firm, had been at HUD in the Carter administration, and had previously directed housing departments in Waltham and Dedham.[8] Coyle was in city hall by the end of June. These were high-quality appointments, capable of bridging the development and neighborhood constituencies.

Flynn's most important initial appointment was his campaign manager, Ray Dooley. He gave Dooley the choice of director of the Boston Redevelopment Authority or director of administrative services. Dooley chose the latter, fateful because it kept him close to the mayor in city hall and gave him the broadest possible scope. Dooley, in the end, both settled the city's finance issues and managed the coordination of interests that Flynn had put together. Other progressives in city hall called Dooley the architect of a coalition of Flynn's South Boston conservative roots and the "Sandinistas" from Fair Share and other leftist-movement organizations.

Dooley had "enormous influence" as director of administrative services, according to Dreier. "He was, in effect, the CFO [chief financial officer] for the entire city government." He was, said Neil Sullivan, "incredibly smart," and he figured out a way to solve the city's financial problems—a "structural deficit" that resulted from the government's dependence on local banking for finance. Dooley, said Sullivan, simply found a way to break the local-finance monopoly by getting loans from New York banks. This was critical for spending programs and other innovations that those on the left supported.[9]

Dreier stressed Dooley's movement style: "Ray was an organizer.... What made the Flynn administration so effective was that it was like a permanent organizing campaign." They looked at issues for their potential to organize support or defeat opposition. They identified targets—"enemies, like the Greater Boston Real Estate Board, or the banks that redlined Boston neighborhoods, or Presidents Reagan and Bush, and allies, working the press, mobilizing people to protest when necessary, etc."[10]

Certainly there was a critical mass from the left that made it possible for Flynn to govern as an organizer, to pursue his development objectives and fulfill other campaign promises in the interest of the city's working-class neighborhoods. One of these was Neil Sullivan, who had recently left Fair Share and involved himself heavily in the mayoral campaign. He was, with Dooley, one of Flynn's first-announced appointments, initially as head of a new Office of Neighborhood Services but soon to be city policy director, chief implementer from the left along with Dooley. He was from Detroit, went to Amherst College, and was working at Fair Share in the late 1970s. He left that organization in 1982 and was introduced to Flynn by the former Fair Share organizer Alex Bledsoe. Sullivan recalled meeting Flynn: "We ended up with a two-hour conversation about Detroit where I grew up and, you know, Mayor Cavanaugh and everything I grew up with as a kid, and he offered me a job."[11]

Another early appointee and important progressive voice in Flynn's administration was Peter Dreier, a journalism major from Syracuse University, formerly an assistant professor of sociology at Tufts, and a lead organizer with the Massachusetts Tenants Organization, one of the main forces in the city's neighborhoods. Dreier attached himself to the Flynn campaign and soon made himself indispensable for his expertise in housing and as a writer of press releases, speeches, and articles ranging from short op-eds to scholarly accounts of what Flynn was attempting to achieve. Dreier, who had recently been the main producer of *Who Rules Boston?*, a programmatic statement released under the aegis of the local Democratic Socialists of America (DSA), was a member of the mayor's "inner circle," Sullivan said, because "Flynn liked him," and because he could "write faster than God."[12]

Development Policy

Flynn had many issues to deal with, but real estate development policy, and the potential conflicts between it and neighborhood people seeking to keep their quality of life up and their rents down, were close to the top of the agenda because of the development boom throughout the 1980s and because Flynn had immersed himself in the issue as a city council member prior to 1983. He had to establish a program that got the support of, or at least defused opposition from, the downtown and business interests; he also had to contend with a city council that was decidedly to the right of his own sentiments and the program his new advisers would want to put in place. Flynn and his staff recognized the potential of the real estate investment in the city's downtown but were also determined to tap that in the interest of the neighborhoods. On the surface, and given the 2–1 majorities for the Fair Share linkage and neighborhood councils referenda, it looked like there would be significant support. But the community organizations were in some disarray after the election. Many had supported King over Flynn. Fair Share was decimated by financial shortfalls. Some of the most capable community activists went to work for the city, leaving their organizations to find new blood.

Flynn pushed ahead with the "populist" strategy as a plausible way to smooth the seams of the racially divided neighborhood constituency: replace talk of racial division with talk of economic division, shift the economic issue from growth *versus* redistribution to growth *with* redistribution.[13] This may have been more subtle than it seems in hindsight. During the campaign, and through the previous White administration, the perception was that the developers simply wanted growth. For decades, the mantra for government interventionists had been a version of "a rising tide lifts all ships." In contrast, what the neighborhood populists saw was "trickle down"—an epithet for promises destined never to be redeemed. For them, the alternative was redistribution, pure and simple, through rent control or public subsidies of various sorts, including for housing the poor.

For a time in 1984, Dreier used his position in city hall to develop a "left" alternative built around the revival of rent control. Had it succeeded, this might have been the leading element in the "redistribution" part of the growth package. Boston had adopted rent control in 1969 for all private rental housing except owner-occupied two- and three-unit buildings. But in 1975 the city had weakened the law by instituting vacancy decontrol, and the number of controlled units fell from over one hundred thousand to fewer than twenty-five thousand by 1983; and condominium conversions and evictions—and landlord-initiated arson—led to tenant protests. Flynn had committed himself to a return to full rent control and either a ban on evictions for condo conversion or a ban on conversions per se. Flynn sought a dramatic package of legislation in June 1984, expanding coverage from twenty thousand to eighty-five thousand units and giving the Rent Equity Board authority to regulate condominium conversions.[14] This would be an uphill fight in city council, which defeated its main provisions early in October.

But by that time, Coyle had become part of the answer. Developers had waited impatiently for the city to find a new director for the BRA, when some resolution could be expected on the eleven "pipeline" projects. Kevin White, the previous mayor, had designated the projects for approval at the end of 1983, and these awaited Flynn's action throughout most of 1984. Developers and others with interests tied to development and construction saw Flynn's decision as a bellwether on whether he would turn out to be an "antigrowth" mayor, so there was a message to be carried. Flynn turned to Coyle, hired in June of 1984, to come up with a recommendation.

Coyle's task was to find a way both to serve neighborhood interests and others (such as preservationists) who opposed the projects and to indicate that at least some of the projects could go ahead. BRA staff reviewed the projects through the rest of the summer of 1984. They spoke to the developers and asked for adjustments in project design and for contributions of various types—in one case receiving a commitment of $750,000, double what would have been assessed under the existing linkage formula.[15] Flynn and Coyle announced their decision at the end of October at a press conference supported by the release of a ninety-one-page BRA report called *Downtown Projects: Opportunities for Boston.*[16] They couched approval of nine of the eleven projects (a tenth would follow shortly) in terms of a social contract: developers would get progress and profits, but they would also contribute to "economic justice." Peter Dreier, looking back on this, saw it as the major starting point for a generally populist policy, as "Flynn emphasized the economic benefits of the projects—particularly the 'linkage' fees that would be gained as a result" at the press conference announcing the approvals, and in later statements, and "sought the business community's support for programs to improve the lives of Boston's poor and working-class residents... in the areas of education, jobs, job training, and housing."[17]

Flynn then presented the "pipeline projects" and the development initiatives they suggested, along with a set of redistributive programs that featured most prominently jobs and training but also linkage as a source of funding; he could also claim a start on affordable housing and tenant protection measures. Progress would be slow, but by the end of 1984 the Flynn administration had laid out a new direction for the city. The elements were:

1. *Jobs.* An expanded version of the Boston Residents Jobs Policy was announced at the same time as the pipeline-project approvals, to ensure meeting an "economic justice" objective: private developers were to make a "best good faith effort to meet goals for hiring construction workers: 50 percent city residents, 25 percent minorities, and 10 percent women." This policy, which originated with organizing by blacks in the 1960s and was carried forward later through the multiracial proposals of the Boston Jobs Coalition in the 1970s, had been adopted by executive order by Kevin White after electoral pressure from King

during the mayoral campaign in 1979. White's version was limited to projects built with city money, but Flynn now imposed the hiring requirements on the ten major projects to be built with private capital but requiring city regulatory permission.[18]

2. *Linkage.* Coyle characterized the pipeline projects as "the first of the linkage generation." Flynn inherited the linkage policy that, after passage of the nonbinding referendum during the November 1983 election, had finally been implemented in a weak form by an amendment to the city's zoning code under outgoing mayor Kevin White. This version, which the new administration inherited, provided for a $5-per-square-foot contribution for office projects of over one hundred thousand square feet, to be paid into a trust fund over twelve years. Linkage proponents wanted the assessment to be at a higher rate, cover more types of development, and be paid over a shorter time period. But Flynn chose not to try to enhance the formula, preferring to wait until it was clear that the first installment of linkage fees was not having the dire consequences on the local economy its opponents claimed it would have. (He was to float the idea of a series of elaborations—including an effective increase in the rate developers would be charged—in the summer of 1985.)

3. *Support for affordable housing construction.* Boston had many community organizations, and several had already begun to operate as community development corporations (CDCs) to produce affordable housing. By 1990 Dreier could cite "ten or fifteen" agencies with substantial capacity to develop affordable housing, and he later wrote that "at the end of Flynn's second term in 1991, CDCs had built or rehabilitated more than 5,000 housing units."[19] But in 1984 only two or three CDCs were doing much in the production of new or rehabbed housing units, and it was to become a main aim of the administration—along with private banks and foundations—to encourage their growth and increased entry into the housing-development field.[20] Dreier made it his goal to promote this. He fastened on the city's policies toward the disposition of city-owned properties, but progress was slow through 1984 and 1985.

4. *Rent control.* By the time Flynn and Coyle were ready to unveil their positive assessments of the "pipeline projects," Dreier's strong rent-control proposals had finally failed in city council. But Flynn was able to secure a compromise set of protections against rent increases, and in 1986 he successfully instituted, through the council, a condominium-conversion and eviction ban, and in 1988 he further extended rent-board authority to regulate conversions and lodging houses.[21]

Retrospectives at the end of 1984 gave Flynn much credit. A centerpiece was appreciation for Coyle's "plan" released in support of the decision to approve the ten "pipeline projects" in October. Planning, per se, struck a chord with *Globe* writers, in contrast to the ad hoc and deal-making approach of the White administration.[22] But it was also the way the plans—and Flynn's "public relations extravaganza" surrounding the announcement—found a way to articulate the goal of "balance" of the growth benefits from the projects—employment and tax base—with benefits targeted to neighborhoods and the working class and middle-income population of the city. *Globe* writer Kirk Scharfenberg summed it up in December of 1984: "One cannot find a politically knowledgeable person who would bet $10 against the idea that he will be re-elected mayor in three years." Scharfenberg's only reservation was that Flynn had done most of this himself rather than stand behind relatively powerful department heads.[23] But this would soon be resolved—with the emergence of Chapnick, Coyle, and city hall staff members like Dooley, Dreier, Sullivan, and others.

City Hall in Start-Up Mode

Still, Flynn's first two years, 1984 and 1985, were more about setting a direction than much accomplishment. The actual performance was uneven. Dreier, in retrospect, realized that the city hall group was not properly organized to succeed with rent control—even if support had been stronger. Overall, he counted many obstacles inside city hall, among them the facts that the BRA was unsympathetic and Flynn would not be able to appoint a majority to the five-member board during his term. The board had agreed to his choice of Coyle as director but was able to force compromises. He had inherited a cumbersome group of city agencies involved in housing that were difficult to coordinate. Particularly galling to Dreier, "the BRA had abandoned neighborhood planning... [and there was no] updated, complete or mapped inventory of city-owned land or buildings."[24]

Dreier wanted to push ahead on affordable housing construction and sought to find a way to coordinate the various city offices with the resources to make that happen. Public housing was not an immediate option—the Boston Housing Authority was in receivership and would not come under city control for several years. There was, on the other hand, a small set of community development corporations that had undertaken to construct and rehabilitate lower-cost units, and there were others that might do the same, with help and time.

The Struggle to Distribute City-Owned Land

The BRA, with its statutory authority over planning and zoning, and the authority to invoke eminent domain to assemble land, had general power to intervene and regulate private developers. But the city's other resources—important especially for any program to support the development of affordable housing—were its inventory of vacant and city-owned land and the authority to dispose of it, and the authority to dispense federal and state housing funds. The former was in the hands of the city's public facilities department (PFD), the latter in the Neighborhood Development and Employment Agency (NDEA). It had been difficult to coordinate these functions, and Flynn and his administrators saw new possibilities: with increased development pressure, the vacant-land inventory had become a resource that could be used, along with federal funding and the powers to build public facilities like police stations, to get private investment in affordable housing.

Peter Dreier, ensconced in BRA but with constant access to Flynn's office two floors below in city hall, made it his project to coordinate the effort to make the city-owned land a viable resource. His vehicle was a Property Disposition Committee, including the heads of the city departments involved. They had to produce an inventory of what properties the city had—initially there was not one available, and compiling it was a project that took over two years—and also to put together a policy for how the city would dispose of the properties. Another piece of the puzzle was how to introduce private financing to the mix required to make affordable housing development feasible for the CDCs. For this, Dreier credits the Boston Housing Partnership. It had been created through the efforts of the director of NDEA, Paul Brophy, one of the few White appointees Flynn retained. It pulled together a number of banks and other entities, and was in principle a source of funding for affordable housing. But, said Dreier, it did not have a clear sense of purpose under White. Dreier's committee "decided its mission was to expand the capacity of nonprofit community development corporations—to get the business community to help the CDCs."[25]

But getting agreement among the departments was difficult—some wanted to continue the earlier practice of auctioning the lots to private builders and speculators. Flynn was frustrated. According to his adviser Neil Sullivan, Flynn finally simply told a deadlocked interagency group, "I'm going to announce that we're going to raise the number of housing permits from 900 to 3,600 next year and that 25 percent of them will be affordable." He told Sullivan: "Tell them, just end the meeting, send them away, tell them I'm going to announce that it's 3,600 and they have between now and next week when I do the State of the City to tell me how many they're going to do."[26]

This was in anticipation of the 1986 State of the City address (the number Flynn announced was actually 3,400). But the logjam had begun to break the previous October when the director of NDEA resigned and Flynn announced the augmentation of PFD, giving it the housing functions of NDEA along with NDEA's control of federal CDBG funds—with Lisa Chapnick the director.

Neighborhood Councils

Flynn had made a commitment to establish neighborhood councils during the campaign and was under pressure from activists, including many in Fair Share, to follow through. Fair Share's successful nonbinding referendum on the 1983 city election ballot, providing for councils with veto power over development decisions, provided some of the impetus. The idea had popular appeal, and progressive mayors and city councils had instituted it—though not with veto power—in several places during the 1970s and 1980s.[27] In Boston, also, the frustrations of neighborhoods facing killing increases in housing prices gave support to the neighborhood-veto idea, and there was a recent experience of neighborhood-level decentralization: health clinics, community schools, and "little city halls" had begun in the 1960s and 1970s, and the first two were still functioning through the 1980s and 1990s.

But progressive mayors usually drew back when they saw the neighborhood councils more popular with neighborhoods dominated by homeowners seeking protection from minorities than in their own electoral base. Neither King nor Flynn had supported the veto provision, saying that there could be citywide interests in neighborhoods that might properly override neighborhood sentiment. Flynn also encountered problems in the minority and racially mixed neighborhoods—especially Roxbury, ultimately the site of special attention from Coyle and the BRA. He nevertheless kept the idea of neighborhood councils alive during his first years in office. But he moved carefully. He did not want to signal an end to development by establishing a neighborhood veto, but he certainly wanted to nourish his electoral base in what neighborhoods he could, and many of them wanted the neighborhood councils.[28]

Rather than appoint councils immediately, Flynn began a series of "town meetings" in the neighborhoods in order to collect comments and sell his plan. The initial proposal for as many as twenty councils, made early in 1984 in a follow-up to his campaign promise, proved controversial. City council members feared the councils would bypass their own representative functions; neighborhood people feared another layer of bureaucracy between them and the power in city hall.[29]

After some deliberation and consideration of experiences other cities had with the neighborhood-council idea, Flynn began to move ahead: councils were to be advisory but listened to by city agencies concerned with development; and Flynn would initially appoint their members, from among a list nominated by neighborhood groups. In a second year there would be elections for half the seats on each council. Council members would be unpaid, and the city Office of Neighborhood Services would provide minimal staffing.

Slowly, a plan for a smaller number of councils took shape. In June 1985 Flynn announced a set of five councils, in the areas of Jamaica Plain, the North End, Chinatown, Dorchester-Codman Square, and West Roxbury. By the end of 1985, his second year in office, these five were in place. In addition, Flynn and the BRA, which needed to update the city's zoning ordinance, announced the creation of Planning and Zoning Advisory Committees (PZACs) that would cover some of the neighborhoods not covered by neighborhood councils. Eventually people in the Flynn administration could claim coverage of much of the city with one or another form of committee or council.[30]

The neighborhood councils were to prove difficult to maintain. On the surface, the most dramatic potential function would have been a legally sanctioned neighborhood veto of proposed development. Neither King nor Flynn had supported this aspect of the Fair Share referendum proposal as candidates, and Flynn never supported it as mayor (with a partial exception, discussed below). But the veto would have entailed more than advisory powers, and the deeper issue was how to constitute neighborhoods with such powers—how to generate citizen leadership and administrative capacities. These questions were more than the Flynn administrators were prepared to confront.

Alex Bledsoe, who ran the Office of Neighborhood Services during 1984 and 1985, exemplified how far they were prepared to go. He thought the veto power for neighborhood councils was a bad idea even from the point of view of neighborhood people interested in empowerment. It would take the pressure off the councils to organize and consult:

> You're trying to develop an organization that has deep roots into a neighborhood, and if they have the kind of roots that they should have, they're going to be able to stop something that . . . doesn't make sense.

If, on the other hand, you empower twelve people [as a neighbor-hood council, they can]...just vote this one down and it won't hap-pen.... There's not going to be any incentive to go out and do approval support, popular support.[31]

Dudley Station and Parcel 18

The issue of "veto power" was particularly fraught in Roxbury and neigh-boring areas along the cleared Route 95 corridor to which the city was preparing to relocate the subway's Orange Line. This exploded in January 1985 when a BRA planner brought a draft planning study for the redevelop-ment of the area around Dudley Station on the soon to be demolished and relocated elevated line to a meeting of UMass Boston students who had been doing their own studies of the area.[32]

Globe writers praised the reintroduction of "planning" in the BRA and Flynn's efforts to deal in the neighborhoods with development decisions that could impact them. Coyle appears to have taken planning and participation seriously. Planning was not restricted only to the project-by-project reviews entailed in the eleven "pipeline" projects; BRA did a series of planning stud-ies, and with the PZACs, joined in the general effort by city hall to provide opportunities for neighborhood participation. But there seemed a contradic-tion—the development pressures were too great, and Coyle too creative and entrepreneurial, for an orderly planning process to prevail.

For Coyle, this contradiction and a different side of his capabilities appeared when the Dudley Station planning study became public. His first response was to promote the plan, preliminary though it was. He was quoted saying the BRA was considering an investment of as much as $750 million in the area, seeing it as good for office development. The reaction from the neighborhood was dismay. Roxbury had experienced the years of top-down BRA development activities in the past and feared that new development car-ried out without its participation would lead to gentrification, as new inves-tors force up housing prices, pushing out lower-income residents. Activists claimed a decade of their own planning efforts was disregarded by BRA. Local responses included the formation of the Greater Roxbury Neighbor-hood Authority (GRNA), which demanded more control than the city had contemplated giving up. GRNA wanted involvement, and a veto, and in any case a lower-impact, more modestly scaled project. Mauricio Gaston and Marie Kennedy wrote that it was "unlikely that a modestly scaled develop-ment of [the project that was evolving in BRA planning] would require the leverage offered by...linkage. However, the type of development the BRA has in mind presumably does require linkage." The GRNA planners, in sum, had a different set of objectives than BRA did.[33]

Coyle responded by taking the neighborhood concerns seriously. At one point he offered to share the "request for proposal" (RFP) responsibility, which would have the effect of defining the project, while retaining BRA control in the selection of the developer. It was in effect half of a veto, or perhaps a "double veto" arrangement. Later in 1985, Flynn, encountering a packed meeting, agreed to support Coyle's proposal, thus going on record modifying his "no neighborhood veto" stance. He was to regret this.

Coyle's initiative and the mayor's initial support bought time. Eventually Coyle and at least some neighborhood interests came to agreement on a project for the area, focused on "Parcel 18"—several blocks away from the Dudley Station area—that threatened fewer residences and (perhaps a disputed claim) had a more widespread neighborhood benefit. It was the first "parcel-to-parcel" linkage project, using financial contributions from the development of a parcel in Chinatown and granting developer status to a group of minority investors. On leaving Boston in 1992, Coyle listed Parcel 18 as one of his proudest achievements, more important than the many downtown skyscrapers that had a more obvious impact.

Coyle had revived the BRA. And proud as he may have been of the parcel-to-parcel linkage effort with Parcel 18, the downtown projects were what got the attention in the city at large and outside the city. They were important, first, for the scale and pace of development. It was noted that "from 1984 to 1990, the city's downtown exploded with more than $6 billion in building activity." Private investment in the downtown also provided the linkage funds that sustained the working-class part of the city economy: if "more than 30,000 people were employed in construction-related jobs," then a portion of those jobs would go to Boston residents and minorities; and if "more than 6,000 units of low- and moderate-income housing were put on the market," these provided the impetus for a series of housing measures.[34] Peter Dreier put the ultimate effect at something like three thousand units per year.[35]

But Coyle was independent. He would get ideas in conversation with developers or neighborhood activists and occasionally make commitments the mayor would have to support or back away from. The famous offer of eminent-domain authority to DSNI was one example of this—though Flynn went to bat for this before the BRA board and made it stick. The offer to share control for the RFPs in Parcel 18 caused consternation in Flynn's staff. But the consensus in 1992 was that Coyle was a bright light in Flynn's administration—many said "the brightest." He was both a planner who considered the many sides of important issues and a negotiator and deal maker who could match wits with the best the business community could put up.

And he appeared to adapt to his political environment. He found that he could not run over neighborhood interests, in the Parcel 18 affair and other cases, and he ended up preaching the mantra of participatory planning—even if his penchant for action got in the way and left activists saying, "he acts like he's God." Coyle quickly found a way to adopt Flynn's policies of extracting a tithe for social justice from developers he was helping profit from the downtown real estate boom in 1984–90. Neither the Flynn administrators in city hall nor Coyle, however, were ready to give a veto to a neighborhood organization. Coyle's offer to GRNA was never accepted by the BRA board. Coyle delayed bringing it up. Flynn, after supporting it publicly in the fall of 1985, ate his embarrassment when it was finally voted down in May of the following year. This soured the atmosphere, at least for those activists who had been involved, for the rest of the 1980s.

In retrospect, Coyle emphasized the importance of participation. After having been the lightning rod for neighborhood protest against large-scale development, he later made statements supporting the interaction with neighborhoods made possible by the NCs, PZACs and other, ad hoc, committees the city put together. From his point of view, it made for better projects. He said,

> I learned on the job because in the beginning I don't think I would have put the process approach...at the top of my list. I'd put results at the top. It took me a lot of head knocking, my head included, for more than a year, to realize if I wanted to achieve any of the things I set out to achieve, there'd have to be one thousand people in that ark rowing, too. And that was the most fun of all.[36]

Neighborhood Pressure—and Its Failures

Flynn emerged from his first two years in office with great popularity and was to win reelection in two successive elections. Not only had he established his bona fides with both developer and at least some neighborhood constituencies but his energy and personal style endeared him to many voters. He could be found playing basketball on the streets and making the rounds of local bars. He was indefatigable, and the city recognized that.

But the first two years, 1984 and 1985, while enough to establish himself as a "progressive" mayor, did not yet add up to significant accomplishments.

For that, he needed to negotiate with—and if necessary defeat—opposition on the city council. That required a neighborhood-based support system to counter the organized pressure that would come from the business community. On the city hall side, this was a challenge that intrigued Peter Dreier, while it also frustrated him. In correspondence, he often warned me not to overestimate the impact of the "Left." "There were too many small groups focusing on narrow issues, with no broad political coalition to hold them together.... The Boston left failed to institutionalize itself politically." Dreier hoped the Rainbow Coalition, after Flynn's victory, would build "a citywide political organization, with staff and members that built on [King's] campaign network, after the election.... In other words, to institutionalize his campaign." He thought it was a "lost opportunity for the left and made my job—and the job of other leftists within the Flynn administration—harder."[37]

But the frustration was as great outside city hall—in the neighborhood constituency—as inside. How this felt, and how it played out, is a big part of the story.

Boston Linkage Action Coalition

Even before Coyle began operations at the BRA, Peter Dreier had laid out a comprehensive housing program that entailed linkage, a four-fold expansion of the twenty thousand units then covered by rent control, and a set of smaller changes. He would not get council agreement on rent control but made progress incrementally on other fronts, particularly linkage. The longer list—even if accomplished—would be only the surface of his accomplishment and the city's experience. Beneath the surface is a story of interaction and frustration involving interest groups and neighborhood organizations that did not imagine leaving the government of the city to city hall.

Of these, Massachusetts Fair Share still held a preeminent position. The organization had been, it later turned out, fatally wounded by financial reverses and defections. But it did not want to leave the field, and it still had thousands of paid members and a few talented organizers who tried to influence city policy. It also had two political investments: the nonbinding "linkage" and "neighborhood councils" referenda on the 1983 ballot that had returned large majorities.

Fair Share also had some new blood. Janice Fine, an organizer who had been working with former Fair Share organizer Tom Snyder in Florida, moved back to take a job with the organization in the fall of 1984. Fair Share had attempted to reorganize itself in the wake of Ansara's resignation in 1983, laying off the majority of its paid staff and putting issues in front of city councils and the state legislature with skeleton support from the few it had left. It still got press coverage. In 1985 Fine was made director of the Boston office.

One of Fine's projects was the Boston Linkage Action Coalition. Fine believed that housing policy was the key issue for Fair Share to focus on. And "linkage" as it had been formulated at the end of the Kevin White administration in 1983 was not the strong instrument the Boston housing advocates had hoped for. The coalition formed as an external pressure group on the mayor, giving him cover to enact a stronger policy, which they thought he was disposed to do in any event.

The linkage coalition began in July 1985 and comprised several groups, some decidedly to the left of Fair Share's majoritarian past: the Massachusetts Tenants Organization (MTO), the Boston Affordable Housing Coalition, City Life, Greater Roxbury Neighborhood Authority, ACORN, and Tenants United for Public Housing Progress. This mix of political position seemed reasonable to Fine, because she came into the situation without the Fair Share "baggage" of standoffishness and occasional conflict with groups to its left.

Flynn had adopted White's linkage formula in 1984, but all these groups agreed on the need to push the Flynn administration toward a stronger position: they felt the original rules were too weak and that the Flynn administration would probably be willing to increase the formula. They also hoped to have some say over how the monies were spent.

The coalition laid out the strongest revision of the White package they could reasonably propose. They sought (a) majority representation on the Neighborhood Housing Trust Fund that would be spending the money, (b) an increased formula, entailing an increase in the fee from $5 to $12 per square foot, (c) payment of the fee up front rather than over a period of years, (d) elimination of the exemption for projects of less than one hundred thousand square feet, (e) a rule specifying that the fees be targeted exclusively to low- and moderate-income people and for some to be put into public housing to bring public-housing units that had fallen out of code back to code; and (f) adoption of an inclusionary zoning provision in the city zoning ordinance.

What was disappointing was the reaction of the Flynn administration, including the officials who had been Fair Share allies. As the linkage coalition saw it, they would make a set of demands for improvements in the ordinance; Flynn would move some distance toward their position; and both Flynn and the coalition members would come out looking victorious. Instead, the city hall group initially refused to negotiate. There was consternation. Looking back, Fine thought it was a learning experience—perhaps on both sides.

Flynn had gotten the BRA board to approve an enhanced linkage package in February of 1986, but it was part of the organizer's mentality to keep plugging away; the coalition's persistence was also reinforced by Fine's optimism and energy, and was encouraged by mentors at UMass Boston, and—despite frustrations—by some within Flynn's city hall offices. The Boston Linkage Action Coalition continued to mount a campaign in 1985 and 1986. They did talk shows and editorials, talking to reporters and trying to get the linkage issue raised again. At the end of 1986, they printed thousands of cards that said, "Merry Christmas, Mr. Mayor.... This Christmas, what you need to give the City of Boston is more affordable housing. We need inclusionary zoning." Each organization in the coalition took responsibility for passing the cards around to specific constituencies.

Later, Fine remembered the relationship in more general but equally frustrated terms:

> The administration had this habit of discounting it all. If it was the GRNA, which I thought was a very exciting development to the black community, that line was "Oh, it's just some Mel King front." If it was us, it was "Oh, you guys, you know, Fair Share's just a shadow of its former self." If it was MTO, "Oh, MTO used to be a real ally of ours but they're getting too independent."

Eventually the coalition was able to make some gains, and managed to get some improvements in the ordinance. Fine felt good about the outcome but was frustrated with the Flynn administrators. "Linkage did expand," she said, "the fee was raised although not as much as we wanted. There was more and more agreement to use it to fund projects that were...affordable and that were going to community development corporations. So I think we got somewhere."[38]

Ansara might have had the most realistic assessment. He said the root problem was that Fair Share, because it had been unable to control its administrative side, had lost credibility, and with that the ability to force accountability from the city. Had Fair Share been less shaky, there might have been a different performance on the part of the mayor and the development of a different sort of approach from his administrators.[39]

CDCs and Community Organizations

Much of the mass organizing that grew so fast in the 1970s abated with the 1983 election, but there was an underlying structure of community organizations that would have persisted with or without that election's outcome, and that was a continuing fact of existence for the Flynn administration. Alan DiGaetano and John Klemanski, in a 1999 political study of Boston, note a community movement that had made the transition from being an opposi- tional force in the 1970s to one that "had begun to develop political skills and resources useful for coalition building around social reform issues." They cited "more than 300 neighborhood and other associations," finding Boston's community movement one that was better organized and "consequently, has wielded greater political clout than in most American cities."[40]

Flynn's mayoralty coincided with a dramatic growth in nonprofit CDCs, particularly those devoted to providing affordable housing. Nationwide the number of CDCs went from a very few hundred in the early 1980s to over two thousand by 1990. In Boston there was similar growth. By the end of Flynn's time in office there were at least twenty community development corporations in the city, producing hundreds of housing units annually, both rehabs and new construction.[41] But in the early 1980s most were doing very little housing. They were a part of a community development move- ment, pressed in different directions. Some had been active since the 1960s: the Massachusetts Association of Community Development Corporations (MACDC) listed housing-unit production for eight such organizations dur- ing 1972–83.[42] They had produced 1,929 units of housing over the twelve- year period, an average of 161 per year among them.

Thus even in 1983 the CDCs were a force. But it was not clear what direction these organizations would take. The MACDC members certainly had committed to housing, among other activities; and perhaps most had resolved to provide services, seeking funding from foundations and elsewhere, and avoiding political involvements that would compromise that funding. On the one side were not only the city government but also national and local intermediaries and foundations, pressing for increased production, par- ticularly of housing units—and this would be a major theme under Flynn. But all needed to maintain a commitment to their clienteles, and that meant at least a sympathetic approach to the causes that took root in these neighbor- hoods from grassroots organizing and advocacy groups, frequently subsisting with practically no funding but playing an instrumental role nonetheless. These latter need a last look.

Neighborhood Opposition: 1986–89

In contrast to the varied but inherently production-oriented work of the community development organizations, and as a counterpoint to the Flynn administration's dogged pursuit of its populist, "pragmatic" program was the remarkable pursuit of neighborhood control. This emerged first as a response to the city's effort to establish neighborhood councils (NCs) and BRA's Planning and Zoning Advisory Councils (PZACs); then as an effort to organize in Roxbury over the initial attempt by the BRA to facilitate development there, led predominantly by people associated with King's Rainbow Coalition; and finally as a quixotic but symbolically effective referendum to establish Roxbury as a separate municipality called "Mandela." Toward the end of the decade, many of these ideas were sifted through and promoted by two "State of the Neighborhoods" conventions organized by the Coalition for Community Control of Development (CCCD).

Neighborhood Councils and PZACs—II

The effort to create a participatory structure through advisory neighborhood councils and PZACs was contested at the outset and uneven in its effects within the neighborhoods. Whatever the benefits in the minds of enlightened administrators like Stephen Coyle, participation absorbed a lot of neighborhood energy, where there might be contests between broadly progressive and more conservative factions. In Chinatown, a progressive slate managed to press for participation but was frustrated by conservative opposition that, they thought, hoped to benefit from BRA-sponsored projects. Later, the progressives boycotted the neighborhood council, and it declined as a legitimate force.[43] In Jamaica Plain, on the other hand, City Life was able to win control of the council for a time, and found it became a more credible force for advocacy as a result.[44]

But City Life, at least, finally concluded that the NCs represented a losing struggle. Steve Fahrer recalled:

> There were way, way too many fronts. It was impossible for anybody, in any neighborhood, to fight on so many fronts. And what we were looking for and what we never got, was a policy...that we felt would be fair, that would dictate some fairness.
>
> They were distributing city-owned properties—buildings, fire stations, police stations, schools—that were surplus or that were abandoned properties. We had joined together in this Boston Affordable Housing Coalition, and what we wanted was a certain percentage of those units set aside to be affordable housing. And in fact, in that case, we wanted all of the units to be affordable housing.
>
> The problem was that the city would never think of doing any of that, and so we and every other community organization in this city, we

were fighting parcel by parcel, plot of land by plot of land, building by building. And there was absolutely no way that we could ever mobilize the people necessary to do that.... I don't think the issue was "veto power" or "not veto power"—the issue was who the city government was going to serve.[45]

The Greater Roxbury Neighborhood Authority

When the BRA plan for Dudley Square leaked in January 1985, one of the reasons for the immediate strong response was a loose coalition of activists that had been organizing and promoting the preservation of community in Roxbury for several years. Prominently associated with them were Mauricio Gaston and Marie Kennedy of the Community Planning program at University of Massachusetts–Boston. Both had been at Urban Planning Aid. Gaston was one of the founding members of City Life. Together they mobilized students in a series of studies of disinvestment and gentrification in Roxbury. They had focused on issues like the relocation of the elevated Orange Line transit on Washington Street scheduled for 1988—it was to be moved a mile north, to the corridor that had been cleared for the cancelled Route 95 (inner belt) link. Kennedy, Gaston, and others foresaw significant development pressure once the elevated line was removed and sought to capture benefits for the community and to prevent the harm that would come from too-fast new construction.

Roxbury, meanwhile, had suffered from disinvestment and had become a difficult neighborhood. Puerto Ricans and Cape Verdeans had moved in, mixing with African Americans and remaining whites; unemployment and poverty were endemic; and absentee landlords were targeting the area with arson. Roxbury became symbolic of the problems impacting many other Boston neighborhoods.[46] A good deal of community leadership had emerged, and when the BRA plan for Dudley became known, that leadership mobilized in a series of meetings. One of their objectives, first floated earlier in the UMass studies and by Kennedy and Gaston, was the creation of a new neighborhood organization with the ability to exert control over development. They formed the Organizing Committee for a Greater Roxbury Neighborhood Authority (OCGRNA) and later the GRNA; that demanded recognition from the Flynn administration as the legitimate neighborhood council with a veto power over development.

In part the community-control movement in Roxbury was fed by the energies and the doctrine of the Rainbow Coalition activists. They knew the experience of displacement in other parts of the city, particularly the South

End. The idea that communities needed to control their own institutions had been the central point of *Chain of Change,* and in this King was reflecting the lessons of the organizers of the 1960s and 1970s in Boston and elsewhere. In the early 1980s the pressures of development on neighborhoods provided concrete foci for organizing. In Roxbury in particular, arson became an instrument for absentee property owners seeking escape from unprofitable properties, and perhaps collecting insurance payments. Eviction was also a threat; eviction protections, long an issue associated with rent-control legislation, had been improved in the city's compromise tenant-protection package passed in the winter of 1984–85, encouraging organizers like those in City Life to mobilize with Roxbury activists around the idea of an "eviction-free zone."[47]

The Flynn administration was at best ambivalent toward these efforts. Early on, in Flynn's first year, the administration realized it had a problem with the commitment to the neighborhood councils. Certainly the city administrators would be cautious initiating contact with the Rainbow Coalition people, who had recently been out to defeat them. But the Flynn people also needed to come to some accommodation in Roxbury. Ken Wade, one of the leaders in GRNA, said, "Flynn basically got less than 5 percent of the Black vote.... [He] started out with a problem in terms of how he builds a relationship [with the black community]."[48] And Steve Fahrer of City Life said, "Because Roxbury was a black community, it was much harder to dismiss what was happening in Roxbury."[49]

So despite the ambivalence, Flynn negotiated with GRNA, which created its own Interim Roxbury Planning Advisory Committee (PAC) at a town meeting in September 1985. Flynn finally recognized the body and agreed to a provision that would have required its approval over major planning and zoning decisions and requests for proposals by BRA. Later, the city appeared to have reneged when the BRA board stalled and finally gave the PAC only "review and comment" and advisory power.[50] Later the PAC, including a majority of mayoral appointees, joined in a lawsuit against the city as a means of pressuring it. Medoff and Sklar quoted Ken Wade to the effect that "to a certain extent... we've won the victory on the principles, for example, the principle of housing affordability."[51] GRNA continued on through the 1980s. It saw itself as an advocacy and umbrella group for other organizations, including not only DSNI but others across the larger Roxbury area. But it could not get enough funding to be the main presence. Medoff and Sklar quote Ken Wade saying this funding shortfall "prevented GRNA from being able to institutionalize the effort in such a way that it could be long-lasting and sustaining.... You create a groundswell, but then you don't have the resources to sustain it."[52]

Medoff and Sklar's comparison of GRNA to DSNI is instructive: "Both had begun organizing to control community development at around the same time. Both made the decision early on to avoid being direct developers or service providers and to concentrate on advocacy and planning. But there were differences. GRNA drew from a much larger area and was already experiencing development pressure and speculation." But also, Medoff and Sklar note, "the GRNA leadership was primarily from Roxbury's African American community, in contrast to DSNI's structured guarantee of equal minimum representation from area ethnic groups. Another difference was that DSNI had substantial involvement by area agencies and significant financial support, while GRNA was never able to develop a solid financial base."[53]

Mandela

In 1986, after the BRA board vitiated the PAC that GRNA thought they had negotiated with Flynn, a public-television producer, Andrew Jones, and Curtis Davis, an architect and urban planner, not leaders in other community struggles, proposed the Greater Roxbury Incorporation Project (GRIP), which would carve out a separate municipality from the Roxbury area, to be named "Mandela."[54] They asked Flynn to hold a plebiscite in Roxbury on the question, and when he refused, gathered the five thousand signatures necessary to put the question on the ballot as a nonbinding referendum.

Their success in getting the signatures in August, three months before the November election, apparently took both the city administration and the black leadership by surprise. Flynn, who hoped to be a racial healer, was disturbed by what he saw as, at the very least, quixotic and distracting, and at most, a fundamental challenge to his notion of one city bound together by rules of fairness without any special status given to race. In public his statement was: "We should not slam the door on the future to make up for the problems of the past." But one black critic of Mandela, Rev. Bruce Wall, was quoted to the effect that "he had never seen Mayor Flynn so angry over an issue."[55]

The black leadership was divided. Many saw the referendum as a losing proposition, simply in the way of gains they could make through accommodation of investment programs and cooperation with city initiatives. Progressives like the leadership in GRNA might well have chosen other issues on which to fight with Flynn. Eventually what they did was try to cast the initiative in terms of the more sophisticated concepts of community control, and support it. Mel King, who had supported the idea of an independent

Roxbury in the past, now came out in favor of the Mandela reincorporation proposal.

All of this had little effect in electoral terms, as the initiative went down to defeat by a 75–25 margin. It had been subjected to an intense campaign against it by the Flynn administration and the *Boston Globe,* which cast the proposal for reincorporation as secession and separatism and did not engage the subtleties involved in the idea of "community control." Marie Kennedy and Chris Tilly reported that "while the *Globe* and the city government spokespeople harped on the racial divisiveness of Mandela, every black leader who spoke on the issue—including Wall and Stith—acknowledged the importance of increasing community control."[56]

Coalition for Community Control of Development

The BRA initiative in Dudley at the beginning of 1985 eventually had repercussions outside Roxbury, as activists in other neighborhoods joined in the Coalition for Community Control of Development (CCCD). The precipitating event—after more than a year of working through the issues—was Flynn's final retreat from the grant of authority that GRNA had negotiated for the Roxbury Neighborhood Council in May of 1986. Like Steve Fahrer of City Life, activists generally tired of having to fight each battle with the city and wanted to institutionalize at least a measure of neighborhood control so that the onus would be on the developers and the city to meet neighborhood needs, rather than on the neighborhoods to fight each incursion as it arose. They wanted "some kind of written system, agreed upon by City Hall and neighborhood activists and adhered to by all parties."[57]

CCCD started operations in 1988 with preparations for the first of two "State of the Neighborhoods" conventions held in 1989 and 1991. It was a one-person office with heavy board involvement. The scope was quite broad, with dozens of organizations from across the city. They were funded by several foundations.

There was obviously a need. The city had attempted city hall–initiated neighborhood organization when Flynn appointed five neighborhood councils in 1985, and Coyle began working with PZACs in other neighborhoods in the course of the zoning revision. But there was dissatisfaction. It was not the surface question of the "veto" over development, though that was one issue. There were just difficulties dealing with city hall. The GRNA group had hoped to get a measure of control through their own council, which they thought they had negotiated with Flynn at the end of 1985, but then hit a brick wall with the BRA board in May 1986. One of their responses was to try for a broader set of rules, if they couldn't get control on their own. In response to city arguments against creating something in Roxbury they would not do elsewhere, the *Globe* reported the general response: "Yeah right, so therefore create neighborhood power in Roxbury *and* everywhere else."[58] Thus the unease was fairly well spread. Recognition of this may have been the cause of the foundation support: Judy Branfman, CCCD's executive director, said the foundations "desperately wanted us to succeed."[59]

GRNA was prominent in CCCD. Chuck Turner, a King ally and former MIT community fellow, was one participant, and Ken Wade, who was one of the founders of GRNA, was a cochair of CCCD. But participation also came from Back Bay, Mission Hill, Jamaica Plain, South End, North End, Dorchester, Fenway, Mattapan, East Boston, and Charlestown, in addition to Roxbury.[60]

CCCD produced a draft of a proposed city ordinance setting up a system of neighborhood councils. In the first version they called for a veto power over development; later they scaled down their proposal, but every version at least provided for some city funding and a requirement that the councils at least review every proposal for development that came before the city.

Never would the city pass the proposals into law. CCCD could not overcome the perception within the Flynn administration that they were basically the enemy. Peter Dreier said in 1990, "The CCCD convention and program was around empowerment and anti-city. We'd rather have them attack the banks."[61] Janice Fine, sympathetic but not a participant in CCCD, said, "CCCD held on to this pure vision. They wanted to have this neighborhood control. And they were right. So there was a left. The inability of Flynn's left to see it was part of the problem."[62]

Relations between CCCD and the city went downhill after a series of defeats in city council that paralleled the earlier disappointments for GRNA over the powers not granted to the neighborhood council in 1986. After a defeat in 1990, the CCCD steering committee concluded: "It seemed clear that the Mayor's opposition to the neighborhood council proposal could not be overcome ... and they sought a vote to put the council on record." The proposal was defeated 8–5, with the bill's sponsor, Rosaria Salerno, noting that "several councilors oppose neighborhood councils because they're afraid they would be a breeding ground for political opponents."[63]

In 1992, CCCD decided to disband. Branfman later gave an assessment: CCCD had achieved a great deal. It captured the involvement of neighborhoods of different stripes across the city, and articulated a vision of neighborhood participation that many supported. But they could not continue. CCCD was fifty grassroots groups, and the problem with being "mostly small neighborhood groups," Branfman said, "is that almost no one had staff and everyone was overwhelmed with work." Nor was there continuing foundation funding. There was money for organizing and for national policy work, but not at the local level. So they could not continue. There was lasting value though: "Relationships were formed—there and throughout CCCD's work—that really crossed some serious boundaries. That's one of the great successes of CCCD."[64]

Flynn's Second Wind: Linkage and the Banks, 1986–92

Regardless of opposition from the left or the right, the Flynn administration simply pushed ahead with its redistributionist strategy, particularly on housing. There were attacks from his left opposition, which argued for a more thoroughgoing populism confronting problems of race and power sharing head-on.[65] But the several initiatives begun in 1984 were bearing fruit by 1986. It was less a rapprochement with the Rainbow forces than an ability to milk the boom in support of those community organizations that had been able to appear "pragmatic" and "productive." Peter Dreier, who was Flynn's main articulator on housing issues, called it a "populist housing policy."

Dreier thought the key to it all was Flynn's efforts to build gradually on the success of the linkage program. As hoped, developers, despite earlier disavowals, found they could pay for linkage. The numbers were dramatic: the "pipeline projects" rollout in October 1984 had projected $24.5 million in linkage payments into the Neighborhood Housing Trust (the linkage fund).[66] This figure was to increase each year through the decade.

But what was more important was the turn in attitudes: if developers were anxious to appear supportive, it became increasingly difficult to attack the principle of exactions or other contributions to neighborhood welfare. By 1986 one developer commented: "There will continue to be linkage in one form or another. We don't disagree with the concept... it's a cost of doing business. No one can argue that housing is one of the most critical needs in the city."[67] What they found was that they could absorb the cost because of the marketability of their properties. In return, what they got was goodwill from the neighborhoods and a predictable development process, mediated by the city.

At least for a while, Flynn could claim a series of effects and build added measures on the linkage victory. As Dreier and others told the story:[68]

- The city promoted affordable housing on city-owned sites, over 80 percent delegated to neighborhood nonprofit developers.

- With the general support of the business and banking community, Flynn was able to take credit for the Boston Housing Partnership, whereby banks provided loan subsidies for nonprofit groups doing affordable housing.
- With the pressure of neighborhood organizations, the city was able to negotiate additional developer contributions: for example, six hundred day-care spaces in a proposed Midtown Cultural Center, and job-training funds earmarked from the expanded linkage fees passed in 1987.
- The city undertook a campaign to force banks to reinvest in Boston neighborhoods, in which the BRA did a study of the proportion of bank deposits that were invested in the areas from which deposits came and enacted a policy of depositing city funds in banks that met local reinvestment standards.
- Parcel-to-parcel linkage was a program whereby, in addition to the regular linkage fee, developers of downtown parcels subsidized development of parcels in outlying neighborhoods, including developments of minority business enterprise.
- There was a partially successful effort to get adoption of "inclusionary zoning," requiring developers of luxury apartments to set aside 10 percent of the units as affordable housing in other parts of the city or on site. Dreier had experimented, in effect, negotiating with developers who—anxious to break ground in a hot market—were relatively easily persuaded to accede to a "voluntary" program. When a court decision suggested developers could oppose a city ordinance successfully, and when the market cooled, the program became moot.

By 1990 Dreier could point to these multiple elaborations of the linkage concept and claim support from both neighborhood and business groups. The result was the claim—perhaps a contested one—to transcend Flynn's white working-class neighborhood base in two ways: he could provide housing in the black neighborhoods as well as the white and get support from the business community as well. There was talk of a new "culture of interaction," and Dreier claimed the creation of a "new growth coalition."[69]

Dreier's claim is interesting in that he could point to a number of interacting elements, even though some, when singled out, had much more impact than others. And yet the whole was greater than the sum of the parts. Linkage itself was a prime example. By one account, it provided for only 6 percent of the city's affordable housing needs, yet it set a direction in 1984 and proved politically durable when Flynn got support for the 1986 enhancements. Moreover, it was possible to press developers for concessions beyond the formula, because once the opposition was forced to retreat (as in the case of the Greater Boston Real Estate Board), developers lined up to make contributions of various kinds. And it is possible that measures that did not directly contribute greatly in terms of quantifiable results still contributed to the atmosphere of moral pressure in other ways. Inclusionary zoning, never passed into law, nevertheless eventually achieved majority support in city council before, faced with an adverse decision in the U.S. Supreme Court, the city withdrew it. Parcel-to-parcel linkage may have had the same effect. The flagship project, Parcel 18, produced little in tangible construction or occupied buildings for nearly two decades but seemed to reflect credit on the city as a good-faith effort.

What did continue to produce tangible results after 1985 were the effort to stimulate private sector investment in affordable housing and the change in the city land-disposition program to improve the chances of CDC developers.

The Community Reinvestment Coalition

In some respects the fallout from linkage transcended the real estate cycle. The Community Reinvestment Act (CRA) movement was instructive. The role of the city was perhaps catalytic and even critical, but the roots of the CRA activism antedated Flynn's mayoralty, included opposition elements, and seemed to have the potential to continue afterward. James Campen provides a good case study: there had been CRA activism in Boston as early as the late 1970s when the federal legislation first passed mandating banks to make loans in the neighborhoods where they extracted deposits. The Community Reinvestment Coalition that formed at the end of the 1980s included such groups as GRNA, DSNI, the Hotel and Restaurant Workers Union Local 26, the Massachusetts Affordable Housing Alliance, and the CDCs Urban Edge and Nuestra Comunidad, and involved associations that reached back more than a decade. When a settlement was reached in 1990 and was announced as a set of bank investments amounting to $400 million (later amended to a claim of $1 billion over five years), it dwarfed the linkage fund. Moreover, the settlement resulted in the creation of new institutions: a Massachusetts Community and Banking Council (MCBC) to oversee provision of basic banking services; a Massachusetts Housing Investment Corporation (MHIC) to administer a $100 million loan pool for construction and rehabilitation of affordable housing; and a Massachusetts Minority Enterprise Investment Corporation to provide equity capital, loans, and technical assistance to minority businesses.[70]

Mark Draisen, the Director of the Massachusetts Association of Community Development Corporations, saw additional long-term results:

> Our organization and a number of other statewide organizations became actively involved in CRA from that point forward; and in fact that is the single thing we spend the most time on, working on CRA agreements. And those agreements have produced very specific and substantial commitments to CDCs and low-income communities in the form of loans, grants, and equity assistance. And when we do our agreements, they are not the big splashy press-release agreements; they are very specific and concrete—specific numbers, specific products, specific places.[71]

This suggests—along with other developments—that a long-term shift in the ground had occurred by the end of the Flynn administration, providing a much more stable basis for CDC initiatives in housing and other activities.

Linkage payments themselves could become problematic. The flow of funds would be cyclical, and there were doubts about how the funds would be administered as the city moved into the 1990s and into a new boom cycle in the mid-1990s. Moreover, there was always a question whether the Boston Residents Jobs Policy was being pursued vigorously. Both linkage and the jobs policy depended on administrative machinery that might or might not remain focused.

But if even some of the secondary financial and other effects Dreier claimed continued, it could be argued that linkage—a battle Flynn fought and won over business opposition in the early to mid-1980s—had done its work, and other institutions would later take on the burden of mediating the allocation of resources between the money machine of downtown business and the employment and population pool in the neighborhoods.

Chapnick, CDCs, and Affordable Housing Production

This seems to be what happened. Under Flynn, Boston became a leader in promoting "affordable" housing production by nonprofits. But it was more complicated than getting financing: Dreier's early efforts to get coordination among the agencies involved with the disposition of city-owned land finally bore fruit when Flynn appointed Lisa Chapnick to direct the augmented public facilities department in the fall of 1985.

Chapnick developed the reputation of being the most hard-nosed of administrators. Flynn first appointed her as director of the traffic and parking department, which seemed a back-office job. But Chapnick made headlines

by announcing drastic increases in parking fees on the premise that downtown space was needed by Bostonians, and suburbanites needed to pay for
the privilege of using the downtown. This was a "progressive" measure that
had been implemented in California cities like Berkeley in the 1970s, but
only on parking meters, never as drastic. At PFD, according to Flynn's policy
director Neil Sullivan, Chapnick was

> one of the strongest willed administrators I've ever met, she's the one
> who united the two sides, the land and the money for us, in public
> facilities. She's the one who dealt with DSNI. I mean, we had this
> crazy idea that we would...give eminent domain to a community
> group....And now, hey, Peter, me, you know all us theory types, you
> know, we were pushing, pushing, we got the vote but—we actually had
> to do it? Lisa did it.[72]

Under Chapnick, PFD took the initiative to implement neighborhood
housing development. She was instrumental in the follow-through with Parcel 18 and the development of housing around Dudley Square, and PFD
took credit for a series of affordable-housing developments throughout the
city. In 1989, PFD issued a report describing the levels of housing starts in
the previous three years: 3,714 in 1986, when Flynn had issued a public
goal of 3,400 units; 4,064 in 1987, the peak of the boom; and a leveling off
to 2,708 in 1988. The proportion of those units "affordable" to low- and
moderate-income families was 29, 45, and 33 percent, respectively; almost all
were done by public subsidy—only a very small portion, 3.2 percent, was
done by private developers in 1988.[73]

The Massachusetts Association of Community Development Corporations (MACDC) provided numbers of units produced by member CDCs.
Its 2006 Historical Real Estate Production Report (cited earlier) listed new
and rehabilitated units produced by its member CDCs—24 in Boston. The
city's Neighborhood Housing Trust (NHT), the linkage fund administered
at the department of neighborhood development, provided historical data on
NHT units produced. A compilation from these two sources—though one
omitted units produced privately and by other nonprofits, and the other
omitted units produced without linkage funds and most certainly duplicated
some in the first set—does provide a sense of change in production over time
(see table 4.1).

The most striking findings in these tables would be the sharp increases
after 1985 and 1986, the drops after 1990 and 1991, and the gradual revivals
in the late 1990s. These reinforce the impression of the stimulus from linkage initiated at the end of 1986 along with other proactive city policies in

Table 4.1   Boston Affordable Housing Production, 1981–99

	MACDC	NHT
1981	147	
1982	311	
1983	225	
1984	150	
1985	115	
Total, 1981–85	948	
1986	385	18
1987	313	1,368
1988	246	550
1989	295	543
1990	807	198
Total, 1986–90	2,046	2,677
1991	85	409
1992	34	59
1993	555	21
1994	56	45
1995	151	151
Total, 1991–95	881	685
1996	123	0
1997	216	766
1998	369	490
1999	771	78
Total, 1996–99	1,479	1,334

Source: The MACDC data are from *2006 MACDC Goals Report,* Historical Real Estate:
Housing, table 28 (Boston: MACDC, 2006). The NHT numbers are in City of Boston,
Neighborhood Housing Trust, n.d., http://www.cityofboston.gov/dnd/pdfs/NHT.pdf.

support of affordable housing; and the figures also point to the vulnerability of the linkage payments when high-volume construction stopped after 1989. But the gradual revival is as important: it reinforces the impact of the larger group of policies and initiatives, particularly the CRA campaign's impact on the reallocation of private banking investments in the 1990s.

It is also noteworthy that these published figures significantly understate the actual construction of rehabilitated and new "affordable" units. Dreier, in correspondence, suggested a figure of several thousand units per year for the late 1980s.[74]

The Boom Ends: Flynn Attempts Economic Policy

Though other sources of housing finance took up some of the slack when linkage payments dropped, and the total capital available for affordable housing was destined to rebound, there would have been no way to be sure in 1991. And in that year, Flynn shifted attention from housing to economic development. At the end of the year, Flynn staged a series of meetings with community and business leaders searching for an economic-development strategy and in anticipation of the campaign for reelection the following year.[75] It was an odd sequence of events, extending into the years after Flynn left office. DiGaetano and Klemanski report the consternation: "The new political consensus that emerged from these meetings ranked job creation as the city's highest economic development priority."[76] They write that "the new governing agenda consisted of four strategic foci: (1) a community-based anticrime program, (2) a broad-based educational reform effort, (3) improvement in community health care facilities and programs, and (4) an aggressive and targeted economic development strategy."[77]

DiGaetano and Klemanski interviewed Don Gillis, director of the previously less-prominent (compared to Coyle and the BRA) Economic Development and Industrial Corporation (EDIC). Gillis, a former organizer, provided a rationale for a different sort of economic-development strategy: CDCs, with housing investment drying up, could be effective agents for economic development.[78]

They report that in spring 1992, Gillis "engineered a new form of collaborative framework, christened the Boston Economic Growth Partnership (BEGP)." That included CDCs, city departments, two foundations, utilities, and banks. The purpose would be neighborhood economic development.[79] But before BEGP could become operational, Flynn resigned; Boston's new mayor, Thomas Menino, never revived BEGP and, rather than relying on the CDCs, he decided to work directly with neighborhood businesses, establishing a "Main Street Program" similar to others around the nation. Menino generally established himself as "business friendly" in contrast to the more abrasive Flynn.[80]

Unbalanced Growth

The question remains whether Boston could have mounted an effective economic-development strategy of any sort in the 1990s. Flynn's frontline administrative leadership was largely gone: Dooley had left in 1989, and Coyle and Chapnick, who had perfected the extraction of housing dollars from the boom, both were gone by 1992—Coyle left in January 1992, Chapnick had moved to direct Inspectional Services in 1991. Dreier resigned to take a position at Occidental College in Los Angeles at the end of 1992.

And it was not just a matter of leadership leaving. Arguably the price of Boston's office-development boom was that it destroyed some of the balance among different ways to "develop" the economy and the population. What kind of boom was it? It was a real estate development boom, one so intense it crowded out other kinds of possible growth and other lines of thinking about how to govern the city.

One thing it crowded out was the economic-development side of the community development movement. In the 1970s King's focus and the purpose of CDFC, CDAC, and CEED had been creating jobs and making them accessible to people of color and others in poor neighborhoods. But by the 1980s there was a shift in perceptions and policy toward housing as the main vehicle and the real estate development sector as the engine of wealth, keyed to the linkage policy and its derivative programs.

As indicated in chapter 3, there had been obstacles to any easy route to enterprise creation, while housing offered opportunities that CDCs, and perhaps eventually private developers, could capitalize on.[81] The result would be ironic. A generation of CDC leaders would become expert at real estate development. They would pay little attention to other sectors of the economy. When they did "economic development," they mainly did so in support of neighborhood-serving business.[82]

The underlying reasons would lie in the relative fortunes of the manufacturing sector, and in the office developments that generated the linkage dollars. The Boston Redevelopment Authority's research division did an analysis of these differences in 2004 that showed a relative increase in "knowledge-based" industrial sectors and jobs during the 1990s. In a comparison of thirty-five large U.S. cities in 2000, Boston had the largest proportion of employment in these sectors—58 percent compared to a range of 18 to 56 percent for the other thirty-four cities. Boston's specialization had been increasing slightly as well; and the absolute numbers of jobs in these sectors had increased from 249,374 to 450,318. Its blue-collar sectors, in contrast, were near the bottom, and declining.[83]

Bennett Harrison, who had been tracking the Massachusetts economy since the 1970s, had seen a hollowing out of the state's economy: (1) the significant growth had occurred during 1975–84 but had come to a standstill after that; (2) the growth had been overbalanced toward the Boston metropolitan area; (3) inequalities in wealth and income had increased; and (4) what growth there was aside from sharing in national trends after 1984 was "concentrated in wholesale trade, business and legal services, finance insurance and real estate and especially construction."[84] In addition to being roughly consistent with the BRA analysis a decade or so later, Harrison's findings supported a city focus on extracting funding to reduce inequalities from the office boom—what the neighborhood organizers had sought since the 1970s, and what Flynn, and later Menino, implemented in the succeeding decades.

Leadership Vacuum?

Though the real estate boom was a factor in the hollowed-out economy Harrison described, there is a deeper issue still: Apart from changes in the distribution of industrial sectors, did the city develop or retain the decision-making capacity to take advantage of what opportunities the economy and the demographics provided it? One can make a few observations:

- Flynn had provided one kind of such leadership: the recognition that growth could be tied to the redistribution of wealth to those populations who did not most readily share in the growth—the main vehicle being housing subsidies.
- Flynn might have had a chance to make policy from a deeper analysis when the real estate boom flattened out at the end of the 1980s. DiGaetano and Klemanski report city hall taking steps from 1991 onward seeking to supplement the linkage strategy with a new kind of economic-development approach.[85] There might have been hope for something different in a small-business development initiative associated with the director of EDIC, Don Gillis, in 1993. But it apparently came to nothing when Flynn moved as ambassador to the Vatican in the summer of that year.
- More fundamentally, there is little evidence that the city hall staff—having begun to lose its best people—had much of an answer. EDIC produced reports on job-training programs; and it continued its programs to lure firms to the city. There was nothing new about either approach.
- After 1993 the new mayor, Menino, went back to more traditional approaches to economic development. The small-business initiative became a "Main Street Program," similar to programs focused on small shopping centers throughout the nation.

It is not clear whether Menino had other options besides simply to listen to the business leadership and do what he could to advance their agenda. To do otherwise would have required an independent economic-leadership presence in city hall and significant staff leadership, reinforced by academic and other intellectual resources. These may not have been available. Most of the "Sandinistas" had already left the government before 1993. Beyond that, news accounts cited a "power vacuum" in Boston's business leadership on the 1990s. The legendary Coordinating Committee ("The Vault") disbanded in 1997. Menino was left to an ad hoc economic-development program. At a 1995 conference that was called to discuss business leadership, keynote speaker and Harvard Business School professor Rosabeth Moss Kantor diagnosed the problem as rooted in the organizational culture of the newly prominent "information industries": she "observed that the Boston business community lacked a 'grand vision' because of the 'rise of growth companies with different priorities.'"[86] The corporate-culture outcome of Harrison's hollowed-out economy had come into being.

Legacy: Menino and CDCs

Flynn, after deciding not to run for governor in 1990, won a third term as mayor in 1991, and then, less than halfway into the term, having held office for nine and a half years, took the position of ambassador to the Vatican in 1993. By that time he had accomplished a great deal, but it was also true that his administration was running out of steam. Key administrators had resigned, the real estate boom had ended, and with it, some of the revenues that had made possible many of the initiatives had dried up. The Stuart murder case, in which a white man had convinced the police that a black man had shot his wife, before he himself came under suspicion and committed suicide, heightened racial tensions and made it difficult for Flynn to maintain his claim to be "mayor of all the people."

Raymond Dooley, who had been Flynn's chief of staff through much of his mayoralty, thought 1989 had been a turning point that marked a decline in the city's civic culture. He said, "Prior to 1989 it was good. Business wanted to be seen as philanthropic. The governor [Dukakis] was a technocratic liberal. The *Boston Herald,* now a right wing force, was regarded as a joke. The onset of economic depression and random violence began about 1989—a real downturn in city spirit." Michael Liu sounded a related note. After 1989, he wrote, "the growth machine reverted to its traditional constituents—developers, bankers, and the construction industry—and refocused on traditional incentive strategies to attract capital. The political opportunity structure that would be available to neighborhoods was now less obvious."[87]

Flynn's successor, Thomas Menino, initially sought to continue Flynn's policies but slowly asserted a different style. Where Flynn had been "populist" to the point of making business elites uncomfortable and could win reelection doing so, Menino tended to stroke both sides. One former Flynn staff member said: "Ray Flynn has this class anger. Menino didn't have that anger. He's much more a man with a big-hearted approach to the world.... Menino's style was less intrusive than Flynn's."[88]

If Flynn's centerpiece was cutting in the neighborhoods for a share of an expanding development pie, Menino's was adapting to some unfinished business left by Flynn: not only economic development, but schools and crime. But the political forces were changing. The once contending parts of Boston's "Left" were on different ground than they had been on a decade previously, when Flynn and Coyle were creating new relationships between communities and the business juggernaut, and while GRNA and the Coalition for Community Control of Development agitated for a larger community voice.

One new thing was that, in terms of organizational and productive capacity, the community development corporations were stronger and more numerous than a decade earlier. MACDC counted twenty-four members, production had increased every year in the 1990s, and the mix of projects had become more diverse, with more home ownership projects and commercial development included.[89] These gains had been achieved because of a combination of state government and city support on the political side, and business and foundation support. State funding had increased from $700,000 at the beginning of the 1990s to $1.9 million in 1999. Strong intermediaries like the Local Initiatives Support Corporation (LISC) and the Neighborhood Reinvestment Corporation were channeling low-income housing tax credits to the CDCs, and a critical development—parallel to the initiation of the Boston Housing Coalition in the 1980s—was the creation of the Neighborhood Development Support Collaborative, channeling funds from several foundations. Moreover, the creation of institutions to channel bank funds to the neighborhoods as a result of the CRA negotiations at the beginning of the decade had become a permanent feature of the landscape.

The other main change was demographic. The numbers were certainly on the side of the communities of color. Non-Hispanic whites had steadily decreased as a proportion of the Boston population (from 67 to 49.5 percent from 1980 to 2000), causing the communities of color to notice their new majority status and to hold conferences to try to capitalize by organizing for voter turnout.[90]

Still, with regard to the political development of the communities of color—which had contributed heavily to the push for community control of development in the 1980s—the situation was somewhat mixed. There was strong disappointment that a charismatic leader—such as King had been—had not emerged, and frustration that Menino had seemed no more willing to nurture independent community movements than Flynn had.[91] There were still those who bemoaned the failure of the Rainbow Coalition to emerge as a progressive organizational force.

But the idea—if not the organization—of the Rainbow Coalition had not died in Boston. King, retired from MIT but running a technology training center near his home in the South End, managed Chuck Turner's successful candidacy for city council in the district that included Roxbury—so effectively that people could talk of the Rainbow as a "machine" in its ability to get out the vote.[92] King thought there was "a lot going on here," listing the vitality of several community organizations and CDCs. DSNI was pushing ahead in Roxbury after a decade and a half of exemplary, multiracial organizing and consensus building.

Meanwhile a number of people had emerged in leadership roles, Latinos and Asians as much as blacks, and were seen as progressives. Nelson Merced—the first Latino elected to the state legislature, in the early 1990s—was followed by African Americans Charlotte Golar Richie and Marie St. Fleur. Richie was then appointed director of Menino's Office of Neighborhood Development in January 1999. Later, Latino Felix Arroyo won an at-large seat on the city council, and African American Andrea Cabral won for sheriff. Organizing and voter turnout in the black and Latino wards increased further after 1999. Turner was encouraged by the "new majority" coalition that held meetings in 2003, with the aim of turning the new demography reported in the 2000 census into voting majorities.[93]

❧ CHAPTER 5

Neighborhood Background
and the Campaign in Chicago

Harold Washington was a well-known African
American mayor, but he was also notable because he was a reform mayor and,
more than that, combined the ideals of reform with a community development program so that reform had a substance it had not had in a century
of previous incarnations. That substance came from the social movements
of the 1960s: civil rights, women's rights, and community empowerment. It
was refined by the experience of diverse community organizations through
the 1970s and was connected to important intellectual and academic support. This substance, when tried out under Washington and connected to the
authority of city government, then rose to a different level.

Political Background and Neighborhood Organizing

Most accounts of Chicago politics stress the long history of its "machine"-
type political organization, longer lasting than those in other large U.S.
cities. The political culture, which had an exemplary spokesperson and theo-
retician in University of Chicago (later Harvard) political scientist Edward
Banfield, held that political values grew out of material self-interest, and
that any overarching aggregation of interests needed to be held together by
mutual gain. Banfield's point, a good one, was that cities tended to have a
fragmentation of formal authority, and the only way overall policies could

be made, or problems solved, was through the aggregation of authority by other means. In the first half of the twentieth century that meant the urban political party, an organization put together to win elections and nourished by the rewards of victory—the "spoils" of political campaigning—in the form of patronage and control of city contracts and other financial resources. Careful distribution of these rewards was the main way to create and maintain such authority. Furthermore, attempts to substitute a "moral" basis for a financial one were not only impractical, Banfield argued, but less representative of the real plurality of city interests than were the concretely ward-based ones.[1]

In Chicago, this view had been reinforced by a political organization—the "machine"—devoted to a similar style of governing: ward bosses had a large hand in controlling development decisions, in particular approval of zoning-change requests, and allocated city jobs as rewards for loyal service, while the longtime (1955–76) mayor and head of the machine, Richard J. Daley, made whatever big decisions were needed but put the purpose of maintaining the organization above all others. Nationally, the machine delivered liberal presidential candidates like Adlai Stevenson and presidents like John F. Kennedy. Locally, it accommodated migrations of southern blacks into segregated neighborhoods, and into segregated but massive public-housing projects, and it co-opted black city council members while resisting serious reforms or sharing of power. Meanwhile, the machine assiduously promoted an image of efficiency. But at its core it was an informal structure, accepted and even celebrated in local opinion: machine operatives in thousands of precincts bringing valuable favors and expecting votes in return.[2]

What was remarkable was how the machine persisted after the 1950s, a decade or more after those in other cities went into eclipse. How this happened is an intriguing story, but simply put, there were two main reasons, one related to the city's black population, the other to Mayor Daley himself. The machine adapted to—cultivated and co-opted—Chicago's black population. Black population increase was startling after the 1930s. As the white population left the city for the suburbs, black votes became increasingly important. Machine recruitment of blacks took a dramatic turn in 1940 when Edward Kelly, then Democratic mayor and machine boss, got black Republican leader William Dawson to switch parties. Dawson remained a power until his death in 1970, all the while operating within the machine culture, delivering votes to the machine. William Grimshaw tells a more complicated story: Dawson never had the empire he sought among Chicago's black voters—he was held in check by Daley and factional competition within the machine. Moreover, while the black population increased, its civic and political organizations declined, leaving it divided and unable to mount a serious challenge to machine control until the 1970s.[3]

Also important to the survival of the machine was Daley's good fortune in coming to power as the city's and nation's growth was peaking in the 1950s. This made it possible for him to undertake a real estate development program that got support from the business community—or rather, the broader "growth coalition." As theorized by John Mollenkopf and others, the growth coalition consisted of a set of interests that profited from growth, especially around real estate development: banks and finance institutions, construction unions, newspapers whose advertising revenues required population growth and sales, architects, lawyers, and other professionals. Partly at their behest, and in response to widespread consciousness of "urban problems" in the form of slums and traffic congestion, federal legislation provided very large subsidies for highways, urban renewal, and housing in the 1950s. In city after city, local and state governments took advantage of the legislation, neighborhoods were razed, and new buildings and street patterns appeared.[4]

In Chicago, these possibilities tied well to the "builder" tradition among machine mayors: big plans, recruitment of financing, developers and contractors leading to the actual construction, then "with luck, the fourth year is ribbon-cutting time...just in time for re-election."[5] Daley was adept at the "builder" role. The result was the accommodation of two quite different political configurations: the ward-based politics of the neighborhoods, and the massive public-works projects and other subsidies devoted to what became known as the downtown growth coalition. For the first, there was the defeat of integrationist goals within the Chicago Housing Authority, so that new public housing was confined to black neighborhoods. For the second, there was the development of O'Hare Airport, the extension of the rapid-transit line to O'Hare and elsewhere, and the building of an extensive system of expressways. There were plans for real estate development and residential gentrification of the Loop and inner-city neighborhoods, though implementation did not gather steam for at least another decade.[6]

Why the projects were oriented to the downtown—as opposed to support for manufacturing interests that might have sustained Daley's working-class neighborhood base for a longer time—is an interesting question. The consequences eventually undermined him. By the 1970s, the machine had lost many of its resources and much of its ability to govern. Part of the reason was the increasing restiveness of working-class neighborhoods and black populations; but equally important was the city's loss of manufacturing jobs and the working-class tax base they supported. The city was left with an economic policy that focused on downtown business interests, to the point where eventually it gave less attention to manufacturing interests and sought to build the downtown with a declining tax base.

The shift away from a manufacturing economy, national in scope, was generally seen as a natural event, but apparently there was more at work, a set of forces and counterforces. The city's 1958 central-area development plan—one that proposed new office and retail space, middle-income residential space, and precious little "light industrial" space, with government and university areas conceived as buffers—separated the inner-loop development from surrounding blight. But the surrounding area contained a substantial portion of the city's manufacturing space and jobs. Joel Rast described the rationale for ignoring these. Ignoring industrial jobs was "remarkably consistent with the economic development preferences of downtown business leaders.... According to these reports, national economic trends were encouraging the flight of industry from cities like Chicago. The decline of manufacturing was inevitable." It was "increasingly unnecessary and futile for city government to make painful choices between support for industrial [versus] commercial growth. Manufacturing was dying or dead."[7] But Rast, describing the crescent of land surrounding the Loop, also noted a distinction.

> The prevailing narrative of urban economic restructuring suggests that the decline of these near-downtown industrial districts was a foregone conclusion.... However, the lure of cheaper land and labor costs on the urban periphery proved sufficient to attract only certain types of central area industrial establishments to new suburban and rural locations. In general, such firms tended to be relatively large, vertically integrated, and producing for national or international markets. By contrast, another class of near-downtown manufacturers—typically small-to-medium in size, engaged in contracting or subcontracting activities and producing for local or regional markets—showed little interest in vacating their existing central area locations.[8]

For whatever reason, these distinctions were unknown to Daley's professionals in city hall and to the downtown and corporate business leaders who supported him, and set in motion the growth of private investment and federally supported infrastructure, whose momentum would continue with little interruption through the following decades.

Eventually something would have to give. Daley, perhaps through force of will and certainly through organizational skill, maintained the machine on this basis longer than had been possible in other cities. But during the late 1960s and early 1970s there were challenges to the machine. Blacks, who had been quiescent and co-opted, became restive after the 1960s and there were some prominent defections from the machine. Independent ward organizations emerged to a greater extent. And more generally the neighborhood movement burgeoned in the 1970s. After Daley's death in 1976, mayors Michael Bilandic and then Jane Byrne tried to maintain a business-as-usual approach but could not satisfy demands for inclusion from working-class or poor black neighborhoods.

But the political culture remained. Political scientist Barbara Ferman described it thus:

> In Chicago, the identification, in the minds of many, of politics with crass material exchange and of government with overt favoritism has bred an atmosphere of cynicism and mistrust. The pervasiveness of this outlook casts a dark shadow over any effort to change the system. Reform in Chicago is often interpreted as rewarding a new set of friends and punishing a new set of enemies. In such an environment it is enormously difficult to mobilize the requisite political support to alter the system.

Ferman thought Chicago's political culture, nurtured by the machine, also made it particularly difficult for the neighborhood organizations to play a role in reform. Its materialism was "much more individualistic than collective in outlook," placing community-based organizations (CBOs) "in a precarious situation.... The media, for instance, often portray CBOs as useless obstructionists."[9]

Social Movements and the Neighborhoods

Alongside the machine, Chicago nevertheless had a history of strong and varied social movements. Part of it was an idealism fed by a middle class shocked at poverty and offended by the working-class political culture that seemed to accept it. This is what characterized the tradition of Jane Addams, founder of Hull House, whose ideas were stated in pieces like "The Subjective Necessity for Social Settlements" and who argued for the self-interest of middle-class reformers in engaging the problems of the poor in the cities.[10] This motivation could be seen in radical movements for long afterwards.

Another sort of tradition—perhaps more attuned to the machine political culture (Ferman thought it contributed to it)—was the organizing of Saul Alinsky, who had started in Chicago's Back of the Yards neighborhood in the 1930s and evolved a disruptive yet oddly conservative political style: organize around issues that match the short-run needs of the people; build from small successes to larger campaigns; avoid political alliances and commitments to office; and choose positions that build power over principle.[11]

Woodlawn

For reasons that combined Alinsky's pragmatism with Addams's commitments to a larger sense of justice, and fundamentally because of the drastic downturn in the fortunes of Chicago's working-class and minority populations, protest organizations began to emerge in Chicago in the 1960s. Some of these organizations were exemplary, and they traced a path over several decades that set the background for later efforts. The first and most famous was in Woodlawn on the city's South Side, immediately south of the University of Chicago campus. There a group of clergy, alarmed at deteriorating conditions associated with the in-migration of poor blacks at the end of the 1950s, began to explore ties with Alinsky and his Industrial Areas Foundation. Expansion plans from the university precipitated action by 1960, and Alinsky and his associate, Nicholas von Hoffman, became organizers for what became The Woodlawn Organization (TWO).

Alinsky brought an approach to organizing that eventually combined with certain uniquely black perspectives in Chicago and were tested first by TWO. The best account is that of John Hall Fish. He described three related dimensions of Alinsky's approach: control, organization, and conflict.[12] First, the problem was best conceived as control from outside. To break this outside control, Alinsky reasoned, the community needed to amass power. This meant, for poor communities, organization: "You [poor people] have to have power," Alinsky said, "and you'll only get it through organization. Because power just goes to two poles—those who've got money, and those who've got people. You haven't got money, so your own fellow-men are your only source of strength."[13]

In order to organize, Alinsky sought to engage in conflict, which he saw as the main way to counter the quiescence of poor people, whose method of survival had been to repress in themselves the sense of injustice that—if they saw their situation clearly—would have motivated them to engage politically. This interpretation led to the institution of the professional organizer, whose main function was not to pursue any particular issue or policy but to build an organization where natural leaders could emerge and decide their own directions. Alinsky and von Hoffman, practical and nonideological to the core, were thus quite prepared to focus on the immediate and mundane concerns of the residents of the neighborhood in order to build the organization and ever ready to scold well-meaning outsiders for a tendency to romanticize neighborhood organizations.[14] They were, on the other hand, unprepared for the fervor that gripped Woodlawn when word of the civil rights struggles in the South came to Chicago through contact with the churches. The precipitating event was the visit of seven CORE Freedom Riders who had been burned out and beaten in Anniston, Alabama, in 1961. TWO scheduled them for a community meeting in June, after which von Hoffman claimed "that he was dumbfounded when the hall was packed with an estimated seven hundred people...[and] said that it was at that moment that he began to realize that there was a 'movement' beginning in Woodlawn."[15]

During 1961, before and after the meeting with the CORE workers, the "undiscovered leaders" who Alinsky theorized emerged. Rev. (later Bishop) Arthur Brazier became the official spokesperson for TWO, a position he enhanced throughout the 1960s and later. The organization sought to become the official representative of the area in city hall and, succeeding in this and supported by energy in the community and federal antipoverty funding from outside, undertook a series of projects in the late 1960s that, perhaps, defined the limits of how far a Chicago community organization could challenge the city political machine for control of its affairs.

It undertook a youth-training and counseling program that enlisted the cooperation of one of the main indigenous organizations in the area, a gang called the Blackstone Rangers, in 1967–68. The program succeeded in creating a truce in gang warfare and violent crime for a time, but from its beginning suffered from police harassment and general official hostility. Police arrested and jailed most of the top leadership in the gang (only one in thirty was finally found guilty), who were the ones most likely to manage the program well, and in the end many of those who had led the effort were rewarded with jail terms.

TWO joined with the University of Chicago in the Woodlawn Experimental Schools Project, designed to introduce parent involvement and blacks into the teaching process, an effort soon defeated by the city school administration. The organization also created an exemplary Model Cities application and plan for the neighborhood that was abandoned when it became apparent they would get no support from the city.

All of these efforts involved a degree of community control and, according to Fish, failed for that reason. Brazier's comment later about the city approach was: "The City of Chicago will resist with all its resources any efforts toward community control," and he interpreted its approach as "help people only if you can control them. If you can't control them, don't help them."[16]

The result was paradoxical. TWO had become the voice of Woodlawn through its organizing earlier in the decade, and the late sixties projected its approach across the city and around the nation. But after the 1960s,

TWO, perhaps feeling its organizing base was secure and concluding it had pushed the limits of community control, adopted more of a service orientation. TWO focused mostly on projects that did things for the neighborhood without challenging city hall's power, a set of activities that were coming to be called, nationally, "community development." The result was a series of concrete accomplishments in the 1970s and 1980s—though modest by the standards it had set for itself earlier. At the behest of the Ford Foundation, TWO created the Woodlawn Community Development Corporation (WCDC) in 1969. WCDC, under the leadership of TWO executive director Leon Finney, was then able to work in alliance with the Daley administration; but this also distanced TWO from its earlier advocacy role. Later, TWO leaders created other organizations: Woodlawn Preservation and Investment Corporation in 1987, and The Fund for Redevelopment and Revitalization in 1992. During this period, however, the area lost population (falling from 81,279 in 1960 to 27,473 in 1990), and TWO adopted a strategy of mixed-income development, meaning an effort to bring middle-class people back to the area. In this strategy they got strong backing from Daley and city hall in the 1990s. Housing developments supported by The Fund in the 1990s included single and duplex units selling for between $97,000 and $142,000 each, but at the higher end in the same area, there were homes in a gated community projected at $249,000.[17]

Thus the 1990s role of TWO seemed to bear out Fish's conclusion—published in 1973—that simply by adapting to the realities of Chicago power and surviving, TWO had created the possibility that its earlier hopes for control might succeed at a later time: "Perhaps in the future TWO would not need to fight City Hall: City Hall might one day need TWO to sustain its own fight for city control."[18]

TWO's new role did not sit well with some of the remaining low-income population or organizations like WECAN (Woodlawn East Community and Neighbors), whose director "asserts WECAN has lost its funding because of its opposition to the Woodlawn mixed-income strategy. It has also had difficulty getting support from the three Woodlawn aldermen."[19] TWO leaders had justified the shift to a services role as a survival strategy. One-time executive director E. Duke McNeil put it this way: "We learned a great political lesson. . . . You can't merely be a protest organization. Once you've identified and diagnosed a problem, you've got to go in and do something. [The transformation of the organization] was a necessary expedient for me and eventually a very painful step."[20]

That the transformation to a services organization would then lead to the "mixed-income" strategy seemed to be part of the scheme as early as the 1970s or early 1980s as well. Leon Finney, who succeeded McNeil, along with the widely perceived dominant force in the organization, TWO's early leader, Bishop Arthur Brazier, responded to criticism with a justification: TWO originally had its roots in the protests of "predominantly middle-class and working-class people aspiring to the middle-class.... TWO was not just built on poor people." In recent years the original base had left the area, and TWO wanted to attract them back.[21]

Finney also justified TWO's transition with a theory of organizing: the changes in TWO's direction came from a "natural evolution." In the earliest phase, "you have to involve yourself in theatrical kinds of confrontations. In the next, 'representational' stage,... you lower your voice and force adversaries to discuss issues, often through the threat of a boycott. [Then,] in the 'brokerage' stage, you're sitting at the table and saying, 'Let's deal.'" Finally, TWO reached an "institutional" stage: "People know you're there and don't want to tangle with you. You are the establishment."[22] By the 1980s, Finney predicted, the cycle of deterioration would have been reversed and outside investment would be coming in.

North Lawndale

There was another possible outcome of TWO's early effort: that it was blazing the trail for other neighborhood organizations in Chicago. This could be true even though most groups would want to improve on the Woodlawn model or reject it completely. An important example was the experience of the North Lawndale neighborhood on the city's West Side.[23] By 1966 conditions there had deteriorated, as in Woodlawn. Robert Giloth, an author and former Chicago community leader, provides figures that document a "blowout," or white-to-black racial transition: from 1950 to 1960 the white population in North Lawndale dropped from 87,000 to 13,000, while blacks increased from 13,000 to 113,000; and from 1960 to 1990 the total population dropped from 125,000 to 47,296. The neighborhood's poverty rate by 1990 was at 48.4 percent, double the city's rate. Meanwhile the economic base of the area was declining: major employment centers like the International Harvester, Sears, and Western Electric sites closed or reduced workforces in the 1960s and 1970s.[24]

By the mid-1960s several bases for community organizing had established themselves in the area. Jack Egan, a Chicago priest who, because of his support for organizers like Alinsky and his propensity to align himself with radical causes, had been "banished" to North Lawndale's Presentation Parish, had started Operation Saturation, bringing in seminarians and volunteers to engage residents in conversations about their lives. They discovered a pattern of redlining of inner-city black communities by conventional banks, the Federal Housing Administration, and by real estate speculators who sold properties on contracts that put buyers at high risk of foreclosure.[25] They thought this could be countered through community organization and developed a pragmatic approach carried out through a new organization called the Contract Buyers League (CBL). The Contract Buyers League litigated and protested. One tactic was rent strikes: in 1968 six hundred contract buyers had put $250,000 in escrow funds. CBL lawyers instituted class-action suits, and the organization researched 475 contract-sale properties. Contract sellers forced twenty-one evictions, but the CBL renegotiated five hundred contract sales for a savings of $13,000 per homeowner.[26]

A parallel effort was the West Side Federation. WSF had been founded by a group of ministers led by the Baptist Reverend Shevlin Hall, and was a coalition of West Side churches. Lew Kreinberg, who was to have a long association with Hall and WSF, recalled that it began out of an effort to gain voice and prominence for West Side blacks in contrast to the more middle-class South Side groups such as had organized TWO; an early organizing effort had been motivated to generate a larger crowd at the Soldier Field rally than the South Side produced. Kreinberg also contrasted WSF with the Contract Buyers League, the Catholics, and the approaches taken by TWO. Hall, he recalled, "believed in maintaining his base, which was West Side blacks. We would work with others—whites, South Side blacks, TWO, the Contract Buyers League—but our priority was our base."[27]

Earlier, Kreinberg had helped mobilize West Side ministers by organizing a trip to Selma, Alabama, and in January 1966 Martin Luther King decided to bring his northern "End the Slums" campaign to Chicago, and the WSF was instrumental; King then rented an apartment in Lawndale a few blocks from Presentation Parish. The results were ambiguous. A rally at Soldier Field and subsequent march on city hall produced a set of demands nailed to the city hall door, chiefly a demand for open housing policies, cited later as instrumental in encouraging middle-class blacks to abandon the inner neighborhoods that organizers were trying to preserve. When King led a march in a white neighborhood, the marchers were "met with rocks and jeering crowds."[28] But King's campaign encouraged other organizations in North Lawndale and was a vehicle for further progress by the West Side Federation.

At the end of 1966 the organization was ready for more organizing. In December the West Side Federation discovered a proposal by a private developer to clear 190 blocks in North Lawndale to create a "new town," including 12,500 units of middle- and upper-income housing and a forty-five-acre golf course.[29] WSF fought this proposal. It capitalized on the local anger with a June 1967 conference on "Today's Lawndale: Black Colony—Tomorrow's Lawndale: New City." The colonial metaphor had become common among blacks and their white liberal allies by about this time. King, preparing his northern campaign earlier that year, said, "The slum is little more than a domestic colony which leaves its inhabitants dominated politically, exploited economically, segregated and humiliated at every turn."[30] References of these sorts are frequent among both white and black Chicago neighborhoods in the 1960s and 1970s.[31]

Out of the conference came a determination to counter the plans of the developers with a community-oriented plan. Organizers attracted funding from the Community Renewal Society and other groups, brought in experts like Jane Jacobs and Charles Abrams, and retained consultant planners who produced plans characterized as "responsible militancy." In effect, the "black colony" rhetoric that had reverberated in Woodlawn, and in the Martin Luther King campaign a year earlier, now generated a concrete remedy: local residents should not simply try to benefit from public policies in their neighborhoods but should own whatever development they decided to pursue.

The vehicles for ownership and control that came out of the June 1967 conference was the merger of four neighborhood organizations (including the Contract Buyers League) into the Lawndale People's Planning and Action Conference (LPPAC) and a new profit-making organization originally called the North Lawndale Economic Development Corporation (NLEDC), later renamed PyramidWest, with control in the hands of a board dominated by neighborhood residents. PyramidWest later gained status from the federal Office of Economic Opportunity's Special Impact Program as a community development corporation. Giloth says that "PyramidWest received more than $18 million of War on Poverty funds, and substantial amounts of categorical funds from the Economic Development Administration (EDA) and HUD, to support its operations and to invest in a variety of promising community development opportunities."[32] The focus of these was on a twenty-eight-block area to be called Lawndale Center, which was to include a shopping center, affordable housing, and a new high school. From Giloth's account, much of the proposed development went ahead, most only after a very long time. A sixteen-acre Lawndale Plaza Shopping Center finally went ahead in 1998; of a proposed 1,600 units of affordable housing, a portion was built, and state funding allowed the renovation of 1,240 units in 1995; the proposed Cal-West Industrial Park on the sixty-acre International Harvester site remained largely empty, and the site was finally sold; the Community Bank of Lawndale opened in 1977 and was spun off to become an independent bank in 1996; of proposed health care and communications ventures, PyramidWest succeeded in establishing a three-hundred-bed nursing home in Cal-West; but it failed in the effort to develop a cable-television franchise.

PyramidWest's underlying development theory for building a new North Lawndale was to become a more self-sufficient economy within the confines of the neighborhood. According to Hal Baron:

> The strategy of North Lawndale Economic Development Corp. is to take the funds that were shaken loose by the great Black protests and political movements of the sixties and to gain the greatest possible leverage from them, i.e., to establish the kind of economic institutions that continuously feed back vitality to the rest of the community's institutions rather than to drain them, as is more typical in the case of a Black ghetto.[33]

Baron then quotes NLEDC's president, Cecil Butler, in a staff memo:

> Of course, in this day and time, it is impossible for any area...to be an independent economy because of the interdependence...among various cities....The best that we can expect to do is to become limited producers of goods that have some value to other areas and to be capable of generating enough income to support the inhabitants of this community. To do this would relieve the area of the stigma of being a welfare-, government-supported poverty area; it would generate the savings and investments required to produce the housing, commercial and business investment that grows from the capacity to save and the expenditure of earnings. Further, it would produce public revenue that would enable the area to claim the capability of supporting its own public and private institutions, industry, schools, public services, charities, churches and the whole range of institutions that supplement and perpetuate the society.[34]

This theory, over time, became more focused: the goal was to undertake land and physical development on a significant scale, assembling and protecting land from other uses. Lew Kreinberg, research director of the NLEDC, said, "We are creating...a community which has never been known in this West Side ghetto."[35]

But Giloth describes a sequence of optimism followed by frustration and organizational decline. Initially NLEDC/PyramidWest was able to sustain itself as an independently conceived response to its image of North Lawndale as a ghetto colony, with a plan for self-sufficiency. A key resource was its designation as a special impact area by the federal Office of Economic

Opportunity: unlike other federal programs, OEO funding did not have to go through city hall,

But over time its CDC, PyramidWest, found that it could not ally with outside capital under the self-sufficiency program: "The Cal-West Industrial Park remained largely empty for years, a result of the market and Pyramid-West's reluctance to sell the land at a low price or to settle on businesses (like warehouses) that were not labor intensive."[36]

A *Chicago Tribune*'s 1986 muckraking series on North Lawndale, published as *The American Millstone,* assigned blame for the slowness of development in North Lawndale, and the community's continued demise, to Cecil Butler, the president of PyramidWest, and the general antibusiness attitude of community control.[37]

Don Kane, a city economic-development official during the period, argues that PyramidWest, as a black-owned development organization, was "swimming upstream to begin with." Butler's refusals to accept deals or to write down the land value ended up scaring investors away, he said. "There's no question about it," Kane said, "that this created a perception among the private sector and the city that they were very difficult to do business with, and ultimately people stopped coming to them."[38]

Giloth found the problem in "the fatal combination of poor market conditions, collapsed urban policy after 1973, changing government regulations, bureaucracy, and high expectations."[39] With the economic and demographic decline, there eventually emerged new plans in the 1980s and 1990s. Other players entered the game, particularly the North Lawndale Christian Development Corporation (LCDC) and the Steans Family Foundation. In 1978 Wayne Gordon, a high-school history teacher and coach who, while a student at suburban Wheaton College, had seen a role for himself in the inner city as a result of his connection to the Fellowship of Christian Athletes, began leading prayer groups at Lawndale High School and founded the nondenominational Lawndale Community Church. Thus connected to a widening circle of local residents, Gordon developed a series of related projects. There was the Lawndale Christian Health Center in 1984: by 1996, he reported seventy thousand patient visits, twenty-nine affiliated doctors, and 120 employees. He also developed the Lawndale College Opportunity Program, and in 1987 the Lawndale Christian Development Corporation (LCDC). By 1997 it had a staff of thirteen and a budget of $550,000 and was rehabbing apartments. Its strategy was to rehab units around the church, a forty-block area, to create home-ownership opportunities for residents.[40] Giloth noted dozens of units by the time he was writing (1997), and grants of $3 million from Neighborhood Housing Services and $3 million from the city. LCDC was also doing economic development: four renovated commercial properties; three for-profit businesses, trying to develop job-training programs; and plans for a day-care building worth $3.5 million, projected to be employing fifty people by 1999.

Giloth lists a number of other initiatives starting in the late 1980s. In 1988 a private developer built Homan Square, mixed-income housing on the old Sears property that, he said, "already contains several hundred occupied units."[41] He recounted many new initiatives in the 1990s: block clubs of homeowners, indigenous rehabbers, a hospital expansion, additional housing, and nonprofit investments.[42] Then in 1994 the Steans Family Foundation made a long-term commitment to community building in North Lawndale. Giloth saw this as a "convening force" to "knit together the activities, leaders and organizations of North Lawndale." Investment was $1 million in 1997, to be repeated yearly, in five-year renewable phases. Money was to go as "flexible, non-categorical dollars."[43]

Giloth, a onetime Chicago organizer and public official who later became an intellectual force in the community development movement with the Annie E. Casey Foundation, found the North Lawndale case paradigmatic, and a conundrum. On the one hand its eventual revival seemed to support a conservative and market-oriented adage proposed by economist Anthony Downs in the 1970s: avoid central planning from city hall; some neighborhoods would simply have to decline until, with disinvestment and depopulation, they again became attractive to investors and relatively wealthy populations seeking to rehabilitate and repopulate areas with locations near inner-city businesses and attractions. But North Lawndale had also gotten constructive attention from churches, foundations, and the efforts of organizations like PyramidWest, in some ways a distinctly liberal, community development initiative.[44]

There was still the question of whether the West Side Federation's analysis of North Lawndale was the correct one and, if so, was the self-determination strategy effective. From the *Tribune*'s point of view, it was not debatable. Giloth refrained from final judgment, noting that eventually, the fact that PyramidWest held out may have benefited the residents who lived in Lawndale at the time—if not the potential middle class that might have been attracted back into the area by outside-financed new development. Kreinberg was at least as positive. "Did anything happen in Lawndale? Yes. We held on to the land."[45]

The Neighborhood Movement

TWO and the North Lawndale CDCs were prototypes, closely tied to the northern arm of the black civil rights movement, originating in protest.

There were white organizers and allies—Alinsky and von Hoffman for TWO, Kreinberg and others in North Lawndale. But black leadership dominated. That the two organizations followed divergent paths in the 1970s and came from divergent class roots was important, but both were different from what came later.

For when neighborhood organizations proliferated in the 1970s and began delivering services in affordable-housing development and economic development, their base had also broadened. Latinos and poor whites formed organizations, and there was a neighborhood movement growing among working-class, typically white populations, especially homeowners. By the later 1970s activists leading a range of groups experiencing displacement—the loss of "affordable" housing units from pressures of various sorts, including the expansion of institutions like universities and hospitals—concluded that they themselves needed to get into the housing business—usually rehabilitation of older structures—rather than limit themselves to protesting or tenant organizing or assuming that either private developers or the city would replace the lost units.

They soon formed networks. One of these activists was Thom Clark, who had been working in the Uptown community. In 1976 he had been meeting with Bob Giloth, then executive director of the Eighteenth Street Development Corporation in Pilsen, a mainly Latino neighborhood. They began meeting on alternate Saturdays, exchanging tips on "which foundations were giving us funky groups money, are there any bureaucrats in City Hall who understand what we are trying to do, do you have any contractors who don't rip you off, and where can you find the cheapest toilet in town. In 1977 there was an offer from the city to form a technical assistance center, and they joined with other to form a nonprofit which eventually became the Chicago Rehab Network."[46]

Meanwhile, activism increased, partly encouraged by developments in the Carter administration in Washington, where HUD had established an Office of Neighborhoods, but also by the early platform promises of Jane Byrne, who won the mayoralty in 1979 on an antimachine, proneighborhood agenda. When she backed away from this on taking office, neighborhood organizations and various other interests, including independent black political organizations, began to mobilize. There was, by the end of the 1970s, a diverse set of coalitions and organizations servicing the community organizations and pressing the city for political advantage on their behalf. Blacks had organized POWER and ICARE around welfare-rights issues. The Associated Colleges of the Midwest was channeling undergraduates into internship positions, and the University of Illinois at Chicago (UIC) was providing technical assistance through its Center for Urban Economic Development.

By 1982, many of these organizations were mobilizing in protest against the exclusionary and business-favoring policies of the old Daley machine. One coalition was organized to fight a proposed World's Fair, on the basis that it would turn viable neighborhoods south of the Loop into a parking lot. Other organizations had formed to do neighborhood planning in opposition to a downtown business-led effort called the Chicago 21 Plan.

There was also a sense that the CDCs, having shifted from advocacy and protest toward the delivery of services—as in the case of the Rehab Network—were moving toward a new level of capacity as potential political actors. Thom Clark recalled getting

> a sense that there were a number of groups reaching the level of sophis-
> tication that went far beyond the rhetoric of we're going to do it
> ourselves and actually begun producing units. We aren't necessarily
> speaking to the cost efficiency... the production efficiency may have
> left something to be desired, but the advocacy and equity that encom-
> passed the efforts of most of those groups and continues today was
> phenomenal, very important, and a very new kind of actor began to
> come into place in this town, so that when a progressive administration
> came into office we were ready to hit the ground running.[47]

Rob Mier and CUED

This broader-gauge approach to community development, with a jobs and business emphasis alongside housing and social services, got strong reinforce-ment from the work of Rob Mier, who had come to the University of Illinois at Chicago (UIC) in 1975 with both an activist interest and an economics orientation. Mier's students took jobs with a set of neighborhood organiza-tions, and Mier quickly sensed an interest on the part of neighborhood busi-nesses in maintaining their neighborhoods, and a sense of the connectedness of housing and business-district welfare. Mier discovered that many small neighborhood businesses had become alienated from the city administra-tion's preoccupation with downtown business, and he found ways to sup-port them:

> Businesses located out of the central area felt ignored by city hall.
> This stimulated the formation of local chambers of commerce, business
> development groups, industrial councils, and eventually the CANDO
> network. In 1977, Mier and some of his students worked with the

Economic Development Commission...doing a survey of manufacturing firms in the Pilsen–Little Village area. These firms were very disenchanted with city hall. This dissatisfaction led to their creation of the Pilsen Industrial Council. This council began to work with the Eighteenth Street Development Corporation. This networking between businessmen's groups and local constituency-based development groups was occurring in many neighborhoods.[48]

In 1978 Mier was successful in getting a grant from the federal Economic Development Administration to start the Center for Urban Economic Development (CUED) at the University of Illinois at Chicago, allowing him to augment student projects with professional staff. Other support organizations for neighborhood groups were the Center for Neighborhood Technology (1976), which published a journal, *The Neighborhood Works,* and such training institutes as the Midwest Academy and the National Training and Information Center. Mier also cited the awakening interest in the late 1970s on the part of civic associations, including the Urban League, Community Renewal Society, Latino Institute, T.R.U.S.T., Inc., and the Jewish Council on Urban Affairs; and foundations such as the Wiebolt, Joyce, and MacArthur foundations, the Chicago Community Trust, and the Woods Charitable Trust.[49]

What developed was a series of transactions between Mier—from his position as professor at UIC and with the resources provided through CUED—and the communities. This had a lot to do with Mier's background and inclinations, which were neither wholly academic in orientation nor wholly community related. He had a technical background—a bachelor's degree in engineering and a PhD in planning. But he wanted more than a technical approach. Part of his motivation came from his experience in the Vietnam War:

> I came back from Vietnam, with my head turned around, and I was still in the military. I wanted to engage in protest...at that point I was an engineer. What I found I was bringing to those community situations was certain technical skills and wanted more, wanted to broaden myself, wanted to understand more about politics and political economy. So I went to planning school. So I went back to Cornell with this strong orientation towards community organization and community development.[50]

At UIC, Mier found himself with students who came out of Chicago community organizations and who later went back to them. This put him in a natural relationship with them, and he soon found it rewarding to engage in two-way learning with them. While many academics—including some of his colleagues at UIC—either had no interest in the community organizations or saw themselves as "experts" with information that could flow mainly at the community, Mier was fascinated to learn from his new colleagues in the neighborhoods.

> I never imposed my definition of problems or my will on the solutions but really engaged with my students, and that's really something that enabled me to maintain a continuing relationship after they had left.... And because of that it became clearer as time went on that that was very important in this community formation and development process, so that I was not taking power from the organizations or using the organizations as a basis for my own personal power but rather was willing to suspend my judgment occasionally. It was clear to me when I started the center that this was a key ingredient in working with the organization.[51]

By 1982 Mier had built up a set of relationships with a network of activists, many of whom complemented housing interests with a neighborhood-based economic program. This was parallel to what Mier had been doing at CUED but was also partly created by him. There was some overlap with the originators of the Rehab Network, but Mier's program was broader than that. Giloth had gone to study at Cornell, but other allies at the Eighteenth Street Development Corporation, like Art Torres, would be involved. Two others, Kari Moe and Donna Ducharme, had gone to study planning at MIT but soon were to return.

One important initiative in 1982 was the Community Workshop on Economic Development (CWED), which organized initially to write a platform opposing enterprise zones, which were key parts of business and real estate proposals central to the fall 1982 gubernatorial race.[52] The CWED platform, which attracted a consensus of many groups, emerged that summer with three main propositions: economic development meant jobs, not real estate; city investments should be balanced between downtown and the neighborhoods; and city economic policy and program delivery should be participatory and shared between city hall and community-based organizations. Thus an agenda came out of the movement before any implementation in city-government policy was a definite prospect.

The 1983 Election Campaign

While the community development groups were beginning to come together in CWED and other venues in the summer of 1982, quite another set of interests were setting sights on the mayor's office: a set of black nationalists who, still smarting from frustrations dealing with Jane Byrne, sought their own candidate. There were several involved, but the most prominent leadership came from Lu Palmer. Palmer, an independent black journalist and political activist, had been meeting with other activists since the end of the 1970s to find and support a candidate for mayor. By the early 1980s he was signing off his radio talk show on black stations with "We shall see in eighty-three." He was tireless and devoted to the cause of independent black politics, a black nationalist who, as he continued to work, devoted himself to creating a coalition among the various factions in black Chicago.

Harold Washington Emerges as a Mayoral Candidate

By 1982 Palmer had trained two thousand black organizers to work opposite machine precinct workers in the 1983 election, and in the summer he organized a meeting of over a thousand blacks, which he billed as a mayoral plebiscite for the election the following year. Harold Washington, now a congressman from the South Side, had been Palmer's focus, and at the end of the meeting a formal vote showed Washington with a lead of over five to one over the next-favored candidate.

Washington had never been close to Palmer, and the relationship was cool. But after some jockeying, Washington did agree to be a candidate for mayor and was gearing up to run by the fall. His candidacy represented pragmatism on the part of Palmer and other black nationalists, as Washington had not been allied with them. Washington had been a machine precinct worker who had at one time been Daley's choice for the important state attorney's job. Proving himself talented but too independent, the machine put him instead into the state legislature where, through the 1960s and into the 1970s, he walked a tightrope between machine loyalty and independence. This became increasingly difficult. In 1969 the police killing of two members of the Black Panther Party, Fred Hampton and Mark Clark, forced a reappraisal for Washington and other blacks in the Chicago Democratic Party. Still he did not break from the party organization. Finally in 1977, after Daley's death, Washington tried a run for mayor against the machine candidate and eventual winner, Michael Bilandic. Washington was defeated soundly, receiving only 11 percent of the vote. That was the end of machine loyalty for him. Gary Rivlin wrote: "Washington did not return to the fold apologetic and contrite. 'I'm going to do what maybe I should have done ten or twelve years ago,' he told a group of black journalists. 'I'm going to stay outside of that damn Democratic organization and give them hell.'"[53]

He then won reelection to his state senate seat over machine opponents, and in 1980 successfully ran for the U.S. congressional seat left vacant after the death of longtime black machine politician Ralph Metcalfe, again over machine opponents.

What were his ambitions and prospects in 1982? Washington had attributes that could be seen in different ways. His experience in the Chicago Democratic Party organization was one of compromise, and neither his distant relationship with the black nationalist organizers nor his substantive positions suggested Washington was anything but a coalition builder. In the campaign, he projected to blacks that he would be a strong representative of black interests. He also promised, citywide, a reform administration—he would end corruption, open up government to all, and run a businesslike city hall.[54]

Community Development Enters the Campaign

In the fall of 1982 Hal Baron, a progressive academic who had channeled activist college students into Chicago community organizations throughout the 1970s for Associated Colleges of the Midwest, became part of Washington's campaign. Baron knew about CWED, having followed the job histories of Kari Moe and other placements, and recommended Moe as Washington's issues coordinator.

As it happened, the CWED ideas had played little role in the gubernatorial race. But while Palmer and other blacks were mounting a registration drive and a search for a candidate, many of the CWED activists then became part of Harold Washington's mayoral campaign when he announced in November 1982. Moe, who had taken a leave from her community job to study for a city-planning graduate degree at MIT, then gone to work with CWED, became the research director for the campaign, rode in the campaign car with Washington, and the CWED platform became the major substance of the campaign, elaborated in *The Washington Papers* as a campaign document.[55] The heat of the campaign tempered the movement agenda: in the terms I have suggested, ideas from the "movement" were transformed to an instrument of "governance." But it is worth noting that Washington did not simply adopt the CWED platform. He adapted it to the specifics of his own experience and connected it to the constituency that eventually elected him. Mier said,

> Washington's performance on the campaign trail was extraordinary. I
> felt that in the campaign we fed him some raw material, and he took it

to a level that was beyond my imagination. When I say he could take it beyond my imagination, we had a plank that we thought really touched the soul of the people the mayor was speaking to because it had come out of them, but his contact with that soul was much deeper. It was apparent to me that he was able to put it into a perspective that was much richer than even my decade of experience in Chicago would have enabled me to do. I couldn't put my finger on what it was at the time. But it didn't take me long after I actually began to work with him to understand it. He could take a current issue and put it into a thirty-year historical perspective that saw that issue in the context of the struggle for black political empowerment, the struggle for community empowerment, for civil rights, for human rights, fairness, labor, and good government. He had this thirty-year history at his fingertips and could relate any current issue to that. In making these historical connections, he was touching in a very fine-grained way on what people were responding to, what they were looking for, who the key actors were, the bases that had to be touched, and so forth.

Moe, who was also present at the interview just quoted, added: "This ability to take our more or less technical contribution to another level is a really important, very significant part of the history of who he was, because the way in which the establishment media, if you will, and the political opposition tried to package him is as a sort of charismatic leader, his victory being somewhat of a fluke, but no one has really addressed—or maybe they intentionally or unintentionally wash it out—the content side of what he really thought."[56]

Mier, Moe, and others worked for a Washington victory. So did many of the people in the neighborhood organizations, including the Latino and white wards, and Moe's role in the campaign car ensured the presence of the community development ideas and those of the CWED platform in the Washington campaign. They surfaced in *The Washington Papers,* particularly the section on "Jobs," produced by Mier and a number of others. But competing ideas also appeared in the campaign—as evidenced later, in March 1983, by the appearance of a business-led Transition Committee, that proposed to influence appointments after the election.

Energizing the Black Vote

The community development ideas energized Washington, but subsequent comment stresses the black vote as the crucial force that won Washington's plurality in 1983. It was a force with the power of a social movement. It was as if the failed campaign of Martin Luther King—marching on Chicago's city hall in an effort to bring the civil rights movement to northern cities in 1966—was finally realized. Melvin Holli and Paul Green saw the election as a "massive, unprecedented and crusade-like folk movement led by charismatics and 'race' men," and he cited exit polls indicating a 98 percent black vote for Washington.[57]

Rehab Network activist Doug Gills described the way it felt on the streets: "There was something beautiful about it, and something that brought the dead to life. People who had been dead since the 1960s, not in a physical sense but emotionally, spiritually dead, came alive! I saw and worked with winos who put on ties and picked up their pens and clipboards and walked precincts during the Harold Washington campaign."[58]

In February Washington won the Democratic primary with 37 percent of the vote, defeating incumbent mayor Jane Byrne (33 percent) and Richard M. Daley, son of the late "Boss," who had 30 percent. In the general election on April 12, Washington defeated Republican Bernard Epton, with 51 percent of the vote. He was to endure a difficult first term, not consolidating control of the city council until 1986. But he was reelected in 1987 with 54 percent of the vote and was on his way toward a position of dominance in city politics when he died of a heart attack at his desk in city hall, the day before Thanksgiving later that year.

✒ CHAPTER 6

Washington in City Hall

Once in office, Washington faced a hostile city council. In a racially charged campaign, he had defeated the machine—still the way of life for the city council and embedded in the minds of the public and the press. The result was a struggle within city hall and with the council, one that hindered what he or his administration could initiate or accomplish. Robert Mier, reflecting on his efforts to initiate new programs in the department of economic development, wrote that "we won the opportunity to drive a 1940s jalopy in a 1980s road race," but "the pit crew was either inexperienced [or] working for the mayor's opponents." Kari Moe said that "trying to get things done was like fighting a war with someone else's army."[1]

Still, Washington's administration went through phases. Most public, for over two years a city council majority (called the "Vrdolyak 29" for the council majority leader, Edward Vrdolyak) engaged Washington in "council wars." A series of minor compromises and public relations successes made things easier by mid-1985, and a definitive break came in the spring of 1986 when, in a special election occasioned by a redistricting suit, Washington gained enough support in city council to control committee assignments, and open warfare ended. Thus there were two main periods for the Washington mayoralty and administration. And the later one could arguably be said to extend after Washington's death through Eugene Sawyer's interim mayoralty into April 1989, because the momentum of things begun were continued, and many administrators stayed on.

First Period, 1983–86

Meanwhile, in the earlier period, although the council-wars spectacle dominated the public's attention, new initiatives began to make their way through city hall. The neighborhood-oriented economic-development program centered in the department of economic development was key, along with a mix of strategic thinking and opportunistic response to crises.

Council Wars

Either the machine or racial antagonism would have made it hard to govern. The two together would produce a spectacle. Observers from other places, or perhaps in a later decade, would have difficulty seeing this. But there is no question about the shock that Washington's election represented to the white electorate. In one account, they heard Jesse Jackson scream on election night, "We want it allllll now!" And "for the machine loyalists and much of white Chicago, it seemed like the coming of a dark age." Most reporting took that viewpoint.[2]

The polarization was so intense that to this day Chicago has two memories, two histories of Washington's mayoralty. This duality and conflict is an enduring part of the story and will be part of what follows: the attempt to win "council wars," the steady progress toward administrative reform, the remarkable innovations in economic-development policy and (to a lesser extent) neighborhood housing and service provision, and later, the aftermath with its competing evaluations of the import of Washington's administration and electoral success.

The new mayor's inaugural address on April 29, while toned down from the fervor of his black supporters, suggested no compromise with the machine. He expected a majority of the council to support his program, and he had conceived a committee structure that would help him achieve it. But by the first council meeting, a week after Washington was sworn in, it was clear he had no majority. Possibly Washington underestimated the resistance he would get from the council. When, seeing this weakness, he adjourned the council, rebellious leadership reconvened the council and established their own set of committees and chairmanships, a situation that persisted until a special election in February 1986. There was a standoff. What seemed like a reasonable compromise to the whites would seem like caving in to Washington's base. One could argue that stubborn holding out served him well in the end. But at the time, the mainstream view of the situation might have been: "Washington is too weak to win, too strong to lose, and too stubborn to make a deal" with his aldermanic opponents.[3]

But from another perspective things were much more positive. The task of a reformer is inherently different from that of a leader who inherits an organization and an established approach to governing. Washington had to (a) combat assumptions about black capacities for leadership, deeply held in Chicago's wards and among its elites; (b) create a new political organization with a new base; and (c) operate within new fiscal constraints.

Administrative Reform

Later observers were divided in their assessments of Washington as an administrator. The majority would probably have agreed with the view expressed by Melvin Holli and Paul Green, who described Washington as "a superb and consummate politician who galvanized the black electorate. . . . He was a below-average and sometimes mediocre administrator and chief for the whole city. The political promise was greater than the mayoral performance."[4] Others complained that Washington "lacked a plan."

Alternatively, considering what Washington confronted, he was as accomplished an administrator as possible. As Washington conceived it, he not only had to deliver "good government" as if he was playing to a broad reform constituency, he also needed to play to his base, a black community that had supported him, which he needed to stay in touch with and responsive to.

Alton Miller, Washington's press secretary for the last three years of his mayoralty, reports a dual approach to organizing city hall. On the one hand, Washington needed to have a well-run, careful administrative approach. For this he had appointed an administratively focused chief of staff, Bill Ware. But he also appointed people whose job was to stay in touch with his constituency. The most controversial was Clarence McClain, a person who had street smarts, who Washington appointed to "be an open ear to anyone who was being 'professionalized' out of City Hall."[5] McClain was later forced out, but numerous appointees reflected Washington's base—not only the blacks but also the neighborhood movement, itself a multiethnic grouping that had built numerous coalitions and bridges in the years prior to 1983. Certainly there were conflicts and jealousies, but there was also great energy. Gary Rivlin, in his book on the Washington administration, noted "scores of people to the left of liberal" along with "businessmen such as Al Johnson . . . were among [Washington's] top advisors."[6]

And Holli, after noting administrative messiness, went on to recount a series of administrative high scores, even in the first year or so of Washington's term, when the city council was blocking many of his appointments:

> On the administrative and managerial side of the ledger, the Washington record was mixed but nonetheless encouraging. In the plus column,

the mayor in the first month symbolized the new austerity by eschewing the use of the city's luxury limousine and taking a 20 percent salary cut. By trimming some of the fat out of city departments and leaving vacant positions unfilled, he balanced the budget, as required by law. In June the mayor pleased reformers by signing the Shakman decree, which banned political hiring and firing. Washington also took the unprecedented step of mandating a freedom-of-information executive order that opened up city records. . . . In addition, the mayor delivered some additional city funds to the neighborhoods and promised that more would follow.[7]

Neighborhood Economics

In retrospect, at least one further interpretation existed, really a deeper one that sprang from the neighborhood organizers and economic-development groups. Like their machine-oriented counterparts, they had an academic support base as well. They would argue that Washington's black base was crucially reinforced by a community development constituency that, while it came partly from a black civil rights movement, had always had allies and participants from other minorities and nationalities and whites, and even in its separatist moments had retained an ethos of mutual tolerance that made coming together, even if only episodic, an occasional force.

Doug Gills, who was part of this community development network and later an academic at the University of Illinois at Chicago, thought the community economic-development group was not only a force that Washington took into his administration but one that had been crucial to his election:

> On the surface it [was] a black nationalist movement. But beneath this was a long-building set of forces and linkages. Many of the most active representatives of CBOs [community-based organizations] in coalitions like the Rehab Network, CWED [Community Workshop on Economic Development], and the Chicago 1992 Committee on the one hand and POWER [People's Organization for Welfare Economic Reform] on the other were active militants in civil rights, black empowerment, and affirmative action movements among the black and Latino communities. These broad associational linkages made possible deep and extensive outreach to constituents who could be politicized and steered into the electoral arena.[8]

After the election, the most important factor launching community development approaches into the city administration itself was the appointment of community activists into jobs in city hall. Notable among these was Rob Mier, who decided after the election to try for the commissioner of economic development position. He thought Washington's victory was mainly about race, but that there was also another substance to it, that of economic development. And Mier had been formulating an approach to economic development for a decade, one that emerged in the CWED platform the previous fall and that Washington had put into practical terms and connected to neighborhood interests during the campaign. Mier formulated it as "jobs, not real estate"; balanced development with direct support to neighborhoods as well as the downtown; and the delivery of economic-development subsidies and services through neighborhood entities, not city hall alone.

Mier had been playing a supporting role in the campaign. His close colleague Kari Moe was in the campaign car briefing Washington, and Mier was "cranking out one-pagers" every day in anticipation of the schedule of appearances. But he had not met Washington.

What brought him to seek the office of commissioner of economic development was the prospect that the policies—those of the CWED platform and *The Washington Papers,* which had been central to the campaign, and which he and his allies had been helping Washington articulate—might get lost when the new mayor got down to administration. Washington had appointed a transition team after the primary election. When it appeared he would win the general election, a number of business leaders got on board with him. Washington, wanting to keep their support, opened up transition-team positions to them. Mier saw that they would try to push economic-development policy in a wholly different direction: "Certainly [the business leaders would have] little sympathy for the ideas that had come out of the CWED conference the previous summer: jobs, not real estate development, balanced development with investments in the neighborhoods as well as downtown, and the delegation of much authority and funding to the neighborhood organizations themselves." He went on to note:

> Some of the [transition] teams, most notably economic development, were used by business leadership to advocate a particular policy position. In a pattern common to virtually every major city that had elected a minority-group mayor, the business leadership began a campaign to move the public development functions from under the control of the mayor into a quasi-public development corporation. They argued that this would provide development with "immunity from politics," but

it was in fact a much deeper struggle over the control of development priorities and resources.[9]

Moreover, Mier was encouraged by a sense that his ideas and those of his neighborhood-oriented allies had resonated with Washington. And it seemed that Moe would go into the mayor's office, so they would have an ally there. Mier saw that they needed to get someone "sympathetic to what we were doing appointed Commissioner of Economic Development . . . and I decided to make a push for it." He made the rounds of confidants of Washington, people pointed out to him, "going and helping them understand the evolution of the ideas that the mayor had campaigned on, where they came from, and juxtaposed it against what was beginning to crop up in the business community."

Mier saw the economic-development job as a way to keep the economic-development agenda at least partly in the hands of the community groups and under the control of the mayor. At some point, Mier said, he wrote a memorandum countering the business-oriented forces and took it to the mayor. Things went well. "The first time I went into meet Harold Washington," he said, "the chemistry was there. . . . The first time I sat down it was clear to me that we were of like mind."[10]

Mier finally took office in August 1983. He found the mayor's sentiments reinforcing, and took a sense of united purpose from them. As he had seen from the way Washington expanded on Moe's briefings during the campaign, there was the prospect for political leadership complementing administrative and technical work, and policy work, of their mutual reinforcement in city hall.

The Neighborhood and Economic-Development Program in Action

Mier's challenge, once in the department of economic development, was to relate the machinery of government to the social-movement base. This could be difficult and might require sustained pressure from outside the government as well as slow persuasion within.

Neighborhood Development

Working through neighborhood organizations had been a central part of Washington's platform. *The Washington Papers* proposed "both a shift in decision-making emphasis from top-down to bottom-up, and a concomitant strengthening of neighborhood organizations' capacities."[11]

After the inauguration, Washington sought to reallocate CDBG funds to neighborhood projects but needed an instrument to do so. The obstacle was the city council, which within a week was contesting the authority of the mayor. But by the end of May there was a compromise on the CDBG funding, with $13 million to be made available.[12]

The creation of the instrument was more complicated. Washington wanted to transform an existing department of neighborhoods into an agency that could bring the activism of the campaign into city hall. The city council blocked this, dismantling the department and firing its commissioner. Instead the council seized on a proposal in *The Washington Papers* that would establish "neighborhood planning boards" with some of the functions of the department of planning and control over CDBG funds. Washington sought to block this as too "liable to be captured by the opposition"[13]

The CDBG-allocation issue reveals the pressures Washington and his administrators felt. One the one hand, the council majority had a different way to handle the neighborhoods. In Rivlin's account, one of their leaders, Richard Mell, spoke for council leader Edward Vdolyak: "Eddie's color isn't black or white but green. All you have to do is give Eddie a little green, and you've got everything else you want."[14] Washington was unwilling to cede control over city jobs to the council, and unwilling to create structural power in the neighborhoods for fear they could be co-opted by the council. This was despite neighborhood support for the idea of neighborhood planning councils. Robert Brehm, executive director of Bickerdike Redevelopment, a Near Northside CDC, thought them a useful experiment.[15] Instead the Washington administration held most authority within city hall and created "delegate agencies" in the neighborhoods. The administration also designated organizations to be cooperating entities, redirected resources, made serious attempts to open up city hall and provide access to information, and tried to be responsive to the energy in the neighborhoods that had become so obvious through the campaign.

Mier's department of economic development (DED) seemed the most thoroughgoing in its implementation of a neighborhood-oriented program. From 1981 to 1992, as the total CDBG entitlement in the city stayed more or less constant, funding for DED delegate agencies increased from $946,000 to $2,349,000, and the number of agencies funded from forty-nine to sixty-six (reaching as many as one hundred in 1987–88).[16]

Perhaps the most complete delegation was DED's Local Industrial Retention Initiative (LIRI). According to Mier, under previous administrations the city already had a policy of supporting development-oriented neighborhood groups, funding some thirty-five groups when the Washington administration began its term in 1983. But the arrangement was a bone of contention. It circumvented the ward organizations, while putting the mayor directly in touch with the grassroots constituency. Previous mayors had sought this despite the discomfort of the council. For Washington, whose base was more directly in the neighborhoods, LIRI was even more desirable, and council opposition more of a challenge.[17]

Under Mier, DED tried to systematize this arrangement so that it could channel more funding to the neighborhoods and deflect opposition from city council. It expanded the numbers of neighborhood groups receiving direct funding from the city to over one hundred and established a four-tiered system so that groups that developed the most capacity were given more funding and DED staffing could pull out of that neighborhood. Another account described the increase as from "fewer than twenty groups" to "about 113," and a budget that went from "less than $400,000" to "over $3 million."[18]

That final stage of development was called the Local Industrial Retention Initiative (LIRI). It was run by Arturo Vazquez, formerly one of the leaders in Pilsen and with CWED, now assistant commissioner for DED's field operations division. DED had identified several local industrial councils it worked with as having the highest capacity to step up their industrial retention efforts.

> The LIRI program originated in the field operations division of DED, run by Arturo Vazquez. It evolved from an identification of the half dozen local industrial councils that had the greatest capacities to undertake industrial retention efforts like deciding what businesses should be approached, carrying out business visitations, figuring out what could be done for them and what the city could realistically do for them. The idea was to "give them more confidence in the city."[19]

Vazquez, who managed the LIRI program, presented it in part as a "good government" initiative, justified not only by the loss of industrial jobs but by the administrative malfeasance of previous administrations: the Daley machine had turned the city over to the downtown growth coalition and there was the problem of shakedowns—"scandals almost every other week about somebody being caught taking money, shaking down a business for money under threat of losing a license. The business community lacked confidence in the city."[20] Vazquez had seen another approach, that of sharing power with the neighborhoods: "I participated in a conference in Florence, Italy, on decentralization, and it was a real eye opener for me....You had locally elected councils in neighborhood areas. The city budget was distributed to these neighborhood areas by formula."

Vazquez decentralized the business-calling function to the LIRI groups. "Every local group had a business constituency and businessmen on their boards, as well as a neighborhood constituency." Thus they both improved the business-calling function and gave local businesses more of a stake in the city's efforts.[21]

The LIRI and other supported neighborhood organizations were often controversial and were scrutinized in city council and HUD audits. Mier and Vazquez tried hard to monitor them by using professional outside evaluations, and in this way they succeeded in deflecting challenges. Vazquez claimed the program was "still in operation [as of around 1992]....The staff we developed to manage it is still in place and is working to keep the program going. So we managed to institutionalize the program."[22]

While DED may have created more neighborhood agencies, or supported more, other administrators made similar claims. One was Robert Giloth, a former Chicago organizer and CDC director who left a PhD program at Cornell to become Mier's director of DED's research and development division (R&D). According to Giloth's review,

> The Department of Human Services shifted $7 million of new and existing resources to support 124 new delegate agencies....The Planning Department initiated a Neighborhood Planning Grant program to support a range of "bottom-up" physical planning efforts....The Department of Housing supported a housing-abandonment-prevention effort that funded thirteen delegate agencies.

And Giloth's own research and development division in the department of economic development "invested $1.2 million between 1984 and 1987 in business incubators, resource recycling, microenterprise, capital pools, sectoral research, and worker buyout opportunities," and did joint projects "focused on building early warning plant-closing networks, industrial displacement organizing, and city purchasing from youth enterprises."[23]

All this was consistent with Washington's campaign rhetoric and general policy. He had signed the Shakman decree soon after coming into office, a consent decree that settled a court case by reducing the number of city patronage appointments drastically, proclaiming that "the machine, as we know it, is dead." Some thought that Washington intended eventually to replace the machine-based allocation of city resources through the aldermen with an administration-based allocation system through the community organizations.[24]

Planning: Chicago Works Together (CWT)

There was the exercise of doing the CWT plan in 1984.[25] This was a matter of the mayor (and Mier) extending his administrative base and, later, reestablishing community involvement around the goals of the plan. Initially the ideas of the CWED platform and *The Washington Papers* in no way extended throughout the administration, which in many cases included professionals who had been hired from elsewhere and had little or no contact with the neighborhood movement. Some were sympathetic but needed to reflect on concrete ways to apply decentralist ideas. Others were simply uninformed about the broader policy issues around them and brought essentially specialist and technical perspectives to their departments.

As Mier described it, Washington sprung the idea of a plan on him. He woke up one morning to hear on the radio that the mayor would release his development plan in about sixty days. Arriving in city hall, Mier went to Washington and asked, "What is this development plan I hear about? The mayor quietly beamed with the smile he wore when he was about to ask for something impossible with the complete confidence it would somehow get done. He said, 'I figured you'd fill in the blanks.'"[26]

Mier then called each of the relevant department heads and gave each a copy of *The Washington Papers,* saying, "This is your bible. The Mayor wants you to read it, and come to a retreat to discuss how your department can implement its ideas." The retreat was held at a suburban motel one weekend, and the plan resulted.

Later, neighborhood people complained at their lack of inclusion in the process; and in November of 1985 the city embarked on an eighteen-month process that led up to a revised plan and the 1987 reelection campaign. Neighborhood representatives got more access to that process.[27] But the first version of the plan was initially an internal-administration affair—though no less important for that.

Mier was fond of recounting the way the Washington administration's economic-development policy emerged from a set of metaphors rooted in the community organizations and activists who assembled in August 1982 to formulate a response to the federal and state enterprise-zone proposals. Most simply put, they proposed a policy that favored jobs over real estate, promoted balance between the Loop and the neighborhoods in development investments, and emphasized the role of neighborhood organizations designing and delivering programs. These core ideas, Mier noted, reappeared in the central campaign platform document, *The Washington Papers;* in the 1984 development plan, *Chicago Works Together* (CWT), put together by the key agencies of the development subcabinet; and in *Chicago Works Together II,* an updated 1987 plan that emerged after the eighteen-month review process that involved a large number of participants.[28]

CWT, several would argue, was a key event in the council-wars period of the Washington administration. Giloth and Moe described a document that, over several iterations, with increasingly wide involvement, put together a constellation of ideas to counter and challenge the nearly hegemonic position of the business community and its machine allies.

They asked the question one always asks about this sort of exercise: What did CWT accomplish?

1. Like the Cleveland Policies Plan, CWT reaffirmed the redistributive functions of city government against the emerging business and mainstream consensus that the main issue should be growth. CWT did not even address growth, according to Giloth and Moe.[29]
2. Washington's administrators put more emphasis on the jobs goal. Giloth and Mier said the goal was important. In their conception, the jobs goal was more than a symbol; it was, rather, a theory of local intervention in the economy that emphasized manufacturing, balanced development, neighborhood jobs, service delivery, and small-business development. A focus on jobs meant communicating a different policy argument about municipal economic development, developing plausible strategies and projects, and holding developers as well as the public sector accountable for their commitments.[30]
3. Chicago's neighborhood activists and administrators had, by the time they formulated the CWED platform and *The Washington Papers,* a sophisticated understanding of the "mainstream" approach to economic development.

David Moberg, a Chicago journalist of note and one of the city's more acute observers, later contrasted two visions prevalent in the city:

There's a fundamental thread running through this neighborhood politics: a belief that it is possible for the city, with many small, well-calculated interventions made in cooperation with community groups, to revitalize Chicago's neighborhoods and economy by building on what is already here and serving people who already live here.

This outlook contrasts with the pessimistic philosophy dominant among many politicians, businessmen and opinion makers who have written off Chicago's traditional economy and many of its neighborhoods, along with their inhabitants, as hopeless millstones, dragging down the city. They see Chicago's salvation in new megaprojects, new service and financial industries, new neighborhoods, and new—whiter, more middle-class, or professional—people, all focused on a booming downtown. They think that government should not try to make the marketplace serve community needs better. Instead, they believe in a minimalist government that defers to investors and other powerful business interests to determine the future of the city according to their own, often short-term profit calculations.[31]

DED's Research and Development (R&D) Division

Late in 1983, Mier took steps to establish a new research and development division within DED. In January 1984, having been charged with the Chicago Works Together project, he arranged the transfer of Kari Moe, who had moved from the campaign car into the mayor's office, into DED as assistant commissioner to direct the new division. Moe then became the main staff person working with Mier on the plan. But the R&D division branched in many directions.

Mier also spoke with Robert Giloth, his former student at UIC and a neighborhood organizer, who was at Cornell at the time. Giloth joined the new division in March 1984 and succeeded Moe as director in mid-1985. He recounted its conception as one of several "centers of progressive innovation" in the Washington administration.[32] Mier also was solving his own problems within DED. He sought to replicate Norman Krumholz's arrangement in Cleveland a decade earlier: hoping to innovate in the rigid bureaucracy he had inherited, Krumholz put a group of young planners in a separate space and told them to come up with something new. Mier had a similar bureaucracy with its own rigidities.

Giloth, like Moe and others in DED and in the "centers of innovation" he describes, was a veteran of the community development movement in Chicago. He had come from one of Chicago's western suburbs, gone to college at the University of Colorado, and dropped out and moved to Chicago in 1970. After working a series of jobs—janitor in Chicago, bookstore worker in Philadelphia—and finishing up at Colorado, he enrolled in the graduate planning program at the University of Illinois at Chicago. Mier arrived there soon after, and Giloth became one of his students, working back and forth between neighborhood organizations and the university. His main commitment soon became the Pilsen neighborhood, and later he was executive director of that area's Eighteenth Street Development Corporation, a CDC that "rehabilitated abandoned buildings by working with former gang members, providing them with jobs and training."[33]

Giloth and Moe, teaming up with Mier, provided research and other support for Mier's commissioner role. The R&D division embarked on a series of efforts that successfully helped launch initiatives outside DED: they formulated the city's response to the Playskool issue, helped launch the general obligation bond campaign in early 1985, and supported the Westside Jobs Network that made possible the Playskool negotiations. (Each of these is discussed later in this chapter.)

But, Giloth wrote, the R&D role within DED was not satisfactory. The original approach had been for R&D to work with other DED units on innovative projects. But these units resisted, according to Giloth. His retrospective account described the efforts to get other DED divisions to work on new issues like first-source hiring, microloans to small businesses, and minority- and female-owned business development. In the end these initiatives did not work. Early on, the line divisions did not have the right personnel to pursue the new projects, and there was a cultural divergence: "Line divisions wanted R&D to design parking program evaluations and program application forms; R&D wanted to launch demonstration projects or to study business needs."[34]

By 1985, when Giloth became director of R&D, the division adopted a "theory and practice of special projects that did not depend upon the resources or participation of the line divisions and that became more externally focused." Giloth later elaborated a theory. R&D would find community partners, or other partners outside city hall, and work with them to devise approaches to problem solutions. They found various partners. One was the Westside Jobs Network that had been started when Mier let contracts to both the Midwest Center for Labor Research and CUED to devise ways to anticipate and head off plant closings, and that played a role in the Playskool plant closing negotiation and its aftermath.[35]

Establishing the Jobs Policy

Whether the R&D unit made all the difference, it certainly helped as DED put together a series of initiatives and policies that established Chicago's new economic-development policy, which sought to retain manufacturing jobs while involving and serving the city's working-class neighborhoods. R&D did other things as well, but certainly during the time Giloth was involved, it was able to aggregate staff time and top-level attention on related and, one must conclude, mutually reinforcing efforts: the plant-closing "early warning system" demonstration in the city's West Side neighborhoods during 1983–85; the Playskool plant closing and city lawsuit and negotiated settlement in 1984–85; the Steel Task Force that operated in 1984–87; and the establishment of planned manufacturing districts—a process that lasted and was elaborated on through the first years of the Richard M. Daley administration.

Westside Jobs Network

One of the early initiatives from Mier and the neighborhood economics activists in the Washington administration was the implementation of "early warning systems" to counter plant closings. Manufacturing-plant closures had become widespread in the Midwest by the 1980s, and activists were trying several tactics to mitigate their effects on employees and neighborhoods. One approach was to somehow counteract the element of surprise on the part of management. Labor activists were becoming aware of a few patterns in management approaches: (1) closings were not market driven, though falloffs in demand were typically cited by management as closings were announced; (2) management statements of intent were unreliable: the pattern was to precede closings with avowals of intent to remain in business for the long haul; and (3) management often sought subsidies from localities and givebacks from labor in the form of wage and other concessions as a condition for remaining in business.

Rather than rely on management statements, labor activists saw that it was possible to discern early warning signs of impending closings by observing patterns at the shop-floor level. These signs might include a change in ownership, the failure to modernize capital equipment, or other signs best discerned at the shop-floor level. By the end of the 1970s, labor activists had begun to see that contacts among workers over plant-floor changes might anticipate closings and give cities and other interested parties a chance to prepare negotiations with these firms and either avert closings altogether or demand conditions that would mitigate the impacts on workers.

Mier had been aware of these sorts of activities, and when he became commissioner of economic development, the task of coming up with some kind of early warning system was on his agenda. Activists and researchers outside of city hall had been developing the topic. Dan Swinney, who had founded the Midwest Center for Labor Research in 1982, sought to organize an early warning system. Another was David Ranney, Mier's colleague at the University of Illinois–Chicago and at the Center for Urban Economic Development. Mier eventually let contracts to both of these units, and out of that emerged the loosely organized Westside Jobs Network (WJN). A retrospective account of the network is that of Giloth and Rosenblum, who reflected on the role of WJN in the Playskool and other plant-closing incidents in the 1980s.[36]

Playskool

Many examples illustrate the ways the Washington administration tried to implement the jobs goal. Mier at one time thought the most important early move by the Washington administration was the aggressive pursuit of the Playskool case in 1984, where a firm employing several hundred workers, after taking a city grant premised on the retention of these jobs, announced it was moving its operations to another state. The city sued Playskool, ultimately winning several concessions for the employees (in the end, however, the Chicago Playskool plant closed), sending the message that Washington was serious about saving jobs and neighborhoods whose economy depended on plants like Playskool, and setting the stage for a number of other policy initiatives.[37]

The reason the city was as effective as it was in winning a somewhat better outcome for the employees and the neighborhood was that there was in place—in large part with city support—the Westside Jobs Network described above. Its members monitored plants for signs of disinvestment so that when a firm like Playskool made moves that might be the preliminary steps toward a closing, they could be ready to spread the alarm. This was the case with Playskool, and within days of the announcement of the closing in September 1984, WJN was ready with a press conference; letters to Mayor Washington and the president of Hasbro, Playskool's parent corporation; and the argument that Hasbro's action was a "breach of trust" implied in the firm's acceptance of a city grant. They played up the dissonance between the effect of the closing on the plant's 750 low-income workers and the toys the firm produced exploiting the Christmas season. By December they had escalated their campaign to declare a nationwide boycott on Hasbro products. In December the city went to court against Hasbro, claiming a breach of contract because of the earlier subsidy and asking for damages. After the press and organizing campaign, both supporters and opponents in city council stood up with Washington on the issue. The dramatization was remarkable, far beyond the immediate outcome—Playskool agreed to establish a $50,000 emergency fund for laid-off workers, keep at least one hundred workers employed in the plant until November 1985, and establish a job-placement program for laid-off workers with a $500 incentive payment to firms hiring Playskool employees. But the campaign publicized the issue of plant closing and made it possible for the city to move ahead with other actions. The city council began looking more closely at the performance of other recipients of city subsidies based on the promise of jobs; awareness shifted from the problem of acquiring firms to retaining jobs. Other early warning networks were investigated around the country—the Playskool incident helped start a national debate about the relative roles of corporate leadership and city governments on jobs issues.

The Task Force on Steel and Southeast Chicago

The Task Force on Steel and Southeast Chicago was put together by DED to save at least some steel-related jobs in the wake of actual and threatened plant closings and layoffs. The immediate and dramatic impact was the closing or threatened closing of five "integrated" mills just prior to 1984, when the task force began its studies. These included Wisconsin Steel, U.S. Steel South Works, and three others.[38] One account put the losses in steel-production employment in Southeast Chicago at fifteen thousand since 1979, with each layoff resulting in further losses of related manufacturing activity and jobs.[39]

The Task Force on Steel and Southeast Chicago was one of Washington's and DED's early initiatives. It was a commitment in *The Washington Papers* during the primary election campaign, and Mier reports the Steel Task Force getting under way early in 1984, along with the Chicago Works Together planning effort.[40] Other task force efforts followed. Steel was arguably the most important, not because of tangible results but for the intellectual capital it mobilized behind the city industrial policy overall.

One can ask what hopes they had for it. Plant closings had been an issue attracting the attention of economists, planners, and activists around the nation. For these, the plant closings revealed a fault in corporate hegemony, a fault in the argument that it "produced abundance" for the nation and its localities. On close scrutiny, plant closings often revealed mismanagement or profit taking rather than simple changes in product demand or changes in technology, though these were also typically part of the picture. Moreover, plant closings were more than an intellectual issue: they caused intense pain where they occurred and required some kind of response. Thus any investigation and policy proposal had a chance to be heard.

But attempts to form task forces had also run into conflict and stalemate, and cooperative approaches were elusive. Corporate leadership in Youngstown and Pittsburgh had proven intractable when activists attempted to counter steel closings with worker takeovers or public interventions. Even when local unions had been able to put together coalitions to acquire or support acquisitions of plants threatened with closure, they would find corporate owners intransigent and unwilling to sell and the international union unsupportive.

Mier and DED went ahead. The task force organized itself during the spring of 1985. It had twelve voting members. DED added four "working groups," on business development, real estate, technology, and the role of steel in the economy. The voting members acted as a "Policy Committee" that would have final say and the only formal standing to issue a final report. Ranney reported the composition as weighted to the disadvantage of the labor and community people, particularly among the voting members, which included four "experts"—in law, real estate, banking/finance, and steel management—plus one member from international union management; there were no workers or local union officers among the twelve. The weighting was more equal in the working groups.[41]

Mier and DED sought to encourage support for the promanufacturing policy, including the retention of steel jobs. In retrospect, there were two main strategies. One of these was to shine the light of day on the dynamics of the steel industry. If management intransigence was ideologically driven—as many critics thought—the city could at least provide a factual basis for an alternative course. Mier sought an industry analyst who combined expertise with a viewpoint independent of industry leadership. He contacted economist Ann Markusen, a University of California, Berkeley, professor, to work as a staff consultant.[42] Markusen, who had worked on steel-industry issues in California, took a leave from her Berkeley job and jumped in with enthusiasm on arrival in Chicago in January 1985. For Markusen, the Task Force on Steel and Southeast Chicago was a chance to extend work she had done earlier in California. There, with Julia Parzen, she had written *A Prototype Industrial Policy Study of the California Steel Industry* and had worked with Philip Shapira and others (Bennett Harrison in New England, Dan Luria in Detroit) on plant-closing issues. And she continued to write on this theme. Clearly she saw it as a national issue, with Chicago as the most prominent case.[43] Mier urged her to complete her report quickly, so that it could impact the task force before its discussions were too far under way and opinions hardened.

The second and complementary strategy was to include receptive people in the task force membership. Mier and Washington thus included a former steel executive and economist, Frank Cassell, on the task force. Cassell, now employed at Northwestern's management school, dissented from the divestment trend in the steel industry. He and Markusen played complementary roles, making the argument for saving a portion of Chicago's steel industry.

DED added other community and union voices, including Stephen Alexander, a former steelworker now on the staff of DED, and Mier's colleague David Ranney at UIC, who had a history of working in manufacturing plants and who was now playing an advocacy research role with Southeast Chicago communities. Ranney played an "outsider" role on the task force, and was quite critical of some of the task force's leadership, including Mier. Josh Lerner, another DED staff member, played a key role with Alexander. These additions were in the working groups. None were included in the key, Policy Committee group of voting members.

Markusen was de facto research director of the task force, working on contract as a consultant for most of two years. She participated in every task force meeting-of-the-whole and in the drafting of the Task Force Report. Perhaps by DED design, Markusen proceeded to pump information into the working groups, and to the Policy Committee. Perhaps the combination of expert opinion within the task force and Markusen's research would uncover perspectives and facts about the industry and the region that would change minds and make possible a cooperative process and productive outcome. For one thing was certain in the minds of researchers who had been observing the plant shutdowns for the past several years: some of the industry perceptions were ideological, not factually driven, and some of the shutdowns were both unnecessary and against the interests of the industries themselves.[44]

Markusen's research, initially collected in a thick volume later in 1985, supported the following conclusions:[45] Contrary to some opinion, including within the industry, steel manufacturing was not a dying industry. Rather, it was going through structural changes, quickened by factors such as a severely over-valued dollar (undermining exports and favoring imports of raw steel and steel-made products). There was a shift of some production from primary "integrated mills" to "mini-mills," essentially recycling scrap. Many jobs were lost as technology improved. There were technologically driven shifts in process, notably to electric furnace processes. There was a drop in demand due to the shift in automobile manufacturing. None of this was fatal for the industry, however, including for the productive apparatus in Southeast Chicago.

Primary production of steel, which still employed as many as 7,074 workers in Southeast Chicago in 1983, was connected to a far greater group of suppliers and purchasers, including secondary producers—of products like machinery and various consumer durables—not just the 15,638 in Southeast Chicago; nearly 300,000 workers was the estimate for the larger region around Chicago.

Markusen et al. indicated a loss of about 10,000 jobs in a "Steel Industrial Complex" of five basic sectors in Southeast Chicago: primary metals, fabricated metals, nonelectrical machinery, electrical machinery, and transportation equipment. The effect is even more pronounced if larger areas are described, for the primary producers in Southeast Chicago can be seen to affect the larger set of industrial sectors throughout the region. Markusen et al. documented a decline in "steel-related jobs" from 514,000 to 327,000 from 1956 to 1982 for the Chicago area defined as Cook and Lake counties.[46]

But if steel production was not dead in Chicago, then the larger "steel industrial complex" was an even more promising resource and productive capacity. And if a reduction in 3,000 "primary metals" jobs in Southeast Chicago triggered a reduction of 127,000 "steel industrial complex" jobs in the region, then would not *saving* that many jobs have a similar positive effect? Whether it was Markusen's data or Cassell's argument from experience, the task force could see the point.

The final step in Markusen's argument was a survey of what might be done. There had been studies of steel production and decline in several different places. Markusen found three responses:

1. What she called "bowing out"—just giving up on producing steel. This had been recommended by some business groups, including members of the steel industry.
2. "Bidding down" the cost of doing business, particularly labor costs.
3. "Building on the basics." Having eliminated or seriously undermined the arguments for "bowing out" or "bidding down," she chose to recommend city support for the maintenance to at least some steel-production capacity.[47]

In the end the task force had not adopted the most dramatic recommendation suggested by Markusen's findings—support for financing to keep at least one of the mills open. As she put it, "It demurred from drawing the analogy between urban renewal, with its strong quasi-governmental development agencies and powers of eminent domain, and industrial renewal."[48]

Markusen's initial report, which she produced as a prelude to the task force's final report, alluded to some of the deeper issues in the steel industry and the regional and interindustry reach of steel in the economy more generally.

A number of relatively more radical solutions were emerging. Staughton Lynd, a labor lawyer who had worked with dissident steelworker factions in Chicago before relocating to Youngstown, Ohio, where three mills closed between 1977 and 1980, had summarized one case as "the genesis of the right to industrial property": workers, because of long personal investment in the job, had a right to challenge management and ownership if it chose to close a mill for reasons of ownership and profit alone.[49]

Markusen's analysis—as she admitted—did not completely carry the day. On the surface one might have attributed this to the differences between business elites and community and labor interests. But there was also an argument *within* the business group, between the real estate people and those who, with community and labor support, sought to support steel manufacturing.

Thus Mier and Washington succeeded in implanting expertise with a community and labor voice in the task force—at least at the working-group level. But the broad range of interests would create difficulty in getting agreement and even in getting steel management to the table. Most important, its leadership was strongly in the real estate sector: Philip Klutznick, Earl Ray, and Leanne Lachman. Markusen commented: "When we started, they just looked at the lakefront property on the Southeast Side and saw condos."[50] Ranney, looking back much later, was struck by the sheer distance between the viewpoints of the city's business leadership and that of community and labor people, and by the DED assumption that the task force, as constituted, could find common ground between "the unemployed steelworker who had lost her or his home and was eating out of garbage cans and millionaire developer Philip Klutznick."[51]

It may be that this did not seem a fatal problem at the time. Markusen was doing her research (and reporting regularly to the task force). There was—after much DED effort and delay—at least some steel-management participation and perhaps a sense that the steel companies would eventually come around. (Stephen Alexander, a key staff member who helped formulate and support the task force, later described the careful efforts DED made to set it up; and Giloth reported that U.S. Steel, in the end, did meet with the task force and at least tacitly accepted some of its recommendations.)[52] But perhaps a fair assessment is that the task force never overcame its messy beginning.

The most poignant failing of the Steel Task Force was one of which Ranney himself was a direct witness: the failure to support the workers at Wisconsin Steel, who thought it would be reasonable to reopen that plant's Southeast Chicago mill. They sought a feasibility study for the idea. Ranney, who was a member of one of the working groups but did not have standing to attend the meetings of the task force's Policy Committee, the group of voting members that had the authority to make the task force's formal recommendations to the mayor, asked Mier for permission to attend. With permission granted, Ranney attended the meeting. Never invited to sit down, he stood to the side of the table around which the nine-member policy group sat and made his proposal. Ranney recounted later:

> When I stated briefly what the workers had proposed, several members of the task force rolled their eyes. One member literally shouted that the idea was absurd and that Wisconsin Steel was a "bucket of rusty bolts." Most of those around the table chuckled and the chairman, millionaire developer Philip Klutznick, pounded his gavel and asked for the next item of business. I was still standing to one side of the conference table (I was never asked to sit down at the table) and I raised my hand to be recognized. I was ignored by the chair so I interrupted, saying that the proposal was for them to do a serious study of the situation before determining the mill was a "bucket of bolts." The chair pounded his gavel...and stated that I was "out of order." I persisted, saying that people's livelihood and lives were at stake and I had hoped that the mayor's task force on steel would have some concern about this. All the while the commissioner of economic development sat silently glaring at me.[53]

Markusen's preliminary report, done under Northwestern University auspices, was high-quality applied academic work and took positions beyond the scope of what a majority of the task force would countenance—for instance, recommending "the traditional limits on public investment must be stretched, if necessary"—a phrase that made it into the official task force report. But it was clear that in the Policy Committee, they would not stretch as far as Ranney's steelworkers' proposal required.

Most discussions of the Task Force on Steel and Southeast Chicago focused, quite naturally, on results. The results seemed minimal. Of five large integrated mills, all had closed or were on the verge by the time the task force began its work. The city did put its available community-development-block-grant money into an effort to keep a portion of U.S. Steel South Works open—the company had announced plans to close—and Mier reported that one thousand jobs remained there as late as the early 1990s. The city did sponsor the Steel Technology conference at Argonne Laboratories. Mier himself noted the task force "failed to ignite a critical level of support."[54]

Retrospectives by some of the participants appeared in subsequent years. One theme was the contribution the Steel Task Force made to the practice of city government: Giloth in particular wrote (in one case coauthoring with Mier) about the task force as a way to encourage innovation.[55] In the case of the Steel Task Force, the differences in the positions taken by the participants were wide, the steel advocates and the real estate people never agreed, and Washington had little control over that, nor was there time to wait for discussion and compromise. He had to do the Steel Task Force, because he had put it in the platform (*The Washington Papers*)—and he had to put it in the platform because the problem was so large and obvious.

But in other respects the Steel Task Force performed well. Using Markusen and Cassell was a demonstration of how expertise could—at least potentially—lead local leaders to positions they would not otherwise have taken. The Policy Committee of voting members did, at least in principle, adopt the positions Markusen proposed to them, and they agreed on the importance of "betting on the basics."

In this, Markusen and Cassell played complementary roles. Cassell remarked on Markusen's stimulating work in a 1987 interview:

> Ann Markusen had views that I had, or I had views similar to hers, except we came from very different backgrounds. I had about 18 years in the steel industry, and knew the industry. And I had been a consultant to European steel companies. She had no experience except for the fact that she had an academic look at them but she was very sharp. So I think the idea that we build on the basics came out of that kind of synergy.

Cassell thought little representation of management was a problem, but that the task force nevertheless did keep in contact with steel management. As a result, he said, "there could have been some real opposition but it never developed."[56] Markusen, viewing the task force's final recommendations in 2008, summarized what she saw as a positive set of developments: "I did insist that the task force keep some focus on steelmaking,... they could see that there weren't a lot of good alternatives for the site. We did keep South Works open another ten years, I think, and we also helped many smaller specialty steel, steel suppliers, and steel distributors stabilize their business. We made a large argument, inevitably, about the manufacturing economy in general, because some of steel's problems were machinery and auto industry problems. You cannot imagine how strong the pessimism was in those days, both on the part of workers and communities and on the part of economists and opinion-makers—they just thought steel was dead! Although the industry did retrench a lot in the 1980s, especially in Pittsburgh, Youngstown, and other landlocked sites, it was far from fatally ill, and I think we made a big difference in the public case for manufacturing. Our work on the commission paved the way, for instance, for the industrial zoning that Chicago pioneered to save many of the other manufacturing establishments along the Clybourn corridor."[57]

One could argue for indirect effects. Mier, who was measured in his own assessment, nevertheless thought the impact of the task force was to reemphasize the city's commitment to saving manufacturing jobs.[58] And that commitment bore fruit in other ways. It followed on the Westside Jobs Network's early warning campaign in 1984, and the Playskool lawsuit and settlement at the beginning of 1985. The Markusen report came late in 1985, and the task force report in 1986. It was much later that the most enduring part of the industrial retention policy came to fruition—the planned manufacturing districts that became the industrial corridors that were implemented under Daley in the 1990s. All this is testimony to how long and hard an industrial policy took to take root—and even in the 1990s it was not the dominant city policy. Perhaps it was worth it. No evaluations, or measurement, have been done.[59]

Planned Manufacturing Districts (PMDs)

Another example of the city's efforts to preserve manufacturing jobs and establishments was the experience of Donna Ducharme, another MIT graduate, like Kari Moe, who led the way to the implementation of the jobs-versus-real-estate idea by helping invent and promote the planned manufacturing district. Her experience illustrates the way social movement, politics, and administration interacted during the Washington mayoralty.[60]

Ducharme had been hired in 1982 as the community development director for an expanded YMCA program north of the Chicago Loop. She had made the connection (it was her MIT thesis project) between unemployed youth in the area and the array of older manufacturing establishments in the nearby Clybourn Corridor northwest of the Loop. She created the Local Economics and Employment Development (LEED) Council, a planning group that included area youth and others, but also a number of manufacturers. Their work was focused early by the threat of displacement of manufacturing establishments and jobs by upscale residential and commercial development, beginning with a project called River North. It was the first time such a diverse group had come together. Certainly businessmen had organized, even manufacturers had. And there had been organizing among unemployed youth. Putting them together around a common goal was what was new.

Eventually LEED fixed on the idea of the planned manufacturing district (PMD), a zoning device that would protect factories and jobs against the influx of wealthy residents and upscale office and commercial development. This concern had been stimulated by a request to change the zoning of an industrial parcel to residential and commercial use. The LEED Council began to organize to fight as this and other proposals came forward that threatened to raise land costs from an average $6 per square foot to $12, or as much as $40, and to force longtime area employers and jobs out of business or out of town.

Advocates of the conversion process argued for the enhanced tax revenues accruing to the city, while opponents argued the costs of job loss in terms of income loss and added welfare costs and the costs of social disorganization. Ducharme's organizing process went through a series of phases. The first, at the ward level, was entirely among the area's businesses and residents. They discovered they opposed the zoning changes and that though they represented disparate social groups, they had a common interest. The second was that as the demands for changes increased within the ward, they undertook a frustrating search for support in the city government. Failing to get consensus in the government (the planning department was attracted to the zoning changes), they were able to get a small foothold in the research division of the department of economic development (DED), which supported a study on the effects of industrial displacement. Finally, with the study in hand and the requests for zoning changes piling up in 1985, they reached a sympathetic political figure in the ward councilman, Marty Oberman. Oberman declared a moratorium on the zoning changes until a solution could be developed. With Oberman's support, the LEED Council got significant political attention. The attitude of DED changed, the city law department got involved, and a PMD was invented for the Clybourn Corridor area.

This was nowhere near the end of the process for Ducharme. First, Oberman left the city council and was replaced in the ward by Alderman Eisendraft. The education process had to start over again. But in the end Eisendraft bought the idea. He had a public relations background and convinced one of the local manufacturers, Finkl Steel, to hire a public relations firm to help publicize its interest. It did so, and this added to the momentum behind the PMD proposal.

In 1986 and 1987 industrial displacement was threatening jobs and getting notice in other parts of the city, and Ducharme began to get requests to speak to other groups and to the idea of the PMD as a general piece of city legislation. In the fall of 1987 the problem had reached a crisis point over the River Lofts' mixed-use commercial and residential development on an abandoned industrial property on Goose Island, a proposed PMD. Proponents of the project were vigorous. The *Tribune* editorialized:

> Mr. Washington has let his economic planners embark on a zany crusade to snuff out commercial and residential growth in areas that they—these insulated City Hall planners—have decreed should be reserved for manufacturing. Investors who want to convert abandoned old factory buildings into job-producing, tax-producing commercial complexes are told no, take your money to some other city. And don't think they won't, if Chicago continues this perverse ideological nonsense.[61]

In November, the city dropped its opposition to the River Lofts proposal, having exacted a set of conditions from the developer, including support for a more general PMD ordinance. But there had been so much debate within city hall and such development of the coalition of manufacturers, labor unions, and neighborhood organizations supporting the larger PMD proposal that Washington came out with support within a few days. After a long silence, this seemed to cement the PMD policy.

In November of 1987 Washington died, having only recently thrown his support behind the idea. Ducharme had been angered by Washington's slowness to support the PMD—she thought they could have had the first PMD much earlier with his support—but later she thought that the delay and the extended period of organizing resulted in a great deal more grassroots support and protected the idea when the Washington coalition began to fall apart under interim mayor Eugene Sawyer. In fact, planning commissioner Elizabeth Hollander and others became strong supporters of the PMD concept in 1988. Charles Finkl, one of the manufacturers whom Ducharme had mobilized in support, was quoted in a *New York Times* story saying, "It's one thing to lose basic industries to international forces beyond our control. But it's another thing to force healthy industries out of the city through unwise and piecemeal zoning policies."[62]

In effect, the long process of discussion within the administration in 1987 and 1988 resulted in a significant alteration in policy, toward support for selected growth-coalition projects like River Lofts and more general support for inner-city industrial retention. Where once there had been simply the growth regime, opposed (ineffectually) by a simple neighborhood advocacy, now there was a more differentiated view with the potential to serve two constituencies. Later, when Richard M. Daley came into office, having attacked the PMD as stopping progress, grassroots support convinced him to retreat from that position. But he now had a position to retreat to, so as to seem to give something to both sides.

The Neighborhood Policy after 1985

The spring 1986 special election that gave Washington a working majority in city council and allowed him to control the finance and other key committees marked the definitive end of the council-wars phase. Washington, no longer reduced to negotiating such a wide variety of issues, large and small, with the "Vrdolyak 29," was able to function as previous mayors had. But Washington had already gained the initiative through a series of smaller victories: the general obligation bond issue the previous spring and summer was one of the important ones.

The 1985 General Obligation Bond Issue

The general obligation bond issue was a proposal to raise revenues for capital spending in the neighborhoods. Washington proposed to distribute the capital improvements in such a way as to replace the council-led pork barrel with a "rational" planning approach. As such, it was a challenge to the white ethnic-based council majority, which—this was the time of the "council wars"—refused to act on it. But Washington had made his proposals in such a way that each ward, including the white ethnic Northwest and Southwest base, would benefit along with the others. Eventually someone in the city government suggested a sales campaign, Washington in a bus, traveling with press and the ward alderman over each pothole.[63] After a few weeks, having gone over the heads of council, Washington was able to get approval, an action which began to unify the racially divided city.

Mier and Moe later saw the successful bond-issue vote as a turning point, and certainly 1986 and 1987 were a new phase. Newspaper and academic comment was that the mayor "seemed to have gotten the hang of it." He had won majority control of the city council in May 1986, and by mid-1986 had supporters in control of most relevant agencies: the park district, the public schools, O'Hare Airport, the Chicago Housing Authority, and the Chicago Transit Authority.[64]

Big-Bang Stadium Deals

Mier was defensive about a series of "big-bang" projects that he spent much time on: lights for Wrigley Field, a new Chicago Bears stadium, and a new White Sox ballpark replacing the old Comiskey Park. As William Peterman argues, much was lost by neighborhood interests in these deals, and in the White Sox case, a developing neighborhood organization was split in two, in part by city hall maneuvering.[65] But Mier argued that the city was under great pressure from "growth" interests to do these deals; to reject them outright would have been a political blow that Washington (even more so, Sawyer) could not sustain. Instead, Mier tried to find ways to bargain for concessions like support for affordable housing for residents displaced by the projects, establishing the principle that there was a social contract associated with any city support. The result was a defeat for neighborhood interests in the White Sox case, a hopeful scheme dashed by the legislature in the case of the Bears stadium, and a useful compromise for Wrigley Field.[66]

Even in 1999, neighborhood spokespeople felt Washington and Mier were compromised by these deals. Thom Clark saw the White Sox deal as a key turning point under Sawyer.[67] (Mier thought Sawyer gave too much.) But a larger view would see the stadium deals in the same light as the River Lofts crisis that helped establish a more nuanced (and permanent) city industrial policy. Growth interests were serviced (the city did not "lose" the White Sox to Florida); but at least some neighborhood values were retained as well.

Linked Development

In 1983 two overwhelmingly white neighborhood federations in Chicago's Southwest and Northwest sides combined into the Save Our Neighborhoods/Save Our City Coalition (SON/SOC) and met with Washington and aides to elaborate a series of proposals asking for assistance from the city. Relations soon soured. SON/SOC people accused the administration of a narrow-minded and condescending attitude toward their proposals; administration people thought SON/SOC overly demanding.[68] SON/SOC published a provocative "Declaration of Neighborhood Independence." Other neighborhood leaders urged SON/SOC to pull back from its confrontationist tactics, but SON/SOC continued. One thousand people attended an April 1984 convention, where committees presented proposals for a home-equity insurance plan, a linked-development scheme whereby a $5-per-square-foot levy on new office structures would be distributed to neighborhood organizations, and several other populist measures.[69] The convention received a great deal of press coverage, and Chicago residents could have been understandably amused at the prospect of a fight among populist factions.

Washington, rather than argue, held out the possibility of compromise and cooperation with SON/SOC. He addressed a second convention in August 1984 and endorsed the principle of home-equity insurance and appointed an advisory committee to look into the linked-development question. Some community development advocates hoped to use the linked-development issue to strengthen ties across race lines, but frustration ensued. City hall relations with SON/SOC became increasingly amicable, but with the real estate developer interests strongly opposed and Washington loath to support the idea in advance of his 1987 re-election contest, little came of the linkage proposals.[70] In this, Chicago failed to match the measures accomplished in Boston, San Francisco, and elsewhere. Mier continued to keep linkage on the agenda in ad hoc, informal ways—not the same thing at all, but something.

❧ CHAPTER 7

Later Developments in Chicago

Key Washington administrators knew they were creating a different kind of city governance. But there was always the question of what would be a lasting change. Washington's unexpected death did signal an end to much of what he had put in place. But it is worthwhile to note—at least from the standpoint of the community development activists inside and outside of city hall—the intriguing periodicity that characterized the last months of Washington's mayoralty, the Sawyer interregnum, and Daley's first years in office.

Professionalism with Diversity

It was not clear whether the political and value positions achieved by Washington and his support base could be institutionalized in professional practice. Was there a new methodology, a new kind of practice? I thought I had detected something of this in other cities, and I asked some of Washington's administrators and planners about this.

Doctrine

On the one hand, a new kind of economic doctrine seemed to be emerging from the Steel Task Force and elsewhere, though it was hard to articulate and its practitioners were only imperfectly conscious of it. It did not come primarily from academics in universities, foundations, or think tanks. In hindsight, what was going on was a basic shift in the popular consciousness of activists. Having identified the "growth coalition" and its ties to the decayed political machine, having revealed its pretensions in the excesses of the plans for the World's Fair and watched its fundamental claims to the provision of economic abundance reduced as manufacturing jobs hemorrhaged from the Midwest, what was needed was a plausible alternative. This was being supplied in popular movements and an increasing barrage of literature. Dissident labor voices were proposing the takeover of major mills, and there were a few successes.[1] Mier, Giloth, and others were aware of all this and found fertile ground to sow the seeds of a different approach. The "jobs, not real estate" plank of the CWED platform of 1982 provided the fundamental rationale. The industrial retention strategies pursued through the Westside Jobs Network early warning system, publicized in the Playskool case, and most dramatically realized through Ducharme's successes with the PMDs, represented the establishment of the doctrine. Markusen may have been the most grounded in academia, and her reports to the Steel Task Force were perhaps the most systematic statements. In later lectures she adapted her analysis of the steel-industry situation for a more general audience. Midwestern city politicians and economic leadership had three strategic choices: bid down the cost of labor, bow out of manufacturing altogether, or "build on the basics" by retaining those manufacturing operations that could be profitable. Similar arguments were made elsewhere.[2] By the end of the 1980s, the arguments of the growth coalition had moderated to accommodate at least a partial acceptance of the new doctrine. Joel Rast, in his discussion of Chicago's industrial policy, makes the case that a new economic doctrine was a major contribution of the Washington administration and the neighborhood-based coalition that it worked with.[3]

Participatory Management

For Mier, particularly during his time as commissioner of economic development, the main innovation might seem to be the participatory approach to management. This had its roots in Mier's academic background and earlier. While he had an early background as an engineer, he also had a nontechnical, people-oriented side. He once said:

> I was as comfortable as [I was] uncomfortable in the traditional system of people. I was comfortable because I had been an engineer and

a technician and I could master—it was a real challenge to organize your thoughts to eight layers deep and present a compelling argument. . . . At the same time, there was something artificial about that. I did not like to walk away from a three-hour class and realize I had split up my own thought. . . . So I experimented with different things, it kept me more off the pedestal and on a more even level.

He had acquired some of this insight earlier:

Actually I think the other thing that affected me was my Vietnam experience. I saw more than my share of big shots going back in a body bag. . . . There were some great equalizers out there, and in fact, if anything, the people that stayed connected with their fellow men survived more than those that had themselves up on a pedestal. When they were up on a pedestal, they were pretty visible and they got their ass shot. All people are equal, that's predominantly what I brought back from Vietnam, although it had its roots in my Catholic upbringing as well.[4]

At the Center for Urban Economic Development (CUED), Mier had implemented a collaborative approach with the community organizations he recruited as clients, and he assembled a staff of professionals and academics who shared that approach. The high point of that collaborative approach might have been the emergence, at a large community meeting, of the Community Workshop on Economic Development (CWED) platform. Mier described the way the CWED platform emerged as a positive twist on a program that polarized the crowd (the Heritage Foundation idea of "enterprise zones" that was being debated as part of the Illinois gubernatorial campaign) and as if it came from the floor. But Mier was running the meeting and managing the discussion. Probably the main points were a joint product. Later, Mier, Wim Wiewel, and Arturo Vazquez retreated to write up the results of the discussion, so it was not purely a matter of ideas coming from the floor. There was some interpretation involved. But the platform was certainly ratified by the participants. Mier remembered the following:

I was playing a facilitator role at this meeting of community leaders to discuss enterprise zones, and there were about three hundred people there, and it got heated, and I was being an exceptionally good facilitator that day and I realized in the midst of it that I had an opportunity to steer this process in a direction it would not otherwise have gone. . . .

There was a real tension between those two courses [for the Reagan version of the Enterprise Zone, or against it]. I recognized that tension and I took the path right down the middle, which was okay, to accept the fact that tension exists and exploit it for our own purposes. I sort of drew out of that meeting a commitment for people to say, Well, hell, the problem is what we're groping for is some public policy that will facilitate what we're doing, and this and this ain't it, and what should be it? They accepted out of Reagan the fact there is a need for public policy, they rejected that particular one.[5]

Later, as commissioner of DED, Mier spoke often of the need to get the participation of the lower-level workers on board with the Washington program, and he devised procedures to do that. Mier writes of an "organizational culture" that he tried to instill in DED, using regular staff meetings, for example, to praise the kinds of behavior he tried to foster, and consistent scrutiny of hiring by his deputies to be certain that an equal-opportunity hiring procedure had been followed. But he was not focused only on participatory processes. One of the great lessons people learned from Mier was from his hard-nosed awareness of structure: the use of office to insist on allocations of authority and resources prior to embarking on negotiations. He once spoke of the outcome of the Steel Task Force in these terms:

> The critical question is always whether or not you've brought people to the point where the quality of that struggle is different. What we've done has been to be able to impose a balance of power on that so that the business people have had to deal with the community people as equals, not because either party believes they are equals but where we're saying it's got to be.[6]

Inclusion

The most important structural issue, for Mier and others in the Washington administration, was race, usually stated in terms of "inclusion." Down to administrative detail, and beyond the broad-brush rhetoric of racial empowerment that polarized the city—as in the case of the SON/SOC controversies—this is the least written-about feature of the city's experience under Washington. One example of how inclusion was practiced in the administration was the emergence of an inclusionary-meetings rule, described by Mier (and Hollander):

> I now find it impossible to approach an economic development challenge without immediately seeing the race and gender dimensions of it, especially those of African-Americans. Thus it is impossible to see that

situation as anything less than an opportunity to pursue social justice. My ex–City Hall colleague, former Planning Commissioner Elizabeth Hollander, says it clearly: "I can never again walk into a room without being constantly aware of who's there... and who's not there. It makes all the difference in the world."[7]

The most extensive account of the Washington administration's movement toward racial inclusion is by Xolela Mangcu, who described the law department and the implementation of targeted purchasing and contracting under law director James Montgomery.[8] In a pattern that repeated the situation of some other "progressive city" administrations, Montgomery—like Mier and other department heads—inherited an operation that was so egregiously inefficient and badly run that it was ripe for reform; in the course of fixing inefficiencies, Montgomery was able to implement changes in direction as well. Some of the practices he eliminated included hiring badly trained lawyers as political payoffs managed from the mayor's office; and a pattern of double job holding, where lawyers working for the city put in appearances in the morning, then retreated for private practice the rest of the day. This had earned a bad reputation for the law department, and the city was seen as not well represented legally.

Mangcu found Montgomery to be the "second most powerful" person in city government, who set for himself the task of "break[ing] the feudal control" of the mayor's office. With Washington's support,

> he prohibited outside employment for attorneys working for the city. Following this prohibition large numbers of lawyers left the department—sensing a loss of the lucrative deals they had controlled and dispensed to their firms. As a result of these actions by Montgomery the budget for outside counsel declined from $2.3 million in 1982 to $280,000 in 1992.[9]

Within the law department, Montgomery instituted management reforms: a hiring committee to recruit women and persons of color according to merit criteria, a system of evaluation, a structured review process. One result was an increase in the proportion of women and minorities from ten percent and "almost nonexistent" to 52 percent and 21 percent, respectively, from 1983 to 1993.[10]

Montgomery had the authority to sign off on all city contracts and purchases and soon began to institute reforms in the department of purchasing and contracts. With the appointment of new people in 1985, the city was able to implement steps to achieve some targeting of contracts to and purchases from firms headed by minorities and females. And, Mangcu pointed out, the Washington administration claimed it did not compromise efficiency in getting equity: past abuses had been so great that there was room for improvements simply by focusing on the new pool of vendors and contractors represented by minorities and women. (This is the implication I take from Mangcu's analysis.)[11]

Montgomery's example and detailed implementation had ramifications throughout the Washington administration and in the private sector. According to Mangcu:

> Gradually, the city's private sector began to emulate the public sector's affirmative action programs. A partner at Skidmore, Owings and Merrill [explained this], "Relationships developed through the partnership in the public sector are bringing about natural associations on the part of larger firms with minority companies in private sector work."[12]

Marc A. Weiss and John Metzger reinforced this with their conclusion that "perhaps the most significant economic development accomplishment of the Washington administration was in stimulating minority business growth through city contracting policies."[13] Certainly the commitment to diversity permeated the administration. Kari Moe said:

> I listened as [Washington] worked to develop the imagery of the city's diverse people needing to live together. I heard the mosaic speech, or the tapestry speech, or the we're all in this together speech countless times but it never failed to bring tears to my eyes. Harold—from his staff appointments, to the young political leaders he mentored, to the exhausting schedule he kept—lived this theme of respect for distinctiveness and diversity. He did his utmost to preach this vision from pulpits in every corner of the city. One measure of his success was Mayor Daley's description, shortly after his inauguration in 1989, of his newly appointed cabinet as a "rainbow."[14]

These doctrinal and procedural changes were not simply a new administrative idea; the practices had been prefigured in the social movement itself—in the multiracial makeup of organizations like the Rehab Network and CWED, and in the hiring practices of such organizations and their self-consciousness about inclusion and participation. And they were strong preoccupations at the political level among Washington and others, if not always successfully executed. Initiatives like the Latino Commission, representing a group that felt itself left out of hiring and appointments, exerted a continual pressure from outside the individual departments and from outside the mayor's office, with some success not just for Latinos but for general procedures in the government.

External Relations

There was more than one progressive city, and it was a long-range goal of movement people, city officials, and administrators to support one another across the nation and internationally. The form of support and interaction evolved over time.

In the 1970s several national support networks developed for neighborhood organizers—such as National Peoples Action and Citizens Action—and affiliated training institutes like the Midwest Academy. The idea of a special center for the local officials and activists of "radical" or "progressive" cities also had a dramatic, if short-lived, embodiment in the Conference on Alternative State and Local Policies (described in chapter 2), before it reduced its operations in the 1980s.[15]

By 1983, interactions among progressive city activists, officials, and mayors became more ad hoc; Washington spoke at the meetings of the U.S. Conference of Mayors, and he, Mier, and other officials made appearances at other conferences, but they were for the most part not specifically oriented to the more progressive cases. Progressive approaches and issues were certainly considered, but they were on the back burner and addressed informally. Speaking engagements and publishing now began to broadcast the message in the context of a diminishing field of action and amid the national perception that liberal and radical approaches were a thing of the past. Washington's mayoralty opened eyes but did not stem the tide of reaction. What he did was create a record that something different was possible, a sense reinforced by Mier and other administrators, who wrote extensively in professional journals. By the end of the 1980s, there were proposals for what we might term a "progressive" or at least "community-based" urban policy, even though—in contrast to Jimmy Carter's proposals as he took office in 1977—little was reflected in presidential campaigns. Despite the promise of these activities and the need for a larger support network, the potential remained largely unfulfilled.

Community Development after 1987

Washington died in November of 1987, having been in office four and a half years. Eugene Sawyer succeeded him, creating an interregnum until May 1989 when Richard M. Daley, son of the old machine mayor, won a special election to fill the vacancy. Sawyer, an African American city council member, had been drafted to the mayoralty, reluctantly, in the chaotic aftermath of Washington's death when neither the old "council wars" majority nor the new Washington coalition were able to put forward a candidate with majority support. Sawyer was conciliatory and did not rock the boat among Washington's appointees, and there was a good deal of administrative momentum that enabled him to continue parts of Washington's program until Daley assumed control in 1989.

Sawyer's Interregnum

With significant capacities within the Sawyer administration and a political coalition in the field, progressives tried to maintain what they had gained under Washington. Within the Sawyer administration, neighborhood-oriented officials and bureaucrats tried to consolidate what was just coming to fruition. Mier stayed in the mayor's office overseeing economic development and several other departments, a position he had assumed under Washington after the 1987 election.[16] Hollander and others spearheaded the push to finish the establishment of the PMDs.

Many others continued in office, but Sawyer proved to be unable to hold together the Washington coalition and was defeated by Daley. After that many Washington appointees, including Mier, were forced out or resigned. Mier received word by phone on the Friday after the election that he needed to be out by Monday, and spent the weekend removing dozens of boxes of records. He apparently had hung on to the hope that there would be at least be an orderly transition. Other changes were not so abrupt. Some Washington appointees—like Greg Longhini and David Mosena in the planning department—stayed on and lent familiarity with what had been going on earlier.

Daley in Office, 1989 and After

When Daley, on taking office, fired almost all of the Washington appointees who had stayed with Sawyer, including Mier, the prospects were for a clean sweep of policies as well. But it was not clear-cut, as there remained countervailing forces in the neighborhoods, and there had been controversy and constructive coalition building during the Sawyer period.

Daley had made no bones about his support from the downtown-oriented real estate development interests, and there had been, starting in 1988, a more or less continual campaign in the press and elsewhere to discredit the neighborhood-oriented policies and reassert the political culture. One land developer said most emphatically:

> We're tired of the anti-development posture that has been promulgated at City Hall in the last six years. The extent of the contributions to Daley's campaign by the real estate community, I think, is clearly making that message known. In Daley we see someone whom we believe is capable of seeing the bigger picture; someone who is capable of solving problems in a more logical way; someone who won't seek taxes [on development] without first establishing a dialogue with the real estate community.[17]

In fact, significant parts of Chicago had never seen Washington as Mier and other neighborhood activists had. Bill and Lori Granger, in a book released in 1987 but presumably written before Washington's death, characterized him thus:

> Harold Washington was a cold, casually indifferent man who could be a forceful speaker when he tried and who had a cutting edge to him. He was careless and lazy. He had no time for details. Friends and co-workers remembered him as always late. A bachelor, he balanced his checkbook in mornings over coffee in a shop on Hyde Park Boulevard down the street from his apartment.
>
> He also had a disregard for the law.... In 1972, he was convicted of failing to file federal income tax returns. For four years. He explained in court that it had slipped his mind.... He served forty days in the county jail.... This singular man whose best friend at the time was...a convicted pimp whom he made his legislative assistant, was the great hope of the black community.[18]

But the most thorough attack on the neighborhood policies came from *Tribune* columnist John McCarron in August 1988.[19] McCarron, in a lengthy series of articles, made two related points. First, activists in the neighborhoods played on a well-founded fear of displacement by upscale investments. But rather than support the reintroduction of middle-class households and commercial ventures (some of which might even include measures to compensate them for rent increases, higher taxes, and housing prices), they tended simply to oppose new development. And McCarron was not restrained about pointing out the self-interest of the neighborhood leadership, often with a racial tinge:

> Chicago is being paralyzed by a self-serving political movement fueled by the fear of displacement and orchestrated by leaders determined

to stop change in neighborhoods that need change the most. . . . One by one, projects and programs vital to the city's future are being shouted down or delayed to death by an assortment of inner-city politicians, preachers, professional organizers and populist ideologues in key positions.

Tim Evans . . . has managed to block nearly all private development initiatives in the poorer sections of his ward—the sections he relies upon to produce the votes he needs to get re-elected. . . . Sometimes the turf guarded from change is a critical city institution. When efforts to reform the Chicago Public Schools were debated this summer in Springfield, elected representatives of the inner-city blacks—those most victimized by the failures of the school system—were instrumental in blocking the most thorough plan for overhaul. . . . In the end, black legislators from Chicago acted to protect the interests of a black-controlled school bureaucracy and teachers union.[20]

McCarron's second main point was that bureaucrats in city hall, rather than counter this misguided or self-serving opposition in the neighborhoods, were using and even encouraging it. The chief theorist, McCarron thought, was Mier.

Back at City Hall, the anti-development crusade is being led by thinkers like Robert Mier, a former college professor who is putting his social theories to work as the city's top economic development official.

Mier is convinced that Chicago's unskilled poor aren't served by downtown's booming service and financial sectors. Even if they were, he argues, the new white- and pink-collar jobs don't pay enough.

So Mier has promised the city's poor that he will bring back low-skill, high-pay, blue collar employment. To that end, he has pushed the new zoning restrictions that would prevent developers from converting vacant factories into condominiums or shopping malls. The old buildings are to be saved for the return of industry. . . . Mier's crusade to bring back old-fashioned jobs is reinforced by a small army of community groups, many of them propped up by federal funds funneled through his office at City Hall.

But, wrote McCarron, the idea of inner-city industrial renewal was hopelessly idealistic: "Few of the crusaders seem aware that, during Mier's five-year reign, the city has continued to lose 15,000 manufacturing jobs a year, or that Chicago's inventory of empty factory floor space has soared beyond

23 million square feet."[21] In a subsequent article, McCarron cited confirmation of his critique:

> "It's an illusion that keeping an old factory will somehow produce hundreds of metal stamping jobs," said Marvin Kosters, director of economic policy studies at the American Enterprise Institute in Washington. "That's the new conventional wisdom," Kosters said when advised of Mier's thoughts.... "What's new is this romanticization of blue-collar work in certain academic circles. How many of these people have ever worked in a factory?"[22]

A (not unkind) journalistic response suggested McCarron wrote out of deep conviction, whatever the uses his article found. At least some of his ideas had been endorsed by progressives like Monsignor John Egan with the words "it needed to be said." And McCarron was quoted saying there was a separate story that needed to be told, about affordable housing.[23] But whatever truth there was in McCarron's argument was probably lost in the eyes of neighborhood activists, who saw political motivation. Wim Wiewel and Phil Nyden thought that

> the series seemed to be aimed at influencing the agenda for the special 1989 mayoral election. This included discrediting those who had provided many of the ideas for Washington's neighborhood and economic development policies, as well as driving a wedge between the various components of Washington's coalition: community organizations, leaders of grass-roots movements in the African-American community, African-American political leaders, and the progressive white community.[24]

Progressive Forces Fight Back

But there was a long denouement rather than a clear-cut end to the progressive movement in Chicago. Daley did not succeed with major "big-bang" projects of his own: a third airport in Southeast Chicago, a gambling casino. Instead he had to expend energy and resources to mollify, and in some respects embrace, parts of the neighborhood movement. Initially this unfolded with vigorous activity in the neighborhoods and within the Sawyer administration during 1987–89.

PRAG

While the McCarron series in the *Tribune* in August 1988 signaled a renewed offensive in the media, some of the foundation people worked

to set up a stronger countervailing force. Rebecca Riley, a program officer in the MacArthur Foundation (reportedly angry at being singled out
in the series), moved to host a meeting of grantees that December, to see
whether the universities that were working with the community groups
might play more of a role. Two university people, Phil Nyden of Loyola
and Wim Wiewel, director of UIC's Center for Urban Economic Development (UIC-CUED), responded with the suggestion that the community
groups themselves ought to be given equal space to set any agendas. What
followed was a series of planning meetings and, in September 1989, a conference that in turn led to the creation of a Policy Research Action Group
(PRAG) in 1990.[25]

One has to believe that the establishment of PRAG created new life in
the community movement. On the one hand, by giving the neighborhood
organizations an equal voice in planning meetings and conferences, it defused
tensions and led to the release of energies that had been restrained by the
normally tense relationships between university and community. Scars still
remained, for example, from the collaboration in the 1960s and 1970s of UIC
and the earlier Daley regime in the expansion of Circle Campus, which had
resulted in the destruction of the neighborhood around it. As important was
the prevailing insulation of university researchers from their communities.
Their normal mode was to use the community as a site for study but not to
include community people in the design phase of research, nor usually to be
particularly attentive about sharing the results. The record Mier and others
created at CUED in the period around 1980 was an exception, but this sort
of outreach was not the rule. Now, with Wiewel, Nyden, and others, there
was a chance to change the approach, and PRAG was to be the vehicle. Their
first move was to create research assistantships for students and let community
organizations initiate the studies. By the middle of the 1990s PRAG had supported 130 projects around the Chicago area and had received over $4 mil-
lion in funding from the MacArthur Foundation and the U.S. Department of
Education, the bulk of which went to student assistants and "interns" from
the community organizations.

Another initiative was a Community Media Workshop. This was the
creation of two progressive journalists, Hank DeZutter and Thom Clark,
producing copy to make journalists aware of what was happening in the
neighborhoods. The goal of the organization was described in this way:

> The Workshop operates from the vision that while the "news" em-
> phasizes conflict, tragedy and other problems of city life, many Chi-
> cagoans are succeeding at solving urban problems that dominate the
> news through community policing, affordable housing, school reform,

community economic development, youth development and other strategies that rely on community organizing.[26]

Industrial Policy under Daley

The PMD coalition challenged the growth coalition on manufacturing and won a permanent place in city policy. Daley, after some initial uncertainty, found a way—as Washington and Sawyer had—to have both an industrial policy and some "big-bang" and downtown projects. The new mayor, after inheriting the Clybourn Corridor PMD that had been passed under Sawyer in 1988, came around to support two additional PMDs by 1990. According to Rast,

> in June of that year [Daley] made a startling announcement: he had reconsidered his campaign position against planned manufacturing districts and was now prepared to support the planning process for the Goose Island and Elston Corridor PMDs. . . . Later that month, despite strong editorial criticism from the *Tribune* and appeals from property developers urging him to rethink his decision, Daley personally introduced both ordinances into city council. With the backing of both aldermen, the ordinances easily survived a full city council vote later that fall.[27]

Daley then went on to support retention of manufacturing jobs in other ways. He initiated a series of industrial-area plans that identified twenty-two separate industrial corridors in the North, South, and West Sides, and in 1993 hired Donna Ducharme, LEED Council director, as the city's top industrial development officer within the department of planning and development. Ducharme then convened a task force which devised a Model Industrial Corridors Initiative, with the purpose of supporting neighborhood industrial retention organizations that operated under the LIRI program that had been initiated by Mier a decade earlier. By 1997 the city had approved funding proposals from twelve such organizations, which used the money for plans and implementation, mainly around infrastructure needs. Rast reported that under Daley, city capital-budget allocations for infrastructure flowed to these areas to a greater degree than they had under Washington and Sawyer.[28]

Housing Organizations and Other Nonprofits Survived

Neighborhood activists learned they could not rely on city hall. They had known this all along in their heads, even when Washington was mayor.

Under Daley they knew it in a more visceral way. Perhaps the signal achievement of the neighborhood housing movement under the new regime came in the organizing and media campaign put on by the Rehab Network that resulted in an affordable-housing ordinance passed in December 1993. The ordinance, called the Chicago Affordable Housing and Community Jobs Ordinance, had been introduced the previous year by Alderman Arenda Troutman and proposed two main changes: (1) it would focus on lower-income rather than middle-income housing; and (2) it would double annual spending from $100 million to $200 million.[29] Daley eventually agreed to a five-year plan that would amount to half the proposed increase, with 70 percent of the total allocated to low-income families.[30]

But Daley held on to the idea of supporting the middle class: "A pugnacious Daley refused to go along with the advocates' demands that his administration focus the bulk of its housing funds on shelter for the homeless and the very poor. Instead, he said, the city is pursuing a mixed-income housing plan with an overarching goal of revitalizing Chicago neighborhoods.... We cannot only build low-income housing and say we're going to straighten the community out," Daley said. "It has to be mixed income—take care of the lowest income, take care of middle income, take care of the single families, take care of homeless people.[31]

What was most remarkable was that, in addition to getting the city to agree to a gross amount of spending (some of the funding came from federal sources), there was a mechanism for accountability with a community board doing an assessment each year. That assessment would be an occasion for press coverage and pressure, and at the same time the administration could use it to claim successes.[32]

The organizing and media campaign was extensive. One of the keys was that the community activists framed the story not as race or class related but as something that affected the entire city:

> The way we cut the story was that we showed that this housing crisis was not a poor or black and other nonwhite issue, it was an issue that impacted the future growth of the city. We showed that if the housing crisis was not addressed, the tax base of the city would continue to erode, causing major financial problems for all of the citizens, not just the poor.[33]

Moreover, the Rehab Network got a lot of support. There were thirty interns trained and supervised by the Midwest Academy meeting with hundreds of individuals and organizations. The campaign was endorsed by 250 organizations. The UIC Voorhees Center *Housing Fact Book* presented information that showed the dimensions of the affordability problem in each council member's ward. There were eighteen briefings of elected officials.[34]

In 1998 Daley renewed the program for another five years. The fact that the city initiated the program this time, without the main media campaign and neighborhood organizing, led some to suspect the community activists had been co-opted.[35] But the Rehab Network thought the city had moderated and developed its approach. According to Kevin Jackson: "We had built in accountability in the first plan, that had us doing meetings with the chief of staff, who is now the former housing commissioner, so we have someone who knows the situation there. The Rehab Network did an analysis of the first four years. Now we are doing an analysis each year, and we have added to the city's agenda several strategic considerations."[36]

In announcing the city's desire to renew the plan, Daley said, "I want us to build upon the success of the current five-year plan." A Rehab Network person then said, "To have him say affordable housing is important is a great step toward addressing the crisis."[37]

Empowerment Zones

More problematic was the effort—largely initiated from the neighborhoods—to create an organizing effort focused on the Clinton administration's Enterprise Zones initiative in 1993–95. Doug Gills and Wanda White have provided a telling analysis of the tightrope Daley walked between accommodating the neighborhood activists and policy scholars assembled in PRAG, and the needs of the machine and the downtown developer constituency.

The fact that there had been attempts to revive the organizing groups after Daley's election—including the establishment of PRAG in 1990—had given the Chicago activists a head start. After the Clinton election in 1992, Tim Wright, who had been commissioner of economic development in Chicago under Sawyer, became a local liaison to the Clinton transition team and approached Chicago activists about whether CWED and CUED would facilitate a meeting to provide input into the Clinton transition planning. Subsequent meetings produced draft proposals that went through Wright to HUD secretary-designate Henry Cisneros and provided some of the basis for the federal legislation.[38] Later, in October 1993, after the federal legislation was passed, CWED staff met with Vice President Gore to discuss the application process for the empowerment zone designation, and in December CWED used its annual meeting to bring in HUD director of community planning and development Roy Priest, who later served as chair of the Federal

Inter-Agency Task Force on Empowerment Zones, and resolved to organize Chicago neighborhoods to participate in the city's application process.

Thus when Mayor Daley appointed an Interim Empowerment Zone/ Enterprise Communities Coordinating Council charged with selecting the census tracts that were to be included in the HUD application, the community activists were ready, and UIC and CWED contributed substantial input into the selection procedures, while "the Mayor's office and the city council members stayed relatively clear of the selection process, at least outwardly."[39] PRAG encouraged university involvement in the EZ communities, and so there was a larger presence in the process: in addition to UIC-CUED, Gills and White mentioned the Northwestern University Center for Urban Affairs and Policy Research, work by Loyola and DePaul universities, Spertus College, Chicago State, Roosevelt University, Illinois Institute of Technology, and the University of Chicago.

The city administration's census-tract selection process went forward according to the procedures established with the help of CWED and other neighborhood activists. Thirty-three groups of communities submitted applications; portions of eleven were selected for nomination by the city and state. The final map included noncontiguous portions of the West Side, Near West, and Mid-South sides, plus a Southwest Side industrial corridor included to provide an "economic engine."

With many neighborhood organizations involved, what emerged was a set of three "clusters" of organizations within the zone for which the application was being prepared. These groups came together without the aid of the city administration, and after the submission to HUD, the empowerment zone clusters were left largely to their own devices by all but a few institutions. But in the spring of 1994, the city opened up to participation in response to the efforts of the clusters: the "city planners who managed the process, under community pressure, altered their preconceived approach to the development of a standard Strategic Plan," and "the Mayor and the Governor signed a progressive Strategic Plan" approved by representatives of the cluster organizations, believing they had a conception of the governance process consistent with HUD regulations. Gills and White thought "the Chicago Empowerment Zones strategic planning process has been...one of the most inclusive citizen participation processes...in the city's history."[40] But they found that the city administration and aldermen thought otherwise, hoping that the participation process would eventually go away. In May 1995 the city passed a governance ordinance that negated the role of the cluster organizations. Gills and White summarized the situation after designation:

The most disheartening aspect of the governance issue in Chicago is that it began with the most deeply involved and most inclusive community-based process. In the end, however, Chicago remains the only designated EZ city that has failed to acknowledge community structures, such as the clusters, in the formal make-up of the Empowerment Zone governance.[41]

They said:

The mayor resisted the communities' efforts to create a body that would have more than advisory status with respect to City Hall executives and the City Council. The ordinance...did not even recognize a role for the Empowerment Zone clusters at any level of formal decision making. Furthermore, it gave the mayor the power to appoint 37 of the 39 members of the advisory body. It reserved to city administrators the power to hire staff members to the governance body, and it made the City Council the ultimate body for determining resource allocation.[42]

Gills and White's assessment was that most observers had expected the mayor to oppose significant participatory structure but were more disappointed in the ward aldermen, who sided with the mayor against what they thought had been significant community support. But it seemed that "the greatest source of disappointment was the virtual silence from community empowerment supporters in the foundations and the social policy and action research community; they remained mute while the principles asserted in Chicago for nearly two decades were trampled without a word of protest."[43]

Politics under Daley

Barbara Ferman and William Grimshaw, writing of the first years of the new regime under Richard M. Daley, characterized the administration as "contradictory." The machine, they wrote, "is not dead, but it is badly wounded. Internal struggles, external challenges, and a depletion of resources have taken their toll."[44] The progressive reform movement that had surfaced during the Washington administration, while seriously weakened, still had a life in city hall: "Policy issues are a regular part of public debate, community-based organizations have more political influence; 'reform' has worked its way into the vocabularies of most people."[45]

Ferman and Grimshaw found at least a partial reversion to the machine's formula of disjunction between electoral and governing coalition: the former was dominated by "developers, key downtown businesses, attorneys and some party regulars," while governance, without benefit of the huge resources of patronage and federal funding available through the 1970s, was required to curry favor with neighborhood interests. They attributed—to Daley—an impressive list of contradictory process and substantive policy initiatives: creation of inclusionary structures like a Capital Improvements Advisory Committee while allocating the majority of funds by old-style centralized decision; passage of the city's first housing trust fund while supporting a disastrous proposal for a third airport that would displace thousands of families and jobs; and appointment of a neighborhood-based head of the department of housing (Michael Schubert) while imposing his own political appointees in addition, thus hamstringing the agency.[46] Outside city hall, meanwhile, there was the increasing influence of alliances between CDCs, corporations, and foundations in local neighborhood housing policy, as federal funds declined. As a political system, Ferman and Grimshaw found that

> the city is not back to the . . . model of the Richard J. Daley administration. The electoral arena is more organized around the distribution of collective policy benefits. This is particularly evident in the success of the community-based movement which has strong corporate backing and has caught the attention of national policy-makers. During the Washington administration, it constituted the bridge between electoral and policy politics. During the current administration, it is the major force pushing for broader input and more representative policy.[47]

They theorized a disjuncture between the apolitical and materialist political culture of the old Richard J. Daley machine—now partly reestablished in governance and city administration—and the electoral arena that now demanded more substantive reforms, including a neighborhood-based agenda that had been established under Washington.

Richard M. Daley had moved back to the downtown-oriented agenda proposed a decade earlier in the Chicago 21 Plan. He wholeheartedly endorsed real estate developers' proposals for the Loop and for upscale residential growth in the "near-Loop" districts. Against the proposals to serve the working-class and poor constituency of renters, he found the appeal of "mixed-income" housing policies irresistible: they would improve neighborhood stability. He could argue for home ownership programs, the conversion of public-housing projects, better schools, and the reincorporation of the middle class into the city. This appealed to white and minority middle-class voters and, especially, real estate developers. And developers had become the centerpiece of the new machine. David Ranney and colleagues put it succinctly, in a kind of companion piece to Ferman and Grimshaw: "Ironically, one impact of the demise of the political machine which traded jobs for votes...is an even greater influence of real estate developers...a new form of patronage in which subsidies and high profitability sites are traded for campaign funds and the influence needed to stay in office."[48] Daley also supported, or half supported, the neighborhood program. He adopted—or adapted—much of the neighborhood rhetoric.[49] He made school reform—an initiative that had begun in a more populist way under Washington—a central part of his program and got some neighborhood support as a result. One could say that in Chicago the progressive agenda lived in the 1990s, but not as much as previously in city hall; it survived, rather, in the neighborhoods. It had developed there in the 1970s, achieved prominence during Washington's time in city hall, and then reestablished itself in the neighborhoods outside city hall. But it was not as simple as this. The neighborhood movement was embattled and given to protest in the 1970s, encouraged briefly and developing its political clout after Byrne's "betrayals"; it was encouraged and lulled into compliance under Washington, then newly challenged and even invigorated as Richard M. Daley began his mayoralty and tried to consolidate his power in the early 1990s. One neighborhood organizer, looking back in the 1990s, captured the feeling:

> During Washington's administration many community organizers who were strong supporters and had worked hard to get Washington elected were in favor of continuing protest on unresolved issues. This was a difficult position because of pressure from other activists, as well as because of their strong sense of loyalty to and love for the mayor. In retrospect, however, many activists now realize that ongoing organizational efforts would have made the Washington administration a stronger one. Community organizing would have provided a system of checks and balances, which all politicians need. More importantly, continued organizing would have shown that strong support remained for the philosophy and goals on which Washington was elected, and would have given him a stronger position from which to face the opposition.[50]

Later Developments

Daley won his second reelection in 1995, quite easily. After that, the balance of power and—related—the style of interaction between city administration and the community development interests changed. It was already a compromise between what many community development activists would have wanted and the sorts of business elite–dominated policies that had prevailed prior to Washington's administration in the 1980s. But now there seemed to be more of a change.

On the surface, there were sufficient numbers of developments to signal a shift. A relatively sympathetic commissioner of planning and development, Valerie Jarrett, left the government late in 1995 and was replaced by the more skeptical Jeff Boyle. Within months Boyle crossed swords with Donna Ducharme over the industrial-corridors policy, and she left the government as well.

CANDO, the organization of business-oriented community economic-development groups that had been prominent since the end of the 1970s, lost influence after 1995 and, facing a loss of city funding, terminated in 2002.

While the Rehab Network had been careful to set up accountability in the distribution of housing funds, so that the neighborhoods would know what was being proposed and spent and have a chance to pressure the city council if not dictate the distribution itself, the balance of authority seemed to tip toward the council and aldermen and away from the community organizations. Dan Immergluck, in a postmortem on CANDO, referred to a "deal" between the mayor and the aldermen as Boyle turned away from the more neighborhood-friendly policies of Jarrett. He quoted an anonymous source saying that, around 1995

> the mayor's office made some decisions. CANDO and groups like CANDO were not as important as they had been in the past. The mayor's office made the decision that if they wanted to rule effectively, they had to make deals with the aldermen, and they had to find ways to buy off the aldermen and get them in their camp.... So there was a wholesale shift in power from the neighborhood groups and downtown groups to the aldermen.

The result was to shift power a little further away from the neighborhoods, reverting somewhat toward the old machine style, at least as far as the council role was concerned: "In exchange for giving the mayor their votes on city-wide and downtown issues, including the budget, aldermen were given control over most policy and programs concerning their individual wards."[51]

School reform would have been a straw in the wind for community-empowerment advocates. It had begun under Washington and Sawyer with 1988 state legislation that gave significant authority to community boards dominated by parents, and engendered many hopeful developments for democratization of school governance. But there were still problems, and in 1995 Daley stepped in and, with new state legislation, took over the school system, putting members of his own central staff in charge in a dramatic move.[52] Their main policy seemed to be to bring back the middle class, and the aim was to strengthen the central administration of the school system against the community boards.

Other community-oriented initiatives continued into the period after 1995 in a diminished way relative to what the hopes had been when they began. The Rehab Network continued to release reports. PRAG was still active. The Neighborhood Capital Budget Group released a report in December 1998, in time for the February 1999 election when Bobby Rush, a black political figure with more name recognition than any who had challenged Daley in 1991 or 1995, challenged him.

But by 1999 Richard M. Daley's political control was complete. Rush was no match for Daley, and lost by a landslide. Later, in 2003, Daley won again with token opposition. Black political scientist Robert Starks was quoted in the *New York Times* saying, "This is not a democracy, it is a dictatorship."[53]

One did not have to look far beneath the surface to see how this came about. To begin with, Daley was competent. Early on he had been under the shadow of his family—his brother William and other family-connected advisers. But when William Daley went into the Clinton administration in 1993, Richard M. Daley's own impact as mayor was more evident. He moved from the family neighborhood of Bridgeport to an expensive townhouse in a new South Loop development. He balanced the city's budget each year—as tax revenues increased. The latter, fed by an office-construction boom in the 1990s, was remarkable. Dick Simpson listed some of the benchmarks in an article in 2002: assessed valuation had increased from $12 billion in the 1970s to $36 billion in 1999; sales-tax revenue increased from $54 million in 1989 to $145 million in 1999.[54] The operating budget, meanwhile, had reached an all-time high, and Daley had balanced it every year since he took office in 1989.

Daley was able to use these revenues for improvements in the neighborhoods. A *Boston Globe* report said,

> Daley used the city's economic windfall wisely. He initially won with strong support from residents in white working-class neighborhoods and middle-class lakefront wards, as well as those in Hispanic communities. He has since made significant inroads with black voters and the middle-class good-government movement. "Politically he worked hard to co-opt or accommodate his opposition" said Don Rose, veteran political strategist. "The reformers or independents have all received

things for their wards." Many black ministers also received help, including rights to buy cheaply in vacant lots near their churches.[55]

By 1999, Daley had a nearly unanimous support in city council. Many owed him for their initial appointments, made by the mayor when vacancies occurred, sometimes due to resignation occasioned by scandals. He had appointed nineteen of the fifty council members, ten of them either black or Latino. In the final weeks before the 1999 mayoral election, Daley had endorsements from three of nineteen black aldermen and six of seven Latino aldermen, while many others remained neutral.[56] Neither Rush in 1999 nor three relatively unknown challengers in 2003 were able to turn the tide, and it appeared that Daley could now continue as mayor as long as he wanted.

Race

There is a tendency in academic and journalistic discourse to mute the impact of race and speak of race in a relatively detached and academic style. But this is misleading, and particularly so in describing the interaction between the community development and other progressive forces and the city government in Chicago. For race was close to the surface. The first thing for an outsider encountering this to do may be to start as I did at the beginning of this account, presenting the markedly different histories—depending on race perhaps, and certainly the consciousness of race on the part of the authors—of Harold Washington. For whatever his mayoralty did, it caused observers on all sides to take a new look at race. And one of the results was the different histories that emerged later.

I also think it true that among the community development activists who went into the Washington administration, and among many who stayed outside, there developed a different take on race and a set of practices that began to transcend the polarization.

Among those contributing to the history of the Washington administration and election, the most notable has been Gary Rivlin. In *Fire on the Prairie* he saw how cathartic race was, as in his account of the tragic life and 1984 suicide of *Tribune* reporter Leanita McClain.[57] McClain's anguish came from the impossibility of rectifying her ecstasy at Harold Washington's victory with the attitudes of the *Tribune* newsroom and her sense of professionalism in general. In a *Washington Post* article titled "How Chicago Taught Me To Hate Whites," Rivlin reported, she "wrote of the bouts of sullenness the election provoked."

She would stare at her word processor pretending to write as she silently cried....I'm threatening, she told herself in disbelief. Jesse Jackson, Renault Robinson, Lu Palmer—and also Leanita McClain, moderate but also ecstatic about Harold Washington's victory. *And that makes me threatening.* She wrote of white co-workers cutting off their conversations when a black reporter happened by. "I'm no racist, but..." If she heard that one more time, she thought she would explode.[58]

Rivlin used the McClain story as counterpoint to a more general evaluation: on the surface, at least, a black mayor had little immediate effect on political attitudes in the majority of the population: black mayors tended to get 10 percent of the white vote—whether it was Washington in Chicago, Kenneth Gibson in Newark, or Andrew Young in Atlanta—regardless of opponents and circumstances. Philadelphia's Wilson Goode, "as conciliatory as Washington was contentious," would win no greater percentage of the white vote than Washington.[59]

Holli and Green had found similar attitudes in Chicago: "On the issue of racial healing, an astonishingly low 7 percent of whites and only 11 percent of blacks thought the city under Washington was 'less divided racially.'...Some 45 and 30 percent of white and black respondents respectively perceived a more racially divided city."[60]

"Progressives," however, did tend to look for common ground. The group that founded CWED and later spread out through the universities and some of the community coalitions in Chicago were good at this. A key part of it was what Doug Gills called the "Gang of Four": Mier, Moe, Gills, and Vazquez. Mier came from a white working-class background, was educated at Notre Dame, and had a Vietnam experience that "turned his head around" prior to starting an academic career that gravitated toward the Chicago neighborhoods. Moe had come from an army family, stationed in many different environments, before coming in touch with the radical academic, and later senator, Paul Wellstone, who helped point her toward the Chicago neighborhood movement. Gills was an African American who came from North Carolina to study political science at Northwestern in the 1970s. He became a tireless combination of organizer and academic—a powerful speaker and articulate writer. Art Vazquez was a Mexican American who had been touched by Caesar Chavez in the 1960s; later he became a key organizer in Pilsen neighborhood before and after working in the Washington administration. These four had connections spread widely through the city and across race lines.

Mier, the most given to writing, later said about "Race and Planning": "Race is a powerful aspect of most planning situations in urban areas, yet it too often is the *last* way a problem, or especially an opportunity, is framed....I believe it should be the *first* way." Mier thought that both liberals who sought aid for central cities and conservatives who spoke for "empowerment...are selling the same idea: quarantine 'them' in inner city ghettos and barrios away from 'us.' Both ideological camps believe that separate can be made equal." He went on to say, "'Separate but equal' cannot work,...the challenge...is to bring about a more unified social reading of the situations [planners] confront, one that develops the ability to 'see' and buy into appropriate actions."[61] Miers's experience in Chicago's neighborhoods, he thought, suggested the ways that city populations and officials could learn to "see" across race lines. The key point, he thought, was to see the "truth" about race, first by acknowledging its presence, as in Elizabeth Hollander's instant awareness of "who's there...and who's not there."[62]

Mier thought this consciousness that made for the ability to see across race lines was inherent in the neighborhood organizations:

> Community groups are in fact able to see beyond their own geographic and social boundaries and engage with issues of larger civic interest....It is a profound mistake to reduce community groups, especially minority communities, to "interest groups." The concept of "interest group" often cripples understanding of the richness and diversity of citizen efforts.
>
> Grassroots leadership is abundant. Leadership is important, but often what is needed is the cooperative, coalition-building variety....This is precisely the type of leadership often found in neighborhoods, especially minority ones.[63]

Thoughts on Chicago

Perhaps the disappointments about the empowerment zone, school reform, affordable housing, and other parts of the community agenda reflected an inexorable weight that would finally grind down all or most of the program built up in painstaking ways by thousands of people after the decline of the old machine in the 1970s. "Reform" under Richard M. Daley had a much narrower meaning, urban policy a more limited vision.

Another way to look at it was more optimistic. Though Daley's governing group seemed simplistic compared to Washington's, he had found a way to govern while satisfying some of the interests of the neighborhood coalition and some of those of the downtown growth coalition. Washington had done the same; it was just that the mix of policies was different, the tilt now away from the neighborhoods.

What counts in this view is the longer run. Did most of the ideas about neighborhood empowerment survive among the neighborhood activists, if not in city hall? The fact they could complain as loud as they did, while keeping at least some of their programs intact, suggests life for the neighborhood program. Rather than simple victory or defeat for either side, what seemed to exist at the end of the 1990s and after was a more subtle mix. One did not know how the pieces would fit together, but a more diverse set of players was on the field than in the 1970s.

✄ CHAPTER 8

Race, Class, and the
Administrative Struggle

It is remarkable that Boston and Chicago produced progressive governments in the 1980s. No other large city did. There were several minority mayors, but they did not produce participatory and redistributive reforms to the same degree. The smaller cities described in chapter 2—though important precursors—did not generally face the same challenges or scale of problems. San Francisco is a special case, but it did not develop the administrative capacities for progressive government that Boston and Chicago did. Instances of progressive city governments outside the United States, fascinating in themselves, occurred in different political systems and cultures. But in the United States, Boston and Chicago most notably extended the achievements of the smaller cities described in chapter 2.

All of these cities were remarkable, and similar in key respects, but they were "outliers." "Progressive," as I define it, means a willingness to entertain redistributive measures like Chicago's manufacturing retention policies or Boston's linkage and related instruments; it also means a relatively open, participatory administration of government. Furthermore, it means a certain relationship between city hall and the neighborhoods, each responsive to initiatives from the other. Among U.S. cities, Boston and Chicago occupy places at the redistributive and participatory ends of both ranges. Most cities did little or no redistribution and were less participatory; and redistributive and participatory initiatives would have encouraged give-and-take between neighborhood and city hall. Boston and Chicago, and the other cities described in chapter 2, differed from the norm in these respects.

In contrast, most cities—less participatory, less interested in redistribution, less nuanced and practiced in city hall–neighborhood interaction—presented a constellation of obstacles to those who advocated moves in a progressive direction, and these obstacles became more apparent over time. In the 1950s, while New Deal reforms had changed the economy and politics nationally, cities were widely seen as "problems," choked by traffic, burdened by obsolete infrastructure and services, and hampered by political machines that could not provide serious administrative responses to these problems. In contrast to the advances in governance and administration at the federal level, scholars wrote of municipal government as a "lost world."[1] This assessment was quickly followed by optimism, as new federal programs like urban renewal and the interstate highway program stimulated massive real estate investments that changed central city landscapes. That these investments also emptied out working-class white populations and moved factories to suburban locations was unremarked, or even seemed an added benefit, at the time.

But the optimism was short-lived. The new urban policies exacerbated racial divides by concentrating minority poverty in poor neighborhoods. To compensate, the Great Society programs promoted by the Johnson administration in the late 1960s attempted to ameliorate inner-city problems through social services and other federal programs. But by the end of the 1970s, urban policy had encountered a reaction. The civil rights movement devolved into racially charged riots and disorder in many cities. The physical infrastructure programs had caused massive disruptions of poor neighborhoods. Social programs became targets of white reaction. The Vietnam War brought protests, and there were the assassinations of two Kennedys and Martin Luther King. Eventually some cities were forced to the verge of bankruptcy. There was a sense of urban crisis.

It is simplistic—but serviceable for our purposes here—to see "urban policy" facing two choices by the end of the 1960s. One route would be to elaborate inner-city services in order to create a set of communities parallel to the suburban enclaves that were developing, fund them adequately with redistributive measures, and press for administrative reforms like open-housing laws applied nationwide. The other course, largely followed, was to leave the central cities to the real estate market, while directing the main national policies to the already growing suburban and Sunbelt cities. In time, some argued, the central cities might revive as well.[2]

Scholarship

This policy development and its results have been laid out piecemeal in scholarly work, as a general account of the emergence of the "neoliberal city." Jason Hackworth presented a useful summary, beginning with the defeat of Cleveland's progressive mayor Dennis Kucinich in 1979 by elites imbued with "the utterly astonishing rise and reproduction of 'neoliberalism' as an ideology, mode of city governance, and driver of urban change."[3] Hackworth described neoliberalism as a reversion to "classical liberalism" as prominently argued by Friedrich Hayek in his 1944 landmark book, *The Road to Serfdom*. Its key elements included (1) the dominant position of the individual as opposed to "community" or "state"; (2) liberty as more important than equality: that is, equality of opportunity was more important than equality of condition; (3) the government role was to be minimal and noninterventionist—it was to keep order as a service to entrepreneurs and property owners; (4) the economy was theorized to function best in the sense of producing abundance, when coordinated by markets; and (5) planning—in almost any form—was anathema as it would tempt legislators to intervene and thereby destabilize markets.[4]

Hayek's argument, and the later rise of his ideas in the 1970s and 1980s through the advocacy of "Chicago School" economists, notably Milton Friedman, was a reaction to the modifications of classical doctrine that had accompanied the New Deal period in the United States and the roughly contemporary rise of social democracy in Europe. These political movements and associated government-program innovations, occasioned by the Depression of the 1930s, eventually settled on a form of intervention in markets associated with the ideas of John Maynard Keynes. Keynesian theory modified classical economic doctrine but did not seek to abolish markets. It promoted at most a limited version of planning. It envisioned regulation of aggregate demand including subsidies to consumption by such means as home-ownership mortgage insurance, unemployment insurance, and Social Security. This was successful as a theory and basis for government action because it offered, on balance, stable markets for private firms. In the early 1960s there even seemed to be some prospect of a government management of the economy of increasing subtlety and effectiveness, capable of adapting to new challenges.[5]

Keynesian doctrine, which Hackworth called "egalitarian liberalism," failed to survive the 1960s, not just because of urban disorder but also because, in a context of falling productivity and profits, private sector leaders lost faith in the ability of government to control key parts of the political system, particularly labor.[6] In place of the "New Deal order" (a combination of economic stimulus, regulation of business, and safety net), neoliberalism offered an alternative: the market and competition could solve most problems. The neoliberal doctrine achieved "hegemonic status," Hackworth argued, through its promulgation by think tanks and foundations, the Reagan and Thatcher governments, and "large global institutions like the International Monetary Fund, the World Bank, and bond rating agencies."[7]

One strand of scholarship, Hackworth pointed out, is the focus on "understanding the 'actually existing' nature of the ideology—that is, less the intellectual lineage of liberal thought than the way that such ideas permeate and are experienced at various geographical scales." One version described neoliberalism as a dialectical process, with "conflicting tendencies toward destruction and creation." Another suggested a "more linear process" of "rollback" followed by "roll-out."[8]

In retrospect, these ideas seem to have framed the national environment in which the progressive-city activists worked. In the Reagan administration, budget director David Stockman sought to "defund the left," and a drumbeat of attacks on "welfare queens" and public housing became the context for attempts to defeat the Congress, which was dominated at the time by the Democratic Party. The same time period brought "creative" ideas: public-private partnerships replacing municipal initiatives, enterprise zones featuring the removal of regulations and business tax obligations in geographically defined parts of inner cities.

Although the analysis of neoliberalism is extensive and its scholarly permutations can be exhausting, studying "actually existing neoliberalism" gives a sense of the immensity of the forces the progressive-city activists were up against. It was not simply a matter of winning the occasional election through sometimes innovative tactics—though certainly the progressives accomplished this. They also had to govern, and to find a route to reelection. That they frequently did get reelected, and generally maintained their policy approaches, is all the more remarkable.

"Actually Existing Progressivism"

In this book, the focus is less on the obstacles per se than on the ways the progressive-city activists fought ahead regardless. How did these regimes manage, and what were their main accomplishments? Describing this was the burden of the previous chapters. Here my goal is to provide a taxonomy, a list of features and accomplishments that, sufficiently well drawn, might help map the way toward replication or even further steps. I touch briefly on the decision to contest elections. I then focus on the key features of the Flynn and Washington mayoralties, features that had the effect of defining a new approach to city administration.

I see administration as different for the progressives described in these chapters because of their social-movement background and because of the ongoing presence of that movement that I call the *neighborhood base*. This then leads to a further issue: how city administration relates to the movement— mainly, in these case histories, the neighborhoods. This is a rich set of relationships, and we only scratch the surface here. But we do identify a *sequence of development* for these relationships. At least in concept, government was to become less top-down, more relational.

How were they to accomplish this? Administration was a special challenge for progressives. Unlike conservatives, they could not confine themselves to a few policing and management functions on the premise that the main task of government is to facilitate the private sector by leaving it alone. Unlike many liberals, they wanted to go beyond efficient pursuit of the welfare state to target more fundamental changes. A list of the challenges and approaches would include (a) making the decision to campaign, contest elections, or work with candidates with "progressive" agendas; arranging potential new initiatives in some order; (b) relating to the base: deliver services, but also manage a list of issues that would arise as that base made a transition from simple opposition to a more nuanced relationship to city hall; and (c) transcending the base: reaching out to constituencies who might have opposed them, but who had to be part of the more wide-ranging initiatives necessary to implement redistributive and participatory goals. I follow this with additional comments on the neighborhood base and the sequence of change, implications for national policy, the question of "evaluation," and a set of final reflections.

Campaigns and Agendas

To trace what was different about these cities, it is useful to begin with one fateful kind of decision: that of the social-movement activists, in sufficient numbers and with organizational histories, to commit to political involvement by contesting elections or—more typically—joining with political candidates who supported their aims. The latter was the case in Boston, where Flynn was a veteran of the city council who challenged the business leadership; and in Chicago, where Washington was a congressman who had come up in the Daley machine before steering a more independent course.

Much of the scholarship on the "progressive city" has dwelled on electoral tactics and coalitions.[9] But for the progressive activists campaigns were part of a larger process that unfolded in stages. Their motivation came from often long histories of social movement that produced radically different agendas. In Boston and Chicago, these had been bubbling to the surface for one or two decades before 1983.

But these histories alone did not produce a program for governing the city. For this, contesting and winning elections was a distinct further step. It was where the essential character and ideas of the candidate and campaign workers made eye contact and shook hands with the public; in the case of the progressive-city activists, it was where they found a larger public and got some idea of what that public would support.

Something similar happened when movement organizations produced platforms or agendas in anticipation of elections. This would be the case when Mass Fair Share produced referenda on neighborhood councils and linkage in Boston, or when Dreier assembled a set of ideas in *Who Rules Boston?*, after King had formulated *Chain of Change,* and when Mier saw the "generative metaphors" coming out of the CWED Platform in Chicago.[10] These were all cases where ideas that had been gestating for some time came into focus, to be further processed in elections before coming together as doctrine, marching orders for city hall workers. Thus newly ensconced administrators would begin with expansive agendas that had been gestating for two decades in the social-movement environment. The most important innovations in Boston and Chicago—linkage and various industrial job–retention devices like the planned manufacturing districts (PMDs)—literally came from movement organizations or campaigns.

Relating to the Base

One of the great resources Flynn and Washington had on taking office was the complex and capable "base" in the neighborhoods and neighborhood organizations. The base did not have the financial resources and institutions of their vanquished foes, but they knew how to organize and had helped generate the broad outlines of larger city policies. At the same time, these administrations realized that they needed to transcend the base that had elected them; governing was a broader operation than an election. But Boston's broader housing ideas and Chicago's industrial policy had come from grassroots organizations. The problem was how to relate to that base while also reaching out to the city as a whole.

There would be people on the mayor's staff and appointed as department heads who came directly from the base. Thus in Chicago Giloth, Moe, and Vazquez were in the neighborhood movement and, in Moe's case, central in the campaign. Ken O'Hare had worked in city hall under previous mayors but was part of the *Washington Papers* Jobs Committee. Rob Mier was on the UIC faculty, but he had been working with the neighborhood base. There was something similar in the "Sandinistas" who went from Boston's neighborhood movement into Flynn's city hall: Ray Dooley had been an organizer in Allston-Brighton before becoming Flynn's campaign manager and then administrative director. Neil Sullivan had been in Mass Fair Share, and Peter Dreier played a role organizing Boston's Tenant Organizing Coalition.

Other department heads and lower-level hires came from outside the city or outside the community development group. Certain high-profile department heads were "outsiders." Perhaps one could put Elizabeth Hollander in that category. In Chicago she initially related to a constituency that cared more about city planning commission issues and not necessarily local neighborhood ones. Howard Stanback came to Chicago from Hartford to direct the Mayor's Office of Employment and Training. In Boston the highest-profile outsider was Stephen Coyle, hired from a San Francisco architecture and development firm to direct the Boston Redevelopment Authority; Lisa Chapnick was from Long Island by way of Michigan, but had been at the State House in Boston before joining Flynn as a formidable administrator and department head.

One might not have expected it, but "outsider" department heads who might in other circumstances have focused narrowly on technical matters or things specific to professional callings consciously and elaborately spoke of inclusion and participation. Mier, in a retrospective book largely on his time as commissioner of economic development, devoted a surprising proportion of space to this. Coyle emphasized it in an interview after he had left Boston.[11] Hollander spoke with admiration of the inclusiveness of Washington's city hall, passing on the experience of meetings not continuing unless the faces at the table included black, white, and brown, male, and female.

Once committed to the campaign and then in office, the new politics and administration had to find ways to adapt to city hall, which had long been accustomed to a more institutionalized form of political constituency and organization—sixteen years under Kevin White in Boston, "the machine" in Chicago—and to adapt city hall to the movement base and community-based organizations.

This would not be easy. Progressive-city activists, inside and outside city hall, would point to lessons learned. First among them was that tensions were inevitable. The relation between progressive government and the progressive base tended to be fraught and tense. This was the reality. From the standpoint of the progressive administrations and politicians, there was the question of how to regard the neighborhood activists, from whose ranks many had come. Were they a "movement," and if so, who was in charge? Political candidates represented a movement. But once in office, Washington and Flynn each had to reach out to groups that had not originally supported them, and this worked against continued use of movement style. When he was speaking to the white ethnic neighborhoods, for example, it would do Washington no good to employ the symbolism of the Task Force for Black Political Empowerment. What did work was talking about street improvements from the general obligation bond initiative. Flynn adopted a stance of supporting "responsible" CDCs and neighborhood groups. Dreier referred to a "pragmatic left."

Another lesson learned by activists-turned-administrators was the nuances of friendship with their friends still on the outside. These friendships could be an advantage: asking a neighborhood organization to avoid opposing a city position that it otherwise might have, for example. But resentments could follow. The best course seemed to be to keep official business formal, and old friends at arm's length at times. This lesson was typically learned imperfectly. Time and experience would help, but there was not always time.

It was an advantage to have former activists in city hall staffs, but administrators, looking back, commented that it was a mistake to hire too many, since that could immobilize the neighborhood organizations and make them less effective allies. Dreier was certain of this, and it was a common observation among veterans of Harold Washington's administration.

Neighborhood councils were typical platform elements for progressive mayors, but they were never implemented in Chicago and were fraught with difficulty in Boston. Mayors were tempted to use the councils as they seemed to offer a direct channel to a constituency that was normally in the hands of—often hostile—city council members. Washington, facing majority opposition, could not implement neighborhood councils and sought to connect by other means. Flynn's efforts were problematic despite the referendum mandate, in part because city hall had inherent difficulties dealing with the relatively fragile and fledgling neighborhood councils, and also because some neighborhoods insisted on more independence than city hall wanted to allow. They complained that Flynn wanted "control" and was not good at sharing power.

Both city halls found it easier to promote concretely materialistic redistributive measures than to share power. Boston went to great lengths to stimulate the production of affordable housing, including supporting and subsidizing community development groups' efforts to produce affordable housing. Chicago was less effective with housing, but focused instead on its "jobs, not real estate" economic policies and delegated significant funding to as many as one hundred local economic development agencies.

Activists also learned that relationships evolved. The relationship between city administration and neighborhoods could change and develop. It helps to see a progression in the relationship, from the coarse to the fine grain of city policy, which may extend from city governance and administration to the movement itself. During Chicago's council-wars phase, both movement and administration were coarsely grained and polarized. At first Washington saw the conflict as a matter of principle, perhaps a personal challenge—a fight between himself and the old machine. But this relationship eventually moderated, the machine group undermined by Washington's midterm electoral gains and the softening induced by the general obligation bond campaign. The Playskool negotiations went this way as well: a lawsuit by the city, then compromise. Flynn, at the outset, sought improvements in rent control, then simply implemented the existing linkage rules and, finally, devised refinements that came later, notably Dreier's CRA campaign. In both places, over time, city administration and politics became more differentiated. There also began to be greater differentiation in movement demands; the movement became more subtle and complex.

Transcending the Base

Once in office, elected officials and administrators found they needed to move beyond their initial support group. In addition to "relating to the base," they had to garner support from, or at least neutralize, constituencies that had been on the fence or even opposed. This occurred during the electoral process and later. If we categorize by race and class, two main steps for progressives were (1) making peace with groups that could be formally seen as part of the class base, but were alienated—usually by race; and (2) reaching across class lines to a business constituency.

RACE

The progressive cities present a set of fascinating contrasts in how they addressed issues of race. Washington won election with massive support from black voters plus some whites, notably those known to Chicagoans as the "lakefront liberals." By 1987 he had solidified his hold by attracting Latino votes and council support. Flynn won by appealing to a populist white working-class base, plus a scattering of other support.

Washington had to reach out to the white and Latino working-class and white middle-class wards simply to get a working relationship (and eventual majority) in the city council. He managed this with tactical moves. For the most part these were pragmatic, made with great care. Washington, unwilling to circumvent the Shakman agreement, simply refused to extend patronage or otherwise cede control to the white wards when suggested by the Vrdolyak forces immediately after the 1983 election. He temporized with the linked-development proposals supported by SON/SOC, so that when consensus failed to develop the idea died.[12] His great success was the general obligation bond campaign in 1984–85.

Flynn, having defeated Mel King and the Rainbow Coalition by a large margin, still had to move with care toward black neighborhoods. Like Washington, he used a pragmatic approach and garnered a measure of black support. There were kind words between Flynn and King on election night. But there was disaffection and a continual sense of discomfort on both sides. Flynn adopted a "majoritarian" approach consistent with the experience of many of the "Sandinistas," who had adopted a similar stance with Fair Share: he would favor redistributive measures to right the inequalities among social classes, without reference to race. This may have played well in white neighborhoods, but blacks found it facile: black and white families of equal income and wealth still had unequal opportunity.

Flynn's approach was to work with the "pragmatic" elements in the community development movement, and he sought to move them toward production of affordable housing units. King supporters did organize efforts to press the city—like the Coalition for Community Control of Development—but did not mesh with Flynn's priorities. Dreier, in contrast, wanted more support for the CRA campaign pressuring the banks for affordable-housing investments.

In contrast to their efforts to cross race lines by directly supporting neighborhood projects, Washington and Flynn took more global approaches to challenge and ultimately co-opt business leadership, with linkage in Boston and the manufacturing-oriented industrial policy in Chicago. The most important "transcendence"—a bridging of both race and class lines—would have been the forging of a détente, if not overt alliances, with segments of the business community. The business community was the natural enemy of a populist movement. One would expect business to oppose, and then attempt to co-opt, any populism, as had been the pattern with many populist mayors.[13] Thus, what is remarkable is the success that Flynn and Washington had, not their frustrations.

LINKAGE

With federal aid and city budgets shrinking in the 1970s and 1980s, progressives in and out of city government sought alternative funds. One approach was to tap real estate development, which, in many cases, was the object of significant investment. Even with the manufacturing base disappearing, investors saw ways to profit from projects related to upscale housing, retail, offices, or tourism. One approach was to expand the concept of "exactions," whereby a city could extract payments if it could show that the proposed development impacted the city budget in some specific way—say, street improvements or added fire service—that would not be compensated for by property taxes. This was roughly the basis for innovations like inclusionary zoning, where developers would be required to supply low-cost housing to balance more expensive units—the added cost justifying the exaction was the burden of housing poorer families elsewhere. It was but a marginal extension from this to the sorts of development agreements imposed on developers in Hartford in the 1970s, and later in Santa Monica: major office developments, for example, would impose costs for day care and added congestion on adjacent homeowners. Boston and San Francisco extended the idea by codifying it as rules that would apply to all development of a certain size, with fees assessed on a square-foot basis.

While linkage did not originate with Flynn or Coyle, they elaborated it. It was first proposed and passed at the end of the Kevin White mayoralty after being advocated by neighborhood groups and promoted by Fair Share. But Flynn and Coyle developed the idea and bore the criticism of developers and others who protested that it would "kill the goose" of real estate development investment. When they stuck to their guns and development continued, the case was made, not only for the specific legislative device of linkage, but the more general principle that real estate investment created a large flow of capital that could be tapped. As Dreier noted later, a significant set of other devices (listed in chapter 4)—much of what was remarkable about the Flynn mayoralty on the community development front—then became justifiable and feasible.

One of the criticisms of linkage—that it was tied to a real estate boom that could not last—missed the larger point: that the principle underlying linkage—that real estate investment could be tapped up front, rather than mainly as a long-term source of tax revenues—spread to other sources of funds as well. CRA protests followed a similar logic, for example, and they resulted in very significant diversions of capital into affordable housing.

INDUSTRIAL POLICY

Chicago's industrial policy was a more fundamental challenge to private sector values than Boston's linkage scheme was. It implied not just that investors should be constrained from maximizing development profits in a parcel, but also that manufacturing investments were to be valued over housing and other investments in some cases. This choice of one sector (manufacturing) made it an *industrial* policy. As Mier had deduced during the CWED platform discussions, the policy should favor "jobs not real estate." This bucked a sea change in finance, national in scope, which favored short-term returns, and a bias against the manufacturing sector generally.

Compared to the Flynn/Coyle initiatives in Boston, Washington and Mier were playing for higher stakes in Chicago. In challenging investor preferences to move capital out of manufacturing, they were attacking a climate of opinion that operated at a national, not just a local, scale. CEOs in manufacturing firms, not disposed to take Washington seriously in the first place, were perhaps swept up in a different set of problems, such as stockholders looking for short-term profits and acquisition by conglomerates formed to shift capital out of manufacturing and into sectors with quicker returns. Thus any gains in Chicago had to occur around the edges of the main investor decisions. Small manufacturers could support the PMDs; but there was little chance of success with Wisconsin Steel or U.S. Steel. Did Mier and Washington perceive this early on in the operations of the Steel Task Force? Possibly, but they pushed on anyhow, setting the stage for the more localized PMD efforts later—particularly given the support drummed up by Ducharme's tireless efforts.

This suggests a point about Chicago's manufacturing retention policies, one that is still debated. In 1999 Joel Rast published a book-length argument for the manufacturing policy in Chicago, and its grassroots support, and saw the possibility, with strong—presumably mayoral—leadership, of an "alliance between neighborhood producers, workers, and community residents" that could develop "flexible, innovative networks of production." But his book was treated with skepticism locally. David Perry, who had inherited some of the leadership functions at UIC, thought Rast's argument was overstated:

> Frankly, when compared to the magnitude of the redevelopment and gentrification efforts of the downtown property-based growth regime, City Hall's implementation of a few planned manufacturing districts and industrial corridors is hardly evidence of a powerful "new regime" of neighborhood manufacturers and workers.[14]

But manufacturing retention did not unequivocally fail in Chicago. In the face of a tidal wave of plant closings, it saved some factories and jobs, and it continued to do so well after the Washington administration. Like Boston's housing policies, it had many parts: the early warning system experiments, the Playskool lawsuit and settlement, the Steel, Apparel, and Printing task forces, and the PMDs and later industrial-corridor programs.

And if the Daley administration compromised the manufacturing policy, it was at least partly because of the strong demand for more upscale housing, which Daley, like Menino, encouraged as part of a policy of bringing the middle class into the city through "mixed-income" developments in former public-housing sites and elsewhere. This policy—when applied in Boston—benefited from linkage dollars there. In Chicago it was financed by Daley's increasing use of tax increment financing (TIF), a device for tapping anticipated tax revenues from urban renewal subsidies.

One of the great ironies is the relative disappearance of industrial policy compared to the hardy survival of linkage in at least a few cities.[15] The effort to recast the economic framework for city policy—Mier's insistence that economic development meant "jobs, not real estate"—may have been the biggest casualty of the Daley administration. It was never a prominent idea in Boston.

On the disappearance of Chicago's industrial policy, the key word is "relative." On the one hand was "failure" of the Steel Task Force early in the Washington administration. Ann Markusen, as consultant to that body, and in a number of presentations and publications, argued that cities and business elites faced three options with regard to manufacturing: "bow out, bid down the cost of labor, or build on the basics." Along with many activists in the unions and allied with the neighborhoods, she thought that manufacturing decline was far from inevitable and that, by examining industrial sectors closely, it would be possible to save at least the more viable portions of basic industry. Countering these ideas were a defeatist attitude within some sectors and the enticement of capital to other sectors, like real estate development. This provided short-term advantage to some business-elite segments while destroying plant capacity and skills in the labor force. The question was how to promote these ideas to get at least a fair debate among those who controlled the resources. Real estate leaders on the Steel Task Force resisted consensus on Markusen's key point, the viability of continued steel production, and so the Task Force report had limited impact.

The national climate for discussion was parlous. National-level business leadership, which had found a way to work with labor and New Deal politics from the late 1930s into the 1960s, was casting about for a new formula.

What it seemed to settle on was disaffection from government in general. Ideas like "industrial policy" that might have helped in Chicago and elsewhere, after a brief revival in the early 1980s, were abandoned when business activists threatened to attack them. The Republican Party seemed taken over by ideas that Lewis Lapham, quoting Lionel Trilling, characterized as "irritable mental gestures which seek to resemble ideas."[16] Markusen nevertheless spent several years arguing her points to any audience of business elites and politicians she could find.

MAJOR ACHIEVEMENTS IN SMALLER CITIES

There were significant innovations in places smaller than Boston and Chicago. They were of smaller scope because "transcending the base" in a smaller city was generally not so enormous an effort.

Rent control in Santa Monica, where there was a large majority of renters, was significant because it brought city policy in general more in line with the natural spectrum of interests. Once rent control was established, it was relatively easy for SMRR to do redistributive housing policies—for example, catering to middle-income homeowners through development agreements and what was called the "housing element" of the general plan. This widening of city policy was relatively easy once the redistributive principle was established and no really viable opposition appeared, as attested by the long-term dominance of SMRR in local politics.

In Burlington, Vermont, the city's Progressive Coalition built a dominant political base around housing policy, using the land-trust model to subsidize, directly or indirectly, 20 percent of the city's housing units. The Fair Representation Ordinance in Berkeley and the eventual emergence of the Cleveland Housing Network long after Kucinich's mayoralty are other examples of progressive city achievements. A full account of the administrative impact of progressive city government would describe at least these in some detail. These accomplishments were dramatic and fundamental, but as in Santa Monica, "transcending the base" in smaller cities did not entail facing the complexities, nor in most cases the class and race divisions, of the larger cities.[17]

Linkage in Boston and manufacturing retention in Chicago were major achievements because they effected a degree of income and wealth redistribution to the have-nots at a time when structural biases in local and national economies were pushing in the opposite direction. Redistributive policies in general had been thought to be most difficult at the local level. If so, these difficulties—embedded in the structure of economies and politics—might be seen to be all the more rigidly ensconced in larger places like Boston and Chicago.

Innovations: The Cascade Effect

Profound as one might think linkage and PMDs were in Boston and Chicago, they were only the tip of the iceberg for what happened in these cities under Washington and Flynn. Looking carefully, one sees many layers.

First, as described in chapter 1, and as I observed earlier for a set of smaller progressive cities, both places engaged in both redistributive and participatory reforms. What was remarkable was that so many reforms presented themselves that there was a cascading effect once public acquiescence to elite interests—downtown developers in one case, corporate capital in the other—was halted. Dreier laid out the list in Boston: inclusionary zoning, parcel-to-parcel linkage, city support for Community Reinvestment Act campaigns to pressure the banks, and so on. These were redistributive policies, but Flynn's effort to support downtown development while accommodating neighborhood participation demands (with neighborhood councils) also ended up creating space for more participation, increasing its base. Exemplary cases of participatory community organizations like DSNI should not obscure other community initiatives that occurred without city hall support, like the Coalition for Community Control of Development and the Greater Roxbury Neighborhood Authority.

The industrial retention efforts in Chicago, likewise, had many facets: the Playskool suit, LIRI, the Steel Task Force, the Apparel Task Force, and the PMDs were repeated many times. The industrial policy in Chicago was followed by efforts on the affordable-housing front too, as reported in the LISC study and monitored by the Rehab Network. These policies provided substance to neighborhood organizations and legitimized them as well, thus expanding a sense of participation opportunities in the city generally. Chicago's inclusionary meeting practices within city hall were striking; and in general there was support for neighborhood organizations, as in the LIRI program, and there were many other examples.

What are we to make of the relative ease with which, once a key innovation like linkage passed muster in Boston, the cascade of other policy initiatives followed? It is hard to avoid the impression that there was an underlying logic all along which its opposition—the "growth coalition" and its allies—had denied while events moved in another direction. The idea that linkage would "kill the golden goose," while an attention-getting metaphor, was contradicted by the fact that developers could afford the fees because their market was strong, and because by participating they could avoid some of the opprobrium and delay that could be leveled by community opposition to development. A similar logic was behind the retention of manufacturing in Chicago: many or most of the threatened firms were viable—even some of the steel producers—and their abandonment by investors, Markusen's "bowing out" option, was not dictated by logic or data but by the convenience of investors who believed the myth that if some manufacturing was moving out, then all must be.

The Neighborhood Base

Even if we built these lists of innovations into the dozens for each place and even if a new kind of administrative practice was codified in textbook fashion, we would be seeing only a partial picture. For while there was a city-government story, there was also the neighborhood story.

The neighborhood story was quite different from the city hall story.[18] In fact, the existence of divergent narratives is a methodological problem, a challenge I have not been able to resolve completely. When I began this study, and also in the previous work it elaborates, my goal was to describe a form of city governance and administration that seemed to be emerging. It was a form, I knew, that came from social movements that existed in city neighborhoods and outside of city hall, and that there would be divergences in different accounts and interviews, but the main stories would come from the perspective of people in city hall. This approach resulted in my reliance on certain key informants within city hall: Robert Mier and a few others in Chicago, Peter Dreier and a few others in Boston. The neighborhood accounts would perhaps be a check, but I would think of them as another, different story, and it would not be my central aim to make judgments about them. I would try, though, to represent different views, without necessarily resolving discrepancies.

Neighborhood leaders had a different standpoint from those in city hall. In some cases they had opposed the new city hall leadership. But even in support, with "friends in city hall," there were distinct capacities and different approaches. These included the following:

- By 1983, neighborhood organizations were a far cry from their modest origins. Many were vigorous and growing, despite an increasingly tight funding environment and hostile federal policies. With the election of new "progressive" mayors in Boston and Chicago in 1983, activists were anxious to engage city government.

- Some had begun to engage in service delivery and affordable housing production, while others held back for lack of funding or to give priority to advocacy and organizing, and there were vigorous debates as to the advisability of one approach versus another.

- Neighborhood organizations were generally wary of city hall, even when city hall offered resources—for example, grants and loans for affordable housing. Neighborhood leaders were averse to the red tape and they remembered cases where promised funds fell through or were so delayed they were of little use. And they felt bureaucrats and politicians were too quick to take credit for neighborhood achievements.

- Neighborhood organizations lacked staff and other resources, and there were great inequalities when community people met with city agencies. City Life's difficulty keeping up with the changes coming out of Boston's city hall, where the BRA and later PFD had dozens of planners to assign to neighborhood projects, was typical.

- Oppositional coalitions of neighborhood organizations formed out of fear of city hall (SON/SOC) or frustration at city hall policies (CCCD), but failed in their main objectives (linked development and a rule-based city development process, respectively) and faded after a few years.

Relation between the Two Sequences

There were two "stories," each describing a sequence of events. But how did the neighborhood sequence and the city hall sequence relate to one another? Was social movement or city administration the best route to a general alternative approach—to the progressive city? These were the questions raised in chapter 1, figure 1.2.

The relationship is certainly more complicated than the diagram suggests. One simple prescription said that organizing and protest—the social movement—was the key to concrete results. This suggests the lower right box in figure 1.2 is the place for activists to put their effort—largely what happened in Boston and Chicago in the 1970s.

Though this may hold water as a simple rule, I think it is too simple. Neighborhood organizations did arise on their own (or due to a confluence of forces in each of these cities) well in advance of city hall encouragement. Moreover, they engaged in overt or more implicit support for political takeovers of city hall—certainly there was such support for Flynn and Washington. What city governments did do, though, was encourage neighborhood organizations to develop as organizations, helping them get the capacity to produce housing units or provide services. The effect of this was controversial, but arguably it created interdependence between the city and the neighborhood organizations, so that the larger neighborhood organizations and their support groups remained as political forces after Flynn and Washington had left the scene in Boston and Chicago.

Some general conclusions about the relationship between the city sequence and the neighborhood sequence are these:

1. Both neighborhood organization and city government went through different phases and learned from them. Neighborhoods (and ethnic minorities) went from accommodation to protest to seeking to own part of city government, as Mel King laid it out for Boston in *Chain of Change*. Progressive city administrations went from being an extension of a social movement to putting together an increasingly competent administration, department by department, to finally implementing coherent policy as suggested by *Chicago Works Together* and linkage as it gradually emerged in Boston under Coyle and Flynn.

2. On occasion it was the neighborhood movement that gave the city administration coherence in its policies. That happened with the introduction of the CWED platform into the campaign car, into *The Washington Papers,* and finally into the two versions of Mier's economic plan; and it also happened with the voter initiatives for linkage and neighborhood councils in Boston. Although these policies could only be implemented by city hall, it was still true to claim they were "bottom up" in origin.

3. City policies encouraged the neighborhood organizations as well: Mier's shifting of DED subsidies to local economic groups based on their performance in the case of the Local Industrial Retention Initiative (LIRI) was a particularly obvious example. New relationships in Boston also existed as time went on. Dreier's effort to promote the Boston CRA protests and Coyle's dramatic opening up of eminent-domain authority to DSNI were important examples. Whether any one of these initiatives successfully stimulated neighborhood organization, much less a movement, is problematic. What does seem clear is that the general approach of the Boston and Chicago city governments created a climate of hope for neighborhood organizations that lasted for a least a time after different mayoralties replaced them.

4. The national environment for city policy mattered. Chicago's industrial-policy emphasis, while it came from grassroots demands, ultimately engaged problems at the national level, especially in the case of the multinational corporations that were shutting down factories for reasons other than effective production. Labor and community pressure was thus less effective in the case of the Steel Task Force than it would be in the 1990s when pressing Daley for a stronger affordable-housing policy. It did find more response in the case of the PMDs aimed at smaller plants. Boston's housing policy and linkage, on the other hand, were easier to achieve, once Flynn and his constituency applied pressure.

5. Chicago progressives found a new base in the small manufacturers they contacted in the push for the planned manufacturing districts, the early warning systems, and some of the task forces. These initiatives put previously less-connected groups together: labor activists, neighborhood organizers, and the factory owners themselves. Dan Swinney and his associates at the Midwest Center for Labor Research carried on the effort through the Daley administration, despite declining city hall interest.

6. The neighborhood groups became an institutional presence as an industry, particularly around housing in Boston and industrial development in Chicago. The organizing around neighborhood housing production was sustained and effective in Chicago after Sawyer's defeat—an attempt to get the most possible from a city administration that was initially hostile. The Massachusetts CDCs were successful statewide and effectively used that as leverage on the city.

7. Neighborhood interest and organization was often fragile—in need of more patience and nurturing than city bureaucrats could offer. The city officials tended to be under pressure themselves, lacking enough time and embattled in conflicts (council wars in Chicago, Dooley's "permanent campaign" in Boston), and their attention was necessarily episodic.

If there is a negative conclusion people have drawn from the experience of progressive cities, perhaps it is a warning about the destructive effect that involvement in city administration has had on community organizations. Leaders often saw their organizations as more fundamental guarantors of the welfare of the have-nots than were political regimes of perhaps temporary occupants of city hall. Thus involvement in progressive politics carried unknown dangers. The most obvious danger had been the siphoning off of neighborhood leadership into jobs in city hall; but another was the increased flow of city money into neighborhood organizations, which could co-opt them or cause conflicts within them as they tried to serve both a neighborhood constituency and city hall. Certainly these things all happened in Boston and Chicago.

But there were other forces at work as well, not all of them negative, and some of them quite long lasting. Most important, the experience of working in city hall created a cadre of leadership that had a new sense of how to work with neighborhoods. Some of this cadre went back to neighborhood organizations, some went to academia or foundations, others to business and finance or other government agencies. All were a resource for subsequent mayors and new generations of neighborhood leadership.

The Rainbow Coalition, GRNA, and CCCD

In Boston, the neighborhood story was embellished by the voices of Mel King and the Rainbow Coalition forces, at variance from the "majoritarian" policies and instincts of the Sandinista group and Flynn in city hall. While Dreier and others in city hall were laying out a convincing narrative for an alternative to the "growth coalition" that had effectively governed the city for three decades, the rainbow group supported a series of initiatives in an attempt to influence city hall policies. The Roxbury group's effort to gain standing as the Greater Roxbury Neighborhood Authority in 1985 and the more broadly based effort to create the Coalition for Community Control of Development in 1988 were the strongest examples. But neither were politically successful. GRNA wanted a partial say over the development issues that began with Coyle's leaked plan for the Dudley Station area and, though the mayor had promised that they would have a say, they were ultimately denied one, despite several years of planning with the aid of Kennedy and Gaston's UMass Boston students. In the end, CCCD simply asked for a set of rules for interaction with the city over development issues to counter the frustrations community groups had over changing city positions, such as the issues noted by Stephen Fahrer of City Life (see chapter 4). This was denied by city council.

The participants on both sides of these issues had ideas as to why these proposals could not be satisfied. Flynn saw himself as a neighborhood-oriented mayor but did not want to lose control over development in these neighborhoods. As Dreier argued, the city had a deal with developers: it would let the developers proceed, and they would in turn give a portion of their profits and prerogatives back to the city. But in Flynn's world, this did not extend to putting developers under the control—even partial control—of a neighborhood group in Roxbury, or in any other part of the city.

A similar logic was at play as CCCD marshaled more general support for development policy across the city, crossing race and class lines. Their neighborhood congresses attracted at least some attendance from city hall officials. But overall, city hall was not supportive. City officials distrusted the Rainbow Coalition, which was prominent, if not dominant, within CCCD. They did not think the "left" forces had a serious "base." Flynn, they said, had worked hard for that base and had received at least modest increases in the black vote in the 1987 and 1991 mayoral elections. Black developers, they noted, opposed some of the community control ideas, and hoped to win some of the affordable housing funds Flynn had tapped through linkage and his pressure on the banks. King, however, "would never support us, whatever we did."[19]

The Rainbow Coalition and Flynn's mayoralty (including his "Sandinista" staff and allies) were very different political phenomena. Marie Kennedy and her coauthors caught the distinction well in the "Tranformative Populism" piece noted in chapter 4. Flynn wanted to redistribute wealth, King and the Rainbow Coalition wanted to generate a transformative consciousness in the neighborhoods.[20] The Rainbow group had history, leadership, and good argument. King had been at the center of organizing in the black community, and in political campaigns in 1979 and 1983 had connected with other constituencies—neighborhoods "of color" and diversity—but also white, middle-class elements and intellectuals attracted by King's community development ideas. King himself was a leader of some charisma, year in and year out speaking for these constituencies. And the "argument"—that communities needed to organize if they were to share in the general prosperity—was of a piece with a great tradition, laid out in *Chain of Change,* but also taught wherever organizers were trained.

Nevertheless it was a hard argument to win with after 1983. The Rainbow Coalition had lost that election by a two-to-one margin, and the city was ready to see what Flynn could do. What Flynn did was spectacular. Buildings went up downtown, and a share of the returns was going to go to the neighborhoods. Transformative populism would be a hard sell when it was up against the promise of hard cash, even with delays and other difficulties with development. And if the issue was race—as it was in many minds—the non-white population of Boston was relatively low (though it was growing; see table 1.5).

There is no easy comparison with Chicago under Harold Washington. Washington won with a tiny plurality in 1983, though the racial balance was much closer and he would win easily four years later. But, given the institutional support for the white population, he had much more need than Flynn to reach out to other groups. Like Flynn, he tried pragmatism: the General Obligation Bond Campaign was his breakthrough, providing resources to every ward as he was, in other ways, building his city council support.

There was little talk of transformative populism in Chicago. Washington might have moved in that direction, but he was putting a different form of transformation in place, one that redistributed material resources toward neighborhoods and industrial jobs. It was less spectacular than Boston's real estate strategy. The housing side was a disappointment, in fact, and did not materialize until the 1990s under Daley.

Urban Policy in General

The nation did not face up to the possibility of a community-oriented urban policy after the 1960s, but the idea of it remained. Bennett Harrison had made the argument for inner-city development based in part on the potential of new community institutions like CDCs. Although these did not immediately bear fruit, the progressive-city activists, after a series of interesting experiments and a few successes in the 1970s, made much more serious efforts in Boston and Chicago. They made the case in two variants.

In Boston, they caught the wave of privately financed downtown real estate investment and tapped it, creating a "new growth coalition" with a chance to provide equity to the neighborhoods and legitimacy to the developers. Several years earlier, a few developers had seen ways to pay the tithe to equity—James Rouse had built the new town Columbia, Maryland, in the 1960s with provisions for race and class diversity—and the idea was successfully pressed as legislation in places like Boston and Minnesota.[21] But Stephen Coyle, paired with Flynn, implemented these sentiments still further.

Chicago presented a second, complementary approach, focusing on industrial structure. The question was whether cities—these or ones like them—perhaps in coalition but still mainly local, could build momentum enough to turn the tide for the nation. Certainly Washington and Mier had ambitions for national policy changes. Mier made the argument that a city-based policy—because it would be forged out of the conflicts and interactions of real neighborhoods and real factories—would have a validity not as likely in Washington: "National industrial policy should be developed in localities and should involve local actors. We argue that a political constituency for national industrial policy must be built on a constituency for local economic development planning."[22]

But there were weaknesses. The Boston strategy depended on the real estate investment cycle. Coyle had looked at history and, seeing a "five- or six-year" window, looked for a city with the prospect of doing something with it.[23] Was there a way to harvest enough during the cycle to have a lasting effect afterward? The progressive-city activists in Boston learned that there would be, and that the linkage funds were only the surface. They had set a new precedent, showing how city hall and the real estate developers could work in a complementary fashion; and how, once established, that experience could pay off in other respects—the CRA pressure that produced over a billion dollars in mortgage money from the banks, and the more or less permanent shift in priorities that affected the city later.

While Chicago's industrial strategy made little impact on the largest plants and firms, it did protect a number of smaller ones. The several task forces and other initiatives introduced questions of jobs and industrial structure into public debate. They convinced themselves, at least, that much could be done, given time. Swinney concluded that, of hundreds of small factories surveyed in Chicago, "eighty percent could have been saved." Markusen found many ramifications supporting the retention and growth of manufacturing throughout the Midwest. Giloth and Moe wrote that the targeted jobs focus, implanted in city policy and absorbed by voters and institutions outside city hall, became a permanent feature of the city's character.[24] Together, their many initiatives under the jobs umbrella—the campaign, *The Washington Papers,* the *Chicago Works Together* plans, the industry task forces, the early warning projects, the PMDs, the local purchasing from and targeting of women-owned and minority-owned firms—identified new constituencies that had not previously been engaged in city policy and now were engaged to the point where Daley, despite conflicting interests and his support for the real estate development interests, tried to accommodate them as well.

For the nation, these experiences might have raised questions to follow up on, if not then, later:

- What would be the conclusion if industrial policy were to be debated openly in public and scholarly venues rather than kept off the table by the assumptions of economic fashion? An approach to this debate might be to exploit the natural curiosity raised by the experience of government subsidy during 2008 and after in the auto industry and other sectors.
- What are relative merits of the jobs strategies like Chicago's, and the "milk the real estate boom" approach taken by Coyle and Flynn in Boston?

- Was there any reason a city could not employ both strategies together? The core resistance was the same—the market orthodoxy that public agencies must not intervene, or even debate, private sector strategies. If this could be relaxed in the real estate sector, why not in manufacturing?
- Would there be an impact on the universities that could soften the orthodoxy of the economist and perhaps take up the questions raised by researchers like Harrison and Markusen?

One could be optimistic about these questions. Consideration of them might lead to a more nuanced approach to collective problem solving for the nation and better prospects for cities like Boston under Flynn, Chicago under Harold Washington, and for urban policy generally.

The Problem of Evaluation

Any assessment of the Boston and Chicago cases presented in these chapters confronts the questions: What was accomplished? What are the numbers? If Boston faced a housing affordability problem and tried to solve it, how many units did it build? Did city policy make a difference, and if so, what was the concrete result in numbers of new apartments and houses? It was difficult to find answers. The census does give numbers of rental and owned units: in Boston there were 218,457 occupied housing units in 1980 before Flynn's election, and 228,464 in 1990, an increase of 10,007, about 1,000 per year. Affordability deteriorated: median rents increased from $189 to $625 in the decade. Average incomes also increased (inflation was a factor) but not as much as housing prices.[25] How much of this came from city efforts is more of a mystery. Chapter 6 includes the information on numbers of units produced by CDCs year by year, and with contributions from the Neighborhood Housing (Linkage) Trust. But there is overlap. Stephen Coyle noted that the Boston Redevelopment Authority completed seventy-seven projects, mostly in the inner part of the city and the downtown, while public facilities and development did forty or so, mostly in the outer neighborhoods.[26] Neither agency had an obviously available set of comprehensive numbers, and I was not able to research the question deeply. At one point I reported an average of three hundred units of affordable housing built per year in the 1980s, but Peter Dreier, reviewing this, thought I was off by a "factor of ten."[27] My impression was that the accounting was episodic, perhaps for the good reason that the relationship between city effort and housing outcomes is difficult to specify.

In Chicago, under Washington, the policy was more focused on jobs than housing, and the parallel unit of measurement would be numbers of jobs created or saved. Robert Giloth and Kari Moe addressed this in a 1999 article.[28] They were able to estimate the effects of job targeting through programs like "minority set-asides" that resulted in clear shifts in the proportions of jobs allocated to particular groups in the population, but they were less successful in getting numbers for the population overall. But they made two observations. One was that progressive administrations, because they set targets at all, are vulnerable to attack from political opponents who can claim it is foolish to try for targets of public policy—the "conservative" could say that it is not government's role to try for specific targets at all; rather it is government's role to facilitate the private sector, thus avoiding the blame when things do not happen.

Progressives like Giloth and Moe also knew something else, something not featured in the public pronouncements of conservatives: there was a bias in the system, in the sense that, left unaddressed, the "natural" forces allocating jobs would favor the white, middle class, better educated, and wealthy. The purpose of the jobs goal, they wrote, was to implant in the city's mind the goals of equity alongside efficiency, fairness alongside the traditional ways that were not so fair. The standard for evaluation of the Washington administration, they thought, was whether those biases changed. They thought the many initiatives, and particularly the prominence they gave to goals and targets even when it exposed them to criticism, put the city on a path to that sort of change. But change was a matter of much more than the four and a half years of Washington's mayoralty.

New Demographics

The irony was that, in both cities, the demographic profile changed, and with that the political mix of forces. Menino and Daley, in some ways, had it easier. One facet was the shift in race and class. The striking increases in poverty (in Chicago, less in Boston) and in the percent of the population that was nonwhite in both places are indicated in chapter 1, table 1.5. There were also changes in education numbers. Between 1990 and 2000, the proportion of jobs in manufacturing decreased in both cities, though there were gains in other sectors so that total employment was stable: up a percent or two in Chicago, down a little in Boston. But the absolute losses in relatively high-paying manufacturing jobs were notable.[29] The demography was equally dramatic. Table 8.1 gives a picture of the population age twenty-five and over in Chicago and Boston in terms of educational attainment, an indicator

Table 8.1.   Educational Attainment, Boston and Chicago, 1990–2000
(percent of total population)

	CHICAGO		BOSTON	
	1990	**2000**	**1990**	**2000**
0–12, no degree	34.0	28.0	24.0	21.0
High school or some college	47.0	47.0	46.0	44.0
BA or higher degree	20.0	26.0	30.0	35.0

Sources: The data are from U.S. Bureau of the Census, *1990 Census of Population,* table P077, Summary File 3; and *2000 Census of Population,* table P49, Summary File 3. The data on educational attainment by race are from 1990 Census table P058, Summary File 3; and 2000 Census tables P148A through P148I, Summary File 3.

of class status. The increase in the percent of people with a BA degree or higher suggests an influx of middle-class and better-off populations in both cities. There were no major inconsistencies with the absolute numbers: the low-attainment groups decreased in numbers, while the middle category remained somewhat the same. Racial groups within the larger populations showed similar changes, starting from lower beginning points.

Reflections and Later Developments

Demography, economic fortune, national politics, and progressive regimes changed between the first progressive city electoral successes in the 1970s—in Hartford, Berkeley, Cleveland, Madison, and elsewhere—and those in the 1980s. Racial divides may have changed and evolved, but they still remained. My tentative assessment is that two things changed most dramatically. One is that the size and composition of the other-than-white populations increased and differentiated in the nation generally, in part through immigration. Africans, Latinos, and Asians became more numerous. The African American middle class increased. Inequality did not appreciably decrease, but it did become more complex.[30]

The other important thing about race was the change in leadership and representation in the government. Carl Stokes's 1967 election in Cleveland had shocked and thrilled the city, but minority mayors were elected with less drama in Atlanta (1973), Berkeley (1979), Hartford (1981), New York City (1989), Cleveland again (1990), and San Francisco (1996). In Boston and Chicago, the iconic presence of Mel King and the inclusionary policies of Harold Washington produced, in different ways, a changed picture, one that neither Daley nor Menino erased.

The starker contrasts between "economic populism" and "transformative populism" faded in Boston and Chicago through the 1990s and later. In part

it was a response to demographics. Mayors hired black and Hispanic administrators to respond to a multicultural constituency; and white administrators
began to speak a different language as well. And all saw the economic straits
the cities and neighborhoods were in.

Another important factor was the increasing efficacy of university support
in both cities. The Community Outreach Partnership program came from
the Clinton administration, connecting university resources to community
organizations. Other support organizations also survived and in some cases
advanced beyond what existed in 1983. By the end of the Washington/
Sawyer period in Chicago in 1989, and the Flynn administration in 1993,
more elaborate support networks existed and a better sense emerged of how
universities might relate to neighborhood groups.

Organizers, city hall people, and connected intellectuals outside these venues would all agree: national policy disenfranchising the cities could make all
of their efforts in vain—local populations, after strenuous organizing, could
again sink into apathy; and the capacities of cities to solve their own problems could erode further. In 2004 Chuck Turner, after making the case for
a possible transformation in Boston politics—a "Rainbow Coalition" with
multiple bases and a new degree of acceptance in city hall—said:

> While it is important to do what we are doing to have this level of
> organization [in the city], we have to realize that unless we can have
> a national movement to press [Massachusetts Senator John] Kerry or
> whoever might be president, the power of the liberal communities and
> the people of color in Boston won't have any translatable impact on the
> lives of people now engaging the system. And if that continues after
> a few years they are going to say, Maybe I was right in the first place.
> That voting doesn't make any difference.[31]

Aftermath

"Transcending the base" was easier for successor regimes, and one could say
the redistributive climate established by Washington and Flynn was temporary and perhaps unstable. Washington and Flynn had concentrated on
a popular base of "have-nots"; Menino and Daley expanded that base to
include the middle class. The focus on crime and schools was key, along
with more emphasis on mixed-income development in neighborhoods. Both
Menino and Daley adapted to national policies promoted by the Clinton
administration and appealed to concerns about the property-tax base and
revived investor interest in the cities. Neither concern had been absent in

the 1980s, but Menino and Daley found they could mix the populist visions of their predecessors with the upscaling pressures that now were felt. This would seem to be a general truth for the progressive cities, as one could discern a similar leveling out in other places.

What role, then, did Flynn and Washington play relative to Menino and Daley? Certainly the former were more uncomfortable for the middle class. But their single-minded focus on redistributive policies made it easier for their successors. More abstractly, they pushed the fundamental structures of economic bias and political power a bit more toward equality in a decade when the nation was moving toward an insupportable inequality. Their programs tended to persist over time—most of them remained in place under subsequent mayors, whether or not "progressive" policies continued to have the same salience in the general local consciousness, and in the face of a general drift away from redistributive or participatory approaches at the national level.

The Long Road to Change

It took a long time to create an institution, and a long time to change it. It took several years and a set of complementary efforts for the manufacturing-support policies in Chicago to establish themselves after Ducharme's initial organizing. Mel King's campaign for black political empowerment in Boston was generational in extent. Dreier, having begun a series of initiatives with the city's populist Left at the end of the 1970s, carried on within Flynn's administration for a decade. The dozens of people talked about in the accounts in this book are remarkable especially for the consistent, dogged effort they put in from top to bottom.

The story goes on. Although many of the most important characters have died—including Gaston in 1986, Washington in 1987, Medoff in 1994, Mier in 1995, Vazquez in 1997, and Dooley in 2006—the survival of some of their ideas is the bright side of an improbable history.

A Real Alternative

Hackworth's exegesis of neoliberalism ended with a series of "actions" that might moderate or replace that evidently destructive approach to managing community and world affairs. Taking a suggestion from Peter Marcuse and Ronald van Kempen, he noted the argument that the biggest obstacle to change is the general belief that "there is no alternative." [32]

The progressive city is an alternative and has much to recommend it: it is local and reasonably accessible to its population so that they can know it. And cities get publicity, so that there is potential to diffuse ideas and devices created in one city to others.

Moreover, their ideas can spread generally upward, from city halls to the level of state or national governments and politics of acting. Mayors, for example, often become governors, members of Congress, senators, and sometimes run for president. This was the hope that Derek Shearer and Lee Webb had for the Conference on Alternative State and Local Policies in 1975, an idea whose time might yet come again.

✊ NOTES

Preface

1. Eve Bach, Nicholas R. Carbone, and Pierre Clavel, "Running the City for the People," *Social Policy* 12 (Winter 1982): 15–23; Pierre Clavel, *The Progressive City: Planning and Participation, 1969–1984* (New Brunswick, NJ: Rutgers University Press, 1986).

2. Pierre Clavel and Wim Wiewel, eds., *Harold Washington and the Neighborhoods* (New Brunswick, NJ: Rutgers University Press, 1991).

3. Joel Rast, *Remaking Chicago: The Political Origins of Urban Industrial Change* (DeKalb, IL: Northern Illinois University Press, 1999). On Boston, see Peter Dreier and Dennis Keating, "The Limits of Localism: Progressive Housing Policies in Boston 1984–1989," *Urban Affairs Quarterly* 26 (December 1990): 191–216; and Peter Dreier and Bruce Ehrlich, "Downtown Development and Urban Reform: The Politics of Boston's Linkage Policy," *Urban Affairs Quarterly* 26 (January 1991): 354–75.

4. Norman Krumholz and Pierre Clavel, *Reinventing Cities: Equity Planners Tell Their Stories* (Philadelphia: Temple University Press, 1994).

1. Introduction

1. In this book I look only at the United States. Outside the United States there were other examples, some of them inspirational to U.S. activists: Bologna, Italy, was an important early example, its features reported in Max Jaggi, Roger Muller, and Sil Schmid, *Red Bologna* (London: Writers and Readers, 1977). There were several in Britain, and in the 1990s in Latin America. See Martin Boddy and Colin Fudge, eds., *Local Socialism? Labour Councils and New Left Alternatives* (London: Macmillan, 1984), and Daniel Chavez and Benjamin Goldfrank, eds. *The Left in the City: Participatory Local Governments in Latin America* (London: Latin American Bureau, 2004).

2. Jonathan Thompson, "Contextualizing Radical Planning: The 1970s Chicano Takeover in Crystal City, Texas," *Progressive Planning* 174 (Winter 2008): 2–6.

3. Doug Gills, "Chicago Politics and Community Development: A Social Movement Perspective," in *Harold Washington and the Neighborhoods*, ed. Pierre Clavel and Wim Wiewel (New Brunswick, NJ: Rutgers University Press, 1991), 59–60.

4. City Planning Commission, *Cleveland Policy Planning Report* (Cleveland, OH: City Planning Commission, 1975).

5. Eve Bach, Thomas Brom, Julia Estrella, Lenny Goldberg, and Edward Kirshner, *The Cities' Wealth: Programs for Community Economic Control in Berkeley, California* (Washington, DC: Conference on Alternative State and Local Policies, 1976).

6. City of Chicago, *Chicago Development Plan: Chicago Works Together* (Chicago: Department of Economic Development, 1984).

7. Pierre Clavel, *The Progressive City: Planning and Participation, 1969–1984* (New Brunswick, NJ: Rutgers University Press, 1986).

8. Jordan Yin, "The Community Development Industry System: A Case Study of Politics and Institutions in Cleveland," *Journal of Urban Affairs* 20 (Summer 1998): 137–57.

9. I am using the idea of the "social base" in the sense meant by Philip Selznick, meaning the external clienteles and support groups that can be mobilized to affect the internal dynamics of an organization or public agency. See Philip Selznick, *Leadership in Administration* (Berkeley: University of California Press, 1957).

10. William W. Goldsmith and Edward J. Blakely, *Separate Societies: Poverty and Inequality in U.S. Cities* (Philadelphia: Temple University Press, 1992), 25 and 27.

11. The year-by-year totals of federal intergovernmental grants to state and local government rose constantly through the 1970s, from $24.1 billion to $91.4 billion in 1980. But as a percent of GDP, the figure began at 2.38 percent, peaked at 3.49 percent in 1978, then fell off slightly to 3.38 percent in 1980. U.S. Bureau of the Budget, *Historical Tables, Budget of the United States Government, Fiscal Year 2009* (Washington, DC: GPO, 2008), table 12.1, http://www.whitehouse.gov/omb/budget/fy2009/pdf/hist.pdf.

12. National Commission on Neighborhoods, Joseph F. Timilty, Chair. *People Building Neighborhoods: Final Report to the President and the Congress of the United States* (Washington, DC: The Commission, 1979); President's Commission for a National Agenda for the Eighties, *A National Agenda for the Eighties* (Washington, DC: GPO, 1981) (the "McGill Report"); and see William W. Goldsmith and Harvey M. Jacobs, "The Improbability of Urban Policy: The Case of the United States," *Journal of the American Planning Association* 48 (1982): 53–66.

13. Eve Bach, Nicholas R. Carbone, and Pierre Clavel, "Running the City for the People," *Social Policy* 12, no. 3 (Winter 1982), 20.

14. U.S. Bureau of the Census, *1972 Census of Governments,* vol. 4, Government Finances (Washington, DC: U.S. Government Printing Office, 1973); also *1982 Census of Governments,* and *1992 Census of Governments;* Council of Economic Advisors, *Economic Report of the President, 2006,* table B-12.

15. Samuel H. Beer, introduction to *New Federalism: Intergovernmental Reform from Nixon to Reagan,* by Timothy Conlon (Washington, DC: Brookings Institution, 1988).

16. John Kincaid, "The State of American Federalism, 1986," *Publius* 17 (Summer 1987): 24–25, 32, cited in Beer, xxi.

2. What the Progressive City Was

1. Melvin G. Holli, *Reform in Detroit: Hazen S. Pingree and Urban Politics* (New York: Oxford University Press, 1969); Tom L. Johnson, *My Story,* ed. Elizabeth J. Hauser (New York: B.W. Huebsch, 1911). For a longer perspective, see Gerald Frug, "The City as a Legal Concept," *Harvard Law Review* 93 (1980), 1057–1148.

2. For much of the discussion in this chapter—on Berkeley, Hartford, Cleveland, Santa Monica, and Burlington—I rely on my own earlier work, *The Progressive*

City: Planning and Participation, 1969–1984 (New Brunswick, NJ: Rutgers University Press, 1986). For earlier background on "liberal" programs in Berkeley, see Harriet Nathan and Stanley Scott, eds., *Experiment and Change in Berkeley: Essays on City Politics, 1950–1975* (Berkeley: Institute of Governmental Studies, 1978); and Eve Bach, Nicholas R. Carbone, and Pierre Clavel, "Running the City for the People," *Social Policy* 12, no. 3 (Winter 1982): 15–23. On the emergence and history of BCA, see David Mundstock, "Berkeley in the 1970s," available on the website http://berkeleyinthe70s.homestead.com/index.html. On Berkeley and other cities described in this chapter, see the website http://www.progressivecities.org.

3. Eve Bach et al., *The Cities' Wealth: Programs for Community Economic Control in Berkeley, California* (Washington, DC: Conference on Alternative State and Local Policies, 1976).

4. For events after about 1985, see Pierre Clavel, "The Decline of Progressive Government in Berkeley, California," *Plurimondi* 1 (1999): 139–48; and Mundstock, "Berkeley in the 1970s" (under "The 80s and 90s in Brief"). I have also benefited from personal communication with Fred Collignon.

5. Eve Bach, personal communication, May 5, 1998.

6. These initiatives are described in Clavel, *The Progressive City.*

7. Clavel, *The Progressive City,* chapter 2; Nicholas R. Carbone, "The City as a Real Estate Investor" (transcript of a lecture given at Cornell University, Ithaca, NY, November 1981). On linkage in general, see Dennis Keating, "Linking Downtown Development to Broader Community Goals: An Analysis of Linkage Policy in Three Cities," *Journal of the American Planning Association* 52 (Spring 1986): 133–41; and Boston Redevelopment Authority, *Survey of Linkage Programs in Other U.S. Cities with Comparisons to Boston* (Boston: Boston Redevelopment Authority, 2000).

8. "Hartford Up-Beat" (newsletter no. 9, of the Conference on Alternative State and Local Public Policies, November 1977), 7, 11.

9. Clavel, *The Progressive City,* 38–39.

10. For an account of these developments in the 1980s and early 1990s, see Louise B. Simmons, *Organizing in Hard Times: Labor and Neighborhoods in Hartford* (Philadelphia: Temple University Press, 1994).

11. These are recounted in Clavel, *The Progressive City,* and more completely in Norman Krumholz and John Forester, *Making Equity Planning Work: Leadership in the Public Sector* (Philadelphia: Temple University Press, 1990).

12. See Krumholz and Forester, *Making Equity Planning Work,* and the website maintained by the Department of Urban Planning, Portland State University, where Bonner was a faculty member while Portland city planning director after leaving Cleveland in the 1970s: http://www.pdx.edu/usp/cleveland_policy_plan.html.

13. Krumholz and Forester, *Making Equity Planning Work.*

14. Norman Krumholz and L. Thomas, "Lessons for Leaders: The Rise of the Cleveland Housing Network" (unpublished manuscript, Cleveland, 2005, in possession of the author).

15. Soglin's radicalism may have been pragmatic locally, but he did claim a certain international cachet, to judge from an online biography that describes him as "the first mayor and the fourth elected public official from the United States to meet Fidel Castro." http://psoglin.typepad.com/about.html.

16. This Madison commentary is based on notes provided by Jonathan Thompson, whose own account is in "Progressive Innovation in the 1970s United States: Madison, WI, and the Conference on Alternative State and Local Public Policies," *Progressive Planning* (Winter 2007): 22–25. Sources on Soglin include various retrospective comments found in news articles. See, for example, "The Third Paul Soglin," editorial, *Capital Times,* August 28, 2002. Thompson has also uncovered additional work on Madison, including Myron A. Levine, "Goal-Oriented Leadership and the Limits of Entrepreneurship," *Western Political Quarterly* 33 (1980): 401–16.

17. On the Madison conference and the establishment of the organization, see Barbara Bick, *Conference Report: Where Do We Go from Here?,* Conference on Alternative State and Local Public Policies (June 13–15, 1975), prepared by Institute for Policy Studies, July 1975, and James Rowen, "The Office-Holding Activists," *The Nation* 221 (July 5, 1975): 19–20. Information for this account also comes from Jonathan Thompson, "Progressive Innovation"; Lee Webb, interview by the author, June 30, 2005; and Barbara Bick and Ann Beaudry, interviews by Pierre Clavel and Jonathan Thompson, Washington, DC, February 2007.

18. The example from the first national conference in Madison is Derek Shearer and Lee Webb, eds., Reader on Alternative Public Policies, Washington, DC: Institute for Policy Studies, 1975.

19. David Smith, "Updating Economic Populism" (newsletter of the Conference on Alternative State and Local Policies, October 1976), 3, 5.

20. Much of the early conference material is collected at Cornell University Library's Division of Rare and Manuscript Collections. The materials are listed on the library's website at http://rmc.library.cornell.edu/EAD/htmldocs/RMA03414.html. The conference materials are further referenced in the supplementary web pages for the Progressive Cities and Neighborhood Planning project, http://www.aap.cornell.edu/crp/research/pcnp/index.cfm.

21. Parallel progressive-city experience occurred in such European cities as London, Sheffield, and other UK places in the 1980s; and Bologna earlier and for a longer time. Latin America had parallel cases in the 1990s, the best known being the participatory budget in Porto Alegre, Brazil.

22. In addition to Clavel, *The Progressive City,* I have relied on Stella M. Capek and John I. Gilderbloom, *Community versus Commodity: Tenants and the American City* (Albany: SUNY Press, 1992); John I. Gilderbloom and Stella M. Capek, "Santa Monica a Decade Later: Urban Progressives in Office," *National Civic Review* (Spring–Summer): 115–31; "Santa Monica Interviews, 1981–1989: The People in the City," compiled by Pierre Clavel and Sharon Lord (deposited in Division of Rare and Manuscript Collections, Cornell University Library, Ithaca, NY); Julie Dad, interview by Anisa Mendizabal, January 2009; and Ken Genser, interview by Anisa Mendizabal, 2009.

23. Howard Fine and Elizabeth Hayes, "People's Republic Is Back," *Los Angeles Business Journal,* August 16–August 22, 1999.

24. In this account I have relied on Clavel, *The Progressive City,* 161–83; Maile Deppe, "Reinventing Local Government: Creating a Culture of Concern, Participation, and Decision-Making; A Case Study of Burlington, VT" (MRP thesis, Cornell University, 2000); Crystal Lackey, "Expansion of the Public Realm in Burlington, VT, 1981–2007" (MRP thesis, Cornell University, 2007); John Davis, "Building the

Progressive City: Third Sector Housing in Burlington," in *The Affordable City: Toward a Third Sector Housing Policy,* ed. John Davis (Philadelphia: Temple University Press, 1994), 165–200; Peter Clavelle, "Creating Sustainable Communities" (unpublished manuscript, ca. 2005); and Steven Soifer, *The Socialist Mayor: Bernard Sanders in Burlington, VT* (New York: Bergin & Garvey, 1991).

25. City of Burlington, VT, Community and Economic Development Office (CEDO), *Jobs and People: A Strategic Analysis of the Greater Burlington Economy* (Burlington: CEDO, 1986).

26. Davis, "Building the Progressive City," 185. Davis, personal communication, May 1, 2009.

27. Davis, "Building the Progressive City," 175.

28. Richard Gendron and G. William Domhoff, *The Leftmost City: Power and Progressive Politics in Santa Cruz* (Boulder, CO: Westview Press, 2009).

29. The two main book-length sources on San Francisco "progressives" differ somewhat. Richard DeLeon saw a progressive voice that had yet to meet the challenge of governing. Stephen McGovern saw an emerging counterhegemony, perhaps a more serious alternative to the growth coalition, and more promising for progressives. See Richard DeLeon, *Left Coast City: Progressive Politics In San Francisco, 1975–1991* (Lawrence: University Press of Kansas, 1992), and Stephen McGovern, *The Politics Of Downtown Development: Dynamic Political Cultures in San Francisco and Washington, D.C.* (Lexington: University Press of Kentucky, 1998). These notes depend mainly on these two sources. I also had the benefit of a communication from DeLeon to Anisa Mendizabal (June 14, 2008); and some of his later work: Richard E. DeLeon and Katherine C. Naff, "Identity Politics and Local Political Culture: Some Comparative Results from the Social Capital Benchmark Survey," *Urban Affairs Review* 39, no. 6 (July 2004): 689–719; and Richard E. Deleon, "San Francisco: The Politics of Race, Land Use and Ideology," in *Racial Politics in American Cities,* 3rd ed., ed. Rufus P. Browning, Dale Rogers Marshall, and David H. Tabb, 167–98 (White Plains, NY: Longman, 2003).

30. DeLeon, *Left Coast City,* 77.

31. McGovern, *Politics Of Downtown Development,* 165.

32. Ibid., 167–68.

33. Ibid., 179–80.

34. DeLeon, *Left Coast City,* 172.

35. McGovern, *Politics of Downtown Development,* 184.

36. Communication to the author, December 21, 2009. Domhoff refers to G. William Domhoff, "Why San Francisco Is Different: Progressive Activists and Neighborhoods Have Had a Big Impact," September 2005, http://sociology.ucsc.edu/whorulesamerica/local/san_francisco.html.

3. The Movement Becomes Politics in Boston

1. For a comparison of King and Flynn, see Marie Kennedy and Chris Tilly, with Mauricio Gaston, "Transformative Populism and the Development of Community of Color," in *Dilemmas of Activism,* ed. Joseph Kling and Prudence Posner (Philadelphia: Temple University Press, 1990), 302–24.

2. Mel King, *Chain of Change: Struggles for Black Community Development* (Boston: South End Press, 1981).

3. *Chain of Change* was in part an account of King's struggles to overcome this. See his comment on page 142: "There was great debate about the importance of supporting Black owned businesses like Freedom Industries, for instance, but the arguments pro and con often centered, I suspect, around some very deep-seated feelings about whether Blacks could successfully operate a business."

4. King, *Chain of Change,* 128–49.

5. Ibid.

6. Ibid.

7. Ibid., 243.

8. Mel King, interview by the author, September 29, 1999; see also King, *Chain of Change,* 202.

9. James Green, "The Making of Mel King's Rainbow Coalition: Political Changes in Boston 1963–1983," in *From Access to Power: Black Politics in Boston, ed.* James Jennings and Mel King (Boston: Schenkman, 1986), 103.

10. King, *Chain of Change,* 221–22.

11. King, interview.

12. King, *Chain of Change,* 251–61; Mel King, "Mandela Proposal" (unpublished manuscript, August 24, 1987).

13. King, "Mandela Proposal," 2.

14. King, *Chain of Change,* 52.

15. David Smith, *The Public Balance Sheet* (Washington, DC: Conference on Alternative State and Local Policies, ca. 1977).

16. King particularly mentions David Smith, Elbert Bishop, and Brad Yoneoka as initial members of the Wednesday Morning Breakfast Group. King, *Chain of Change,* 202. Emily Achtenberg, later an expert on housing issues, remembered Gar Alperovitz, Ken Geiser, and Carl Sussman. On the evolution of community development thinking in Boston, I have relied on Rachel Bratt, *Rebuilding a Low-Income Housing Policy* (Philadelphia: Temple University Press, 1989), particularly pp. 259–72; and Nancy Nye, "Six Years Later: The Experience of the Massachusetts CDFC," *Entrepreneurial Economy* 2, no. 9 (March 1984): 11–12.

17. Bratt, *Low-Income Housing Policy,* 268.

18. Thomas Vietorisz and Bennett Harrison, *The Economic Development of Harlem* (New York: Praeger, 1970). In Cambridge, Harrison contributed widely to local groups—as in his opening address to the Center for Community Economic Development (CCED) Conference on Market Failures (CCED newsletter, April–May 1978, 1–5).

19. The most prominent statement of this sort came from John F. Kain and Joseph J. Persky, "Alternatives to the Gilded Ghetto," *Public Interest* 14 (Winter 1969): 74–87.

20. Bennett Harrison, *Urban Economic Development* (Washington, DC: Urban Institute, 1974), 167–84.

21. Ibid, 179. See chapter 8 in Harrison's book, "Approaches to Rebuilding the Ghetto Economy," which casts the community development corporation as an alternative to "black capitalism" oriented toward individual firms. (Harrison reports a 38 percent success rate on direct business loans.) Harrison's advocacy of CDCs was based on observation of their efforts at collective planning and the mutual reinforcement that suggested. The analysis—and the case examples he provides—give

a snapshot of the optimism that existed in the community development circles at the time, where there were reports of at least initially successful small manufacturing start-ups and networks of independent retailers. All of this was aided by the CDC, developing "community owned or sponsored manufacturing, commercial and service enterprises selected as much for the nature and extent of the on-the-job training they are capable of providing as for the product and profits they would generate.... [But] the CDC will necessarily trade off profits for the sake of community service benefits." Ibid., 175.

22. Rachel Bratt and Kenneth Geiser, "Community-Based Economic Development: The Massachusetts Experience" (unpublished manuscript, Tufts University, 1982).

23. Ann Greiner, *The Housing Affordability Gap and Boston's Economic Growth: Potential for Crisis* (Cambridge, MA: MIT Department of Urban Studies and Planning, October 1987).

24. Chester Hartman, in an autobiographical essay, is imprecise, placing the date at "the mid-sixties." Chester Hartman, *Between Eminence and Notoriety: Four Decades of Radical Urban Planning* (New Brunswick, NJ: Center for Urban Policy Research, 2002), 18–20. A more detailed account is Lily Hoffman, *The Politics of Knowledge: Activist Movements in Medicine and Planning* (Albany: SUNY Press, 1989).

25. The highway controversy is described in Alan Lupo, Frank Colcord, and Edmund P. Fowler, *Rites of Way: The Politics of Transportation in Boston and the U.S. City* (Boston: Little, Brown, 1971). In 2007 Douglass B. Lee, a transportation scholar at a U.S. Department of Transportation unit in Cambridge, told a group of visiting Cornell students that the inner-belt project, had it not been stopped, would have had decisively negative effects on the city. He attributed the cancellation of the project to four persons: among them activist Fred Salvucci; MIT professor and—at the critical moment—state secretary of transportation Alan Altshuler; and the governor at the time, Francis Sargent. Lee addressed the Cornell students on October 6, 2007.

26. Hoffman, *The Politics of Knowledge*.

27. Lee Staples, interview by the author, March 26, 1992. Unless noted otherwise, the following account on Massachusetts Fair Share is drawn from this interview, supplemented by a personal communication, December 28, 2009.

28. Staples, interview. Ansara, who later became executive director of Fair Share, was a longtime leader in Boston, beginning with the Students for a Democratic Society at Harvard.

29. Staples, interview.

30. Michael Ansara, interview by the author, May 12, 1992.

31. Jonathan Kaufman, "Fair Share Faces a Financial Crisis," *Boston Globe,* September 24, 1983. Fair Share continued on after 1983. Mark Dyen took over as director, later Tom Snyder. They finally liquidated in 1988.

32. Frank Ackerman, "The Melting Snowball: Limits of the 'New Populism' in Practice," *Socialist Revolution* 7, no. 5 (September–October 1977): 113–28; Kathy McAfee, "Socialism and the Housing Movement: Lessons from Boston," in *Critical Perspectives on Housing,* ed. Rachel G. Bratt, Chester Hartman, and Ann Meyerson, 405–27 (Philadelphia: Temple University Press, 1986).

33. Steven Fahrer, interview by the author, April 17, 1992.

34. Kathy McAfee, interview by the author, February 26, 1992.

35. Kathy McAfee, "Socialism and the Housing Movement: Lessons from Boston," draft appendix to a prospective revised version of Bratt, Hartman, and Meyerson, *Critical Perspectives on Housing.*

36. Fahrer, interview.

37. The authority on DSNI in general is Peter Medoff and Holly Sklar, *Streets of Hope: The Fall and Rise of an Urban Neighborhood* (Boston: South End Press, 1994). This classic account is my main source.

38. Chapter 4 provides a detailed account of this event.

39. Medoff and Sklar, *Streets of Hope,* 69.

40. Eugene "Gus" Newport, "The Dudley Street Neighborhood Initiative, Roxbury, Massachusetts: History and Observations" (unpublished manuscript, n.d.), 2.

41. Ibid., 5.

42. Derrick Z. Jackson, "Dudley Street's Vision for a Village," *Boston Globe,* July 16, 1997.

43. Xavier de Souza Briggs and Elizabeth Mueller with Mercer Sullivan, *From Neighborhood to Community: Evidence on the Social Effects of Community Development* (New York: New School for Social Research, 1997), chapter 2, "Urban Edge Housing Corporation"; Charles A. Radin, "A Neighborhood Reborn," *Boston Globe Magazine,* 12–35.

44. Radin, "A Neighborhood Reborn."

45. King, *Chain of Change,* 163.

46. "After the votes rolled in, Hicks saw now that 'every time the Negroes demonstrated, they campaigned for me.'" Ronald P. Formisano, *Boston against Busing: Race, Class and Ethnicity in the 1960s and 1970s* (Chapel Hill: University of North Carolina Press, 1991; epilogue 2004), 31.

47. Formisano, 27, 33.

48. J. Anthony Lukas, *Common Ground: A Turbulent Decade in the Lives of Three American Families* (New York: Knopf, 1985), 10.

49. Doug McAdam, *Freedom Summer* (New York: Oxford Univ. Press, 1988).

50. Lukas, *Common Ground,* 650.

51. Green's review of *Common Ground* was particularly penetrating, if ahead of the curve: James Green, "In Search of Common Ground: A Review Essay," *Radical America* 20, no. 5 (September–October 1986): 41–60.

52. Shortly before the October preliminary election, the *Globe* reported that among the candidates for mayor, there was "no businessmen's favorite." A typical quote was: "'I don't know anybody who's sitting up worrying about this election because the candidates are all decent people.'" Some were negative: "'I have observed a fear of either Flynn or King becoming mayor because of a basic lack of confidence in their ability to handle city problems.'" King's views were "not consonant with the city as a whole," and Flynn did not "have the capacity to administer the city successfully without relying on others to guide him." Charles Kenney, "No Businessmen's Favorite: Community Is Split on a Mayoral Candidate," *Boston Globe,* September 30, 1983.

53. Robert L. Turner, "Suddenly, Mel King Looks Like a Winner," *Boston Globe,* October 2, 1983. Turner suggested that King's prospects in the preliminary election benefited from his rivals' perception that he (King) would be easiest to defeat in the runoff. "Said Flynn campaign manager Ray Dooley, 'He (King) can say anything

that comes to mind, and nobody's likely to call him on it.' Also, Flynn and Finnegan probably won't attack King...because they would rather oppose King in the final than each other."

54. David Nylan, "New Players in the Old Game," *Boston Globe,* October 16, 1983. See also James Green, "The Making of Mel King's Rainbow Coalition: Political Changes in Boston 1963–1983," in Jennings and King *From Access to Power,* 99–135.

55. Robert Jordan, "Win for City, Too—King," *Boston Globe,* November 16, 1983. At a gay bar, King once said, "We all have a little bit of gay in us," and he followed a similar path of forthright engagement with feminists and other "rainbow" elements, and even with white ethnics, including a well-publicized foray into a South Boston bar.

56. Janice Fine, "Rainbow Coalition: An Interview with Mel King," in *Building Bridges: The Emerging Grassroots Coalition of Labor and Community,* ed. Jeremy Brecher and Tim Costello, 144–50 (New York: Monthly Review Press, 1990).

57. Ibid., 144.

58. Mike Kane, a neighborhood activist who supported King in the election, nevertheless had respect for Flynn: "He had built up a following—part of it was his own base in South Boston. He pretty much had attracted all the good people in South Boston.... And he had all of those votes with him—kind of a Catholic left undercurrent.... It was not accident that he had a photograph of Mother Theresa on the wall of his city council office. His moral vision was really not that different from Berrigan's. He was really strong on most of the right issues." Interview by Ken Reardon, 1986.

59. David Nylan, "New Players in the Old Game," *Boston Globe,* October 16, 1983.

60. Mary Baker, interview by the author, April 25, 1992.

61. Editorial, *Boston Globe,* November 8, 1983.

62. Fox Butterfield, "Boston Rivals Voice Satisfaction at Election Result," *New York Times,* November 17, 1983.

63. James Green, "The Making of Mel King's Rainbow Coalition," in Jennings and King, *From Access to Power,* 124.

64. James Green, "King, Flynn and Populism," *Boston Globe,* October 28, 1983.

65. Kane, interview.

66. Butterfield, "Boston Rivals Voice Satisfaction."

4. Flynn's City Hall and the Neighborhoods

1. Statement by Neil Sullivan, included in a set of excerpts assembled by Peter Dreier as a memorial after the death of Ray Dooley. Peter Dreier, e-mail posting, April 21, 2006. In another communication, Dreier emphasized "how much the real estate industry controlled the city council.... There were never more than 3 or 4 liberal votes (of 9 and later 13) on the City Council." Personal communication, February 11, 2000.

2. Ed Quill, "Former Foe King Turns Down Flynn Offer of Administration Job," *Boston Globe,* December 31, 1983.

3. On linkage in general, see chap. 2, note 6.

4. Charles Kenney, "2 Referendum Questions Will Be on Tuesday's Ballot," *Boston Globe,* November 12, 1983.

5. Neil Sullivan, interview by the author, June 5, 2009.

6. Dreier has written extensively on Flynn, and much of this chapter relies on his work, along with a series of interviews done in 1990, 1991, and 1992. His most extensive account, written after 1986, is a fifty-page, single-spaced draft that was the basis for several published articles and chapters, was entitled "Economic Growth and Economic Justice: Boston's Populist Housing Policies" (unpublished manuscript). Parts of this appear in more accessible form, including "Urban Politics and Progressive Housing Policy: Ray Flynn and Boston's Neighborhood Agenda," in *Revitalizing Urban Neighborhoods,* ed. W. Dennis Keating, Norman Krumholz, and Philip Star, 63–82 (Lawrence: University Press of Kansas, 1996). See also Peter Dreier and Dennis Keating, "The Limits of Localism: Progressive Housing Policies in Boston 1984–1989," *Urban Affairs Quarterly* 26 (December 1990): 191–216; and Peter Dreier and Bruce Ehrlich, "Downtown Development and Urban Reform: The Politics of Boston's Linkage Policy," *Urban Affairs Quarterly* 26 (January 1991): 354–75. The interviews are accessible in part in "Interview with Peter Dreier," in *Reinventing Cities: Equity Planners Tell Their Stories,* ed. Norman Krumholz and Pierre Clavel, 133–50 (Philadelphia: Temple University Press, 1994).

7. Michael Rezendes, "Top Flynn Aide's Exit Would Shift Balance of Power," *Boston Globe,* June 27, 1990, written on the occasion of Dooley's departure from city hall. Sullivan's sentiments are from the interview cited above.

8. Ed Quill, "New Chief of BRA Promises Master Plan," *Boston Globe,* June 8, 1984; Michael K. Frisby, "Chapnick, McCormack: Women on the Move in Flynn's City Hall," *Boston Globe,* October 18, 1985.

9. Sullivan, interview.

10. Dreier, e-mail posting.

11. Sullivan, interview.

12. Sullivan, interview. Dreier went on to an academic position at Occidental College in 1993, where he continued as a leading figure in the urban studies field—notably for his role as coauthor of *Place Matters,* an influential text published in 2001. Peter Dreier, John Mollenkopf, and Todd Swanstrom, *Place Matters: Metropolitics for the Twenty-First Century* (Lawrence: University Press of Kansas, 2001).

13. Dreier, "Urban Politics and Progressive Housing"; Dreier, interview by the author, August 19, 1991.

14. Dreier laid out a comprehensive housing program for the *Globe,* including not only rent control provisions but also linkage tied to deposits in a neighborhood housing trust and the creation of a "residential property policy board to centralize disposition of abandoned property," which Dreier describes as a "one-stop clearinghouse." *Boston Globe,* "Flynn's Package on Housing Contains Seven Key Provisions," June 19, 1984.

15. Anthony J. Yudis, "$1.3b in Projects Get Flynn Boost," *Boston Globe,* November 1, 1984.

16. Boston Redevelopment Authority, *Downtown Projects: Opportunities for Boston* (Boston: Boston Redevelopment Authority, 1984).

17. Dreier, "Economic Growth," 13.

18. Kirk Scharfenberg, "Resident Jobs Plan Passes a Milestone," *Boston Globe,* July 21, 1985.

19. The "fifteen to twenty" number was given in an interview with the author, 1990. The "5,000 units" is in Dreier, "Urban Politics and Progressive Housing," 75–76.

20. Historical data from the Massachusetts Association of Community Development Corporations (MACDC) indicate five CDCs were producing housing in 1984. *2006 MACDC Goals Report,* Historical Real Estate: Housing, table 28, "Completed Housing Projects" (Boston: MACDC, 2006) indicates an average of perhaps 160 units per year from 1972 through 1985. From 1986, when linkage began to fill the Neighborhood Housing Trust, through 1990 (the end of the boom), the production ranged from 246 to 807.

21. Dreier, "Urban Politics and Progressive Housing," 73

22. Otile McManus, "New BRA Director: City Needs a Plan," *Boston Globe,* November 11, 1984.

23. Kirk Scharfenberg, "Taking Stock of Flynn's First Year," *Boston Globe,* December 29, 1984.

24. Dreier, "Economic Growth," 19.

25. Dreier, interview, 1991.

26. Sullivan, interview.

27. The most striking example may have been the neighborhood councils in Italy. See, for example, Max Jaggi, Roger Muller, and Sil Schmid, *Red Bologna* (London: Writers and Readers, 1977). Neighborhood councils were also begun, usually in attenuated form, in a number of U.S. cities—Burlington, Vermont, was one case. See Pierre Clavel, *The Progressive City: Planning and Participation, 1969–1984* (New Brunswick, NJ: Rutgers University Press, 1986).

28. Flynn's advisers went so far as to engage a consultant, John Alschuler, for a memorandum advising on the question. Michael Ansara, interview by the author, May 12, 1992.

29. Michael K. Frisby, "Flynn Reduces Scope of His Neighborhood Council Program," *Boston Globe,* October 24, 1984.

30. On the initial moves see, for example, Ed Quill, "Flynn Plans Neighborhood City-Service Councils," *Boston Globe,* June 6, 1985.

31. Alex Bledsoe, interview by the author, May 19, 1992.

32. The account of the Dudley plan and aftermath, and of Coyle's modus operandi, is drawn from a set of interviews I did with activists and city hall staff; press accounts in the *Boston Globe;* a set of interview transcripts provided to me by Ken Reardon, who did a preliminary reconnaissance in Boston in 1986; and Mauricio Gaston and Marie Kennedy, "Capital Investment or Community Development? The Struggle for Land Control by Boston's Black and Latino Community," *Antipode,* 19, no. 2 (1987): 178–209. The account of the "leaked plan" comes from Kennedy, communication to the author, February 22, 2010.

33. Gaston and Kennedy, "Capital Investment," 201.

34. The quotations come from a *Boston Globe* article that appeared at the end of Coyle's tenure, as he was leaving the city to take a position with the AFL–CIO Housing Investment Trust in 1992: Michael Rezendes and Don Aucoin, "BRA Chief Coyle to End 7-Year Role: Accepts AFL–CIO Post," *Boston Globe,* December 20, 1991.

35. Peter Dreier, personal communication, April 21, 2006. He wrote: "The first year alone, more than 3,000 were added, and it grew almost each year." Dreier did not specify "affordable" units, and common practice in Boston was to mix affordability levels within projects.

36. Stephen Coyle, interview by Stephen McGovern, May 12, 1992.

37. Peter Dreier, personal communication, September 11, 2000.

38. This account of the Boston Linkage Action Coalition is pieced together from two interviews I did with Janice Fine in April and May 1992, supplemented by press accounts and a transcript provided to me by Kenneth Reardon, who did a set of six interviews in the summer of 1986. See also *Boston Globe*, "Flynn's Package on Housing Contains Seven Key Provisions," June 19, 1984; Daniel Golden and Marvin Pave, "Fair Share Regroups after Crisis," *Boston Globe*, June 22, 1984.

39. Ansara, interview.

40. Alan DiGaetano and John S. Klemanski, *Power and City Governance: Comparative Perspectives on Urban Development* (Minneapolis: University of Minnesota Press, 1999), 199–200.

41. Dreier, interview, 1992. Dreier's figures are roughly corroborated by Mark Draisen, executive director of the Massachusetts Association of Community Development Corporations (MACDC). Mark Draisen, interview by the author, October 5, 1999.

42. *2006 MACDC Goals Report,* table 28.

43. Suzanne Lee, interview by the author, May 22, 1992. See also Michael Liu, *Chinatown's Neighborhood Mobilization and Urban Development in Boston* (PhD diss., University of Massachusetts–Boston, 1999), 104–5.

44. Steven Fahrer, interview by the author, May 17, 1992.

45. Ibid.

46. On conditions in Roxbury, see Gaston and Kennedy, "Capital Investment."

47. Fahrer, interview.

48. Quoted in Peter Medoff and Holly Sklar, *Streets of Hope: The Fall and Rise of an Urban Neighborhood* (Boston: South End Press, 1994), 92. Pages 92–96 are a concise general source on GRNA, and include references to an undated interview with GRNA cofounder Ken Wade.

49. Fahrer, interview.

50. Medoff and Sklar, *Streets of Hope,* 93 (see note 48, above).

51. Ibid., 94 (see note 48, above).

52. Ibid., 95 (see note 48, above).

53. Ibid., 94 (see note 48, above).

54. Marie Kennedy and Chris Tilly, "A City Called Mandela: Secession and the Struggle for Community Control in Boston," *North Star* 5 (1987): 12–18.

55. Ibid., 13.

56. Ibid., 18.

57. Alan Lupo, "Neighborhood Councils?" *Boston Globe,* January 17, 1987.

58. Ibid.

59. Personal communication, November 30, 2009. In a separate communication, January 8, 2010, she listed the foundations: Boston Foundation, Burgess Urban Fund, Episcopal City Mission, Haymarket Foundation, Hyams Foundation, New England Biolabs, Partnership for Democracy, Reebok, RESIST, Roxbury Technical Assistance Fund, Topsfield Foundation.

60. Branfman wrote: "We had a lot of groups who supported us but for one reason or another or fear of being left out to Flynn's largess, they never formally endorsed. Our 1990 fundraising letter was signed by Larry Englisher from Brighton, Suzanne Lee from Chinatown, Rev. Bill Loesch from Dorchester, Fred Mauet from Back Bay, Mary Mercure from Fenway, Margaret Noce from Jamaica Plain, Emilie Pugliano from the North End, Ken Wade from Roxbury, and Rita Walsh from Hyde Park—hardly a bunch of 'radicals' from GRNA!" Personal communication, January 8, 2010.

61. Peter Dreier, interview, 1991.

62. Fine, interview, May 15, 1992.

63. Daniel Hurewitz, "Council Shoots Down Advisory Neighborhood Council Proposal," *Allston-Brighton Journal,* March 29, 1990.

64. Judy Branfman, personal communication, July 25, 1999.

65. The argument from the left is best summarized in Marie Kennedy and Chris Tilly, with Mauricio Gaston, "Transformative Populism and the Development of Community of Color," in *Dilemmas of Activism,* ed. Joseph Kling and Prudence Posner, 302–24 (Philadelphia: Temple University Press, 1990).

66. Yudis, "$1.3b in Projects."

67. E. Bronner, "Opinion Divided over the Impact of Linkage Ruling," *Boston Globe,* April 6, 1986.

68. Peter Dreier summarizes these in "Economic Growth."

69. Ibid. On claims of a new regime, see Dreier and Ehrlich, "Downtown Development and Urban Reform."

70. James T. Campen, "The Struggle for Community Investment in Boston, 1989–1991," in *From Redlining to Reinvestment: Community Response to Urban Disinvestment,* ed. Gregory D. Squires, 38–72 (Philadelphia: Temple University Press, 1992).

71. Draisen, interview.

72. Sullivan, interview.

73. Brian C. Mooney, "Boston Housing Starts Down One-Third in '88, Data Show," *Boston Globe,* February 16, 1989.

74. The Boston Department of Neighborhood Development, which began a comprehensive program of affordable-housing production in the 1990s, was estimating figures substantially lower and advertised a *goal* of 2,100 affordable units for a three-year period after that, an average of seven hundred per year. That estimate would include not only CDCs but other nonprofits and private contractors as well.

75. The *Globe* reported a series of public meetings: Irene Sege, "Flynn Calls Meeting on Local Economy," *Boston Globe,* November 25, 1991; Steve Marantz, "Economy, Lack of Public Funds Will Challenge Next BRA Chief," *Boston Globe,* December 20, 1991.

76. DiGaetano and Klemanski, *Power and City Governance,* 141. They cite Sege, "Flynn Calls Meeting," and interviews with Gillis (1992) and Sullivan (1992).

77. DiGaetano and Klemanski, *Power and City Governance,* 209. citing Sullivan interviews conducted in 1992 and 1994.

78. DiGaetano and Klemanski, *Power and City Governance,* 210.

79. Ibid. citing "Gillis interview June 23, 1992"; and an apparently internal EDIC document titled "Boston Economic Development Partnership—Concept Paper" (Economic Development and Industrial Corporation, 3, n.d.).

80. DiGaetano and Klemanski, *Power and City Governance*, 210–11. citing "Lago interview, Grigsby interview, both 1994"

81. Chapter 3, note 16, cites Rachel Bratt, *Rebuilding a Low-Income Housing Policy* (Philadelphia: Temple University Press, 1989), 259–72.

82. A possible exception is indicated by the work of Michael Porter, a Harvard Business School economist who argued for "The Competitive Advantage of the Inner City" (*Harvard Business Review* [May–June 1995]: 55–71). This may have been a promising idea, but it was also controversial. See Thomas D. Boston and Catherine L. Ross, *The Inner City: Urban Poverty and Economic Development in the Next Century,* New Brunswick, NJ: Transaction, 1997.

83. Yolanda Perez, *Employment Growth and Specialization in the Nation's Large Cities during the 1990s: Boston among 35 American Cities* (Boston: Boston Redevelopment Authority, 2004), 23–25.

84. Bennett Harrison and Jean Kluver, "Deindustrialization and Regional Restructuring in Massachusetts," in *Deindustrialization and Regional Economic Transformation: The Experience of the United States,* ed. Lloyd Rodwin and Hidehiko Sazanami, 104–31 (Boston: Unwin Hyman, 1989). See also Bennett Harrison, "Regional Restructuring and 'Good Business Climates': The Economic Transformation of New England since World War II," in *Sunbelt Snowbelt: Urban Development and Regional Restructuring,* ed. Larry Sawers and William K. Tabb, 48–96 (New York: Oxford University Press, 1984).

85. DiGaetano and Klemanski, *Power and City Governance,* 209–12.

86. Richard Kindleberger, "Lack of Boston Business Leadership Discussed over 250 Attendees Debate, Address Problems at Forum." *Boston Globe,* December 6, 1995.

87. Raymond Dooley, interview by the author, April 14, 1992; Liu, *Chinatown's Neighborhood Mobilization,* 115.

88. Jeanne Strain, interview by Kate Carpenter, September 30, 1999.

89. Draisen, interview.

90. Data on local area race and ethnicity are available from the U.S. Census Bureau website, http://www.census.gov. The city population grew from 562,294 to 589,141 in the same period while losing 93,000 non-Hispanic whites—there was a net gain of other non-Hispanics, including blacks (about 70,000), and of Hispanic whites. The foreign born of all races increased from 87,056 to 151,836 from 1980 to 2000.

91. This was the theme of Stephanie Ebbert's article, "'Grass-Roots' Groups Said to Be Under City's Sway," *Boston Globe,* December 26, 1998.

92. Chris Tilly, personal communication, December 5, 1999.

93. Chuck Turner, interview by the author, October 1, 2004.

5. Neighborhood Background and the Campaign in Chicago

1. Edward C. Banfield, *Political Influence: A New Theory of Urban Politics* (New York: Free Press, 1961); also Banfield and James Q. Wilson, *City Politics* (New York: Vintage, 1963).

2. Bill Granger and Lori Granger, *Lords of the Last Machine: The Story of Politics in Chicago* (New York: Random House, 1987), 103.

3. William Grimshaw, *Bitter Fruit: Black Politics and the Chicago Machine, 1931–1991* (Chicago: University of Chicago Press, 1992), 34.

4. John Mollenkopf, *The Contested City* (Princeton, NJ: Princeton University Press, 1983).

5. Melvin G. Holli and Paul M. Green, *Bashing Chicago Traditions: Harold Washington's Last Campaign* (Grand Rapids, MI: Eerdmans, 1989), 140.

6. Larry Bennett, "Downtown Restructuring and Public Housing in Contemporary Chicago: Fashioning a Better World-Class City," in *Where Are Poor People to Live? Transforming Public Housing Communities*, ed. Larry Bennett, Janet L. Smith, and Patricia A. Wright, 282–300 (Armonk, NY: M.E. Sharpe, 2006). See especially pp. 284–89. See also Barbara Ferman and William Grimshaw, "The Politics of Housing Policy," in *Research in Urban Policy*, vol. 4, ed. Kenneth Wong, (Greenwich, CT: JAI Press, 1992), 105–6.

7. Many have remarked on the shift to downtown-developer interests away from manufacturing. John Mollenkopf conceptualizes the shift toward "growth" policies and away from inner-city manufacturing as the "second industrial revolution" and as one of the central causes of urban problems. He focuses on responses by "political entrepreneurs" rather than those internal to the business sectors involved and pays no attention to the distinction among sectors Rast mentions. Joel Rast, *Remaking Chicago: The Political Origins of Urban Industrial Change* (DeKalb: Northern Illinois University Press, 1999); and Mollenkopf, *The Contested City.*

8. Rast, *Remaking Chicago,* 30, 14.

9. Barbara Ferman, *Challenging the Growth Machine: Neighborhood Politics in Chicago and Pittsburgh* (Lawrence: University Press of Kansas, 1996), 141. Ira Katznelson might have been writing about Chicago when he laid out the characteristics of machine politics in "The Crisis of the Capitalist City: Urban Politics and Social Control," in *Theoretical Perspectives on Urban Politics,* ed. Willis Hawley et al., 214–29 (Englewood Cliffs, NJ: Prentice Hall, 1976).

10. Jane Addams, *Twenty Years at Hull House* (New York: Macmillan, 1910), 67–76.

11. On Alinsky the authority would be Sanford D. Horwitt, *Let Them Call Me Rebel: Saul Alinsky; His Life and Legacy* (New York: Knopf, 1989).

12. John Hall Fish, *Black Power/White Control: The Struggle of the Woodlawn Organization in Chicago* (Princeton, NJ: Princeton University Press, 1973).

13. Ibid., 25.

14. Ibid., 27.

15. Ibid., 49–50.

16. Ibid., 281.

17. Marilyn Gittell et al., *The Politics of Community Development: CDCs and Social Capital* (New York: Howard Samuels State Management and Policy Center, City University of New York, 1999), 29.

18. Fish, *Black Power/White Control,* 284.

19. Gittell et al., 33.

20. Lillian Thomas and Eugene Forrester, "T.W.O.: A One Man Show," *Chicago Journal,* August 11, 1982.

21. Ibid.

22. Ibid.

23. Robert Giloth, "Chicago: Community Building on Chicago's West Side; North Lawndale, 1960–1997," in *Rebuilding Urban Neighborhoods: Achievements, Opportunities and Limits*, ed. W. Dennis Keating and Norman Krumholz, 67–86 (Thousand Oaks, CA: Sage, 1999).

24. Ibid., 70–71.

25. Ibid., 73.

26. Ibid., 73–74.

27. Lew Kreinberg, interview by the author, June 28, 2000.

28. Giloth, "Chicago: Community Building," 72.

29. Ibid., 74.

30. Ibid., citing David J. Garrow, *Bearing the Cross: Martin Luther King, Jr. and the Southern Christian Leadership Conference* (New York: Vintage, 1986), 466.

31. Such references abounded in Woodlawn and Lawndale. See, for example, an article written by Kreinberg and his University of Wisconsin mentor: Lew Kreinberg and William Appleton Williams, "Martin Luther King and the New American Frontier," *Renewal* (June–July 1968): 4–7.

32. Giloth, "Chicago: Community Building," 76.

33. Hal Baron, "Building a Black Community: Popular Economics in Lawndale," *FOCUS/Midwest* 16 (1974): 18.

34. Ibid.

35. R. Casas and T. Colvin, *Lawndale: How Far Is Up* (Evanston, IL: Madill School of Journalism, Northwestern University, 1974).

36. Giloth, "Chicago: Community Building," 76.

37. Ibid., 77. Chicago Tribune, *The American Millstone: An Examination of the Nation's Permanent Underclass* (Chicago: Contemporary Books, 1986).

38. Chicago Tribune, *The American Millstone*, 183.

39. Giloth, "Chicago: Community Building," 77.

40. Ibid., 79; and see Wayne Gordon, *Real Hope in Chicago* (Grand Rapids, MI: Zondervan, 1995).

41. Giloth, "Chicago: Community Building," 80.

42. Ibid.

43. Ibid., 81.

44. Ibid., 83–84.

45. Kreinberg, interview.

46. Thom Clark, interview by the author, June 10, 1987.

47. Ibid.

48. Robert Mier and Kari Moe, "The Department of Economic Development: Decentralized Development from Theory to Practice," in *Harold Washington and the Neighborhoods*, ed. Pierre Clavel and Wim Wiewel (New Brunswick, NJ: Rutgers University Press, 1991), 68–69.

49. Robert Mier, *Social Justice and Local Development Policy* (Newbury Park, CA: Sage, 1993), 51.

50. Mier, interview by the author, June 10, 1987.

51. Ibid. Mier said, "My teaching experience defined the way I experienced [city hall and being commissioner] . . . not the way people normally experience teaching. . . . My teaching experience was extraordinary preparation for the job I'm in now. I've been called upon to use those skills constantly."

52. On CWED, see Mier and Moe, "Department of Economic Development."

53. Gary Rivlin, *Fire on the Prairie: Chicago's Harold Washington and the Politics of Race* (New York: Henry Holt, 1992), 57.

54. Holli and Green, *Bashing Chicago Traditions,* 6.

55. Committee to Elect Harold Washington, *The Washington Papers,* (Chicago: Committee to Elect Harold Washington, 1983).

56. Norman Krumholz and Pierre Clavel, "Interview with Robert Mier," in *Reinventing Cities: Equity Planners Tell Their Stories* (Philadelphia: Temple University Press, 1994), 74.

57. Holli and Green, *Bashing Chicago Traditions,* 17.

58. Doug Gills, "Chicago Politics and Community Development: A Social Movement Perspective," in Clavel and Wiewel, *Harold Washington and the Neighborhoods,* 60.

6. Washington in City Hall

1. Robert Mier, *Social Justice and Local Development Policy* (Newbury Park, CA: Sage, 1993), 93.

2. Bill Granger and Lori Granger, *Lords of the Last Machine: The Story of Politics in Chicago* (New York: Random House, 1987), 211: "Washington's approach [in the 1983 campaign] was like that of the Irish factions.... To hell with the Machine. Grab as much as you can as fast as you can and for as long as you can. On election night... Jesse Jackson literally screamed,...'We want it alllllll now!'"

3. Melvin G. Holli and Paul M. Green, *Bashing Chicago Traditions: Harold Washington's Last Campaign* (Grand Rapids, MI: Eerdmans, 1989), 170.

4. Ibid., vii.

5. Alton Miller, *Harold Washington: The Mayor, the Man* (Chicago: Bonus Books, 1989), 163.

6. Gary Rivlin, *Fire on the Prairie: Chicago's Harold Washington and the Politics of Race* (New York: Henry Holt, 1992), 249.

7. Holli and Green, *Bashing Chicago Traditions,* 164.

8. Doug Gills, "Chicago Politics and Community Development: A Social Movement Perspective," in *Harold Washington and the Neighborhoods,* ed. Pierre Clavel and Wim Wiewel (New Brunswick, NJ: Rutgers University Press, 1991), 50.

9. Robert Mier, videotaped interview, in *Harold Washington and the Neighborhoods: A Videotape,* produced by Wim Wiewel (Chicago: Center for Urban Economic Development, University of Illinois at Chicago, 1992).

10. Mier, personal communication, May 9–10, 1989.

11. Committee to Elect Harold Washington, *The Washington Papers,* (Chicago: Committee to Elect Harold Washington, 1983), 25.

12. "Chicago City Council and Mayor Harold Washington Negotiate Their First Major Compromise, Approving Application for $147 Million in Federal Community Development Funds," *Chicago Tribune,* May 27, 1983.

13. Robert Giloth, "Social Justice and Neighborhood Revitalization in Chicago: The Era of Harold Washington, 1983–1987," in *Revitalizing Urban Neighborhoods, ed.* W. Dennis Keating, Norman Krumholz, and Philip Star (Lawrence: University Press of Kansas, 1996), 85–86.

14. Rivlin, *Fire on the Prairie,* 223–24.

15. Robert Brehm, "The City and the Neighborhoods: Was It Really a Two-Way Street?" in Clavel and Wiewel, *Harold Washington and the Neighborhoods,* 238–69.

16. Robert Mier, Wim Wiewel, and Lauri Alpern, "Decentralization of Policy-Making under Mayor Harold Washington," in *Research in Urban Policy,* vol. 4, ed. Kenneth Wong (Greenwich, CT: JAI Press, 1992), 89.

17. Mier, *Social Justice and Local Development,* 98.

18. Arturo Vazquez, "Interview with Arturo Vazquez," in *Reinventing Cities: Equity Planners Tell Their Stories,* ed. Norman Krumholz and Pierre Clavel (Philadelphia: Temple University Press, 1994), 92.

19. Mier, *Social Justice and Local Development,* 99.

20. Vazquez, "Interview," 89–90.

21. Ibid., 91.

22. Ibid.

23. Giloth, "Social Justice and Neighborhood Revitalization," 86–87.

24. This was Doug Gills's view. He saw the system of community organizations, and administrative support for it, as an alternative to the traditional ward-based machine. Gills, "Chicago Politics and Community Development," 54.

25. City of Chicago, *Chicago Works Together* (Chicago: Department of Economic Development, 1984). See also Robert Mier, Kari Moe, and Irene Sherr, "Strategic Planning and the Pursuit of Reform, Economic Development and Equity," *Journal of the American Planning Association* 52 (1986): 299–309.

26. Rob Mier and Kari Moe, "The Department of Economic Development: Decentralized Development from Theory to Practice," in Clavel and Wiewel, *Harold Washington and the Neighborhoods,* 81–82.

27. Mier, *Social Justice and Local Development,* 118–19.

28. Mier summarized his reflections on strategic planning in *Social Justice and Local Development,* especially chapters 4 and 5.

29. Robert Giloth and Kari Moe, "Jobs, Equity and the Mayoral Administration of Harold Washington in Chicago (1987–87)," *Policy Studies Journal* 27 (1999): 129–46.

30. Ibid., 131.

31. David Moberg, "Daley and the Neighborhood Agenda," *The Neighborhood Works* 12 (June/July 1989): 1, 15.

32. Others were parts of the mayor's office and the Strategic Planning Group in the Mayor's Office of Employment and Training (MET). Robert Giloth, "Making Policy with Communities: Research and Development in the Department of Economic Development," in Clavel and Wiewel, *Harold Washington and the Neighborhoods,* 100.

33. Robert Giloth, *Nonprofit Leadership: Life Lessons from an Enterprising Practitioner* (New York: iUniverse, 2007), 49.

34. Giloth, "Making Policy with Communities," 104.

35. Ibid.

36. Dan Swinney, "Early Warning Systems: A Proactive Economic Strategy for Labour in the Regional Economy," *South Africa Labour Bulletin* (April 1999), http://www.clcr.org/publications/html/SALB.html; David C. Ranney, "Manufacturing Job Loss and Early Warning Indicators," *Journal of Planning Literature* 3 (Winter 1988):

22–35; and Robert Giloth and Susan Rosenblum, "How to Fight Plant Closings," *Social Policy* (Winter 1987): 20–26. A recent review is Sara O'Neill Kohl and Pierre Clavel, "Early Warning and Plant Closings in Chicago in the 1980s," *Carolina Planning* 14 (Summer 2009): 38–46.

37. Mier, *Social Justice and Local Development,* chapter 8.

38. Southeast Chicago had been the site of a complex of large integrated steel mills: U.S. Steel South Works employed over nineteen thousand; Inland Steel was at eighteen thousand, Republic and Jones and Laughlin were at five thousand and sixty-five hundred. Ann Markusen et al., *Steel and Southeast Chicago: Reasons and Remedies for Industrial Renewal; 1985, Report to the Mayor's Task Force on Steel and Southeast Chicago* (Evanston, IL: Center for Urban Affairs and Policy Research, Northwestern University, 1986), 107. Wisconsin Steel had recently closed.

39. Stephen Alexander, Robert Giloth, and Joshua Lerner, "Chicago's Industry Task Forces," *Economic Development Quarterly* 1 (November 1987): 353.

40. Steel was one of several task forces. Washington appointed the Steel and Navy Pier task forces in early 1984 while CWT was getting under way. Mier, *Social Justice and Local Development,* 79.

41. David Ranney, *Global Decisions, Local Collisions: Urban Life in the New World Order* (Philadelphia: Temple University Press, 2003), 109.

42. Markusen, personal communication, March 13, 2008. "I was contacted directly by Rob Mier. I was at UC–Berkeley, but he knew through someone else that I might be interested in coming to Chicago on leave. I signed a contract with the City of Chicago Department of Economic Development... and [was] charged with being the research director for the newly forming... Task Force on Steel and Southeast Chicago."

43. Ann Markusen, *A Prototype Industrial Policy Study of the California Steel Industry* (Sacramento: State of California, Senate Office of Research, 1983). See also Markusen, "City on the Skids," *Chicago Reader,* November 24, 1989; Markusen et al., *Steel and Southeast Chicago.* Also based on Markusen, interview by the author, February 21, 2008.

44. The best-known statement was Barry Bluestone and Bennett Harrison, *The Deindustrialization of America: Plant Closing, Community Abandonment, and the Dismantling of Basic Industry* (New York: Basic Books, 1982).

45. Markusen et al., *Steel and Southeast Chicago.*

46. Ibid., 8.

47. Ann Markusen, "Planning for Communities in Decline: Lessons from Steel Communities," *Journal of Planning Education and Research* 7 (1988): 173–84.

48. Ibid. The final report of the task force, reflecting the conclusions of the policy committee, was *Building on the Basics: The Final Report of the Mayor's Task Force on Steel and Southeast Chicago* (Chicago: City of Chicago Department of Employment and Economic Development, 1987).

49. Staughton Lynd, "The Genesis of the Idea of a Community Right to Industrial Property in Youngstown and Pittsburgh, 1977–1987," *Journal of American History* 74, no. 3, The Constitution and American Life: A Special Issue (December 1987), 926–58.

50. Ann Markusen, personal communication, March 3, 2010.

51. Ranney, *Global Decisions, Local Collisions,* 107–8.

52. Stephen Alexander, "Equity Policies and Practices of the Harold Washington Administration: Lessons for Progressive Cities," in *Economic Development in American*

Cities: The Pursuit of an Equity Agenda, ed. Michael Bennett and Robert Giloth (Albany: State University of New York Press, 2007), 72.

53. Ranney, *Global Decisions, Local Collisions,* 110.

54. Mier, *Social Justice and Local Development,* 158, 159.

55. Giloth, like Mier, took heart from the process. Giloth, "Making Policy with Communities," 118.

56. Frank Cassell, interview by the author, June 1987.

57. Personal communication, March 28, 2008.

58. Mier, *Social Justice and Local Development,* 155.

59. Alexander, a former steelworker, was instrumental in maintaining the DED presence on the task force. See Alexander, Giloth, and Lerner, "Chicago's Industry Task Forces."

60. Donna Ducharme, "Planned Manufacturing Districts: How a Community Initiative Became City Policy," in Clavel and Wiewel, *Harold Washington and the Neighborhoods,* 221–37; Joel Rast, *Remaking Chicago: The Political Origins of Urban Industrial Change* (DeKalb: Northern Illinois University Press, 1999).

61. Rast, *Remaking Chicago,* 123; Editorial, *Chicago Tribune,* September 28, 1987.

62. Rast, *Remaking Chicago,* 127; William Schmidt, "Chicago Plan Aims to Curb Factory Loss," *New York Times,* December 10, 1987.

63. Ken O'Hare, looking back in 2008, thought the idea might have come from someone in the development subcabinet, perhaps public works commissioner Paul Karras. Interview by the author, March 19, 2008.

64. Holli and Green, *Bashing Chicago Traditions,* 184–85.

65. William Peterman, *Neighborhood Planning and Community-Based Development: The Potential and Limits of Grassroots Action* (Newbury Park, CA: Sage, 2000), 91–109.

66. Mier and Moe, "Department of Economic Development," 87–89.

67. Thom Clark, interview by the author, October 21, 1999.

68. Larry Bennett, "The Dilemmas of Building a Progressive Urban Coalition: The Linked Development Debate in Chicago," *Journal of Urban Affairs* 9 (1987): 263–76.

69. Ibid.

70. See also Kenneth Reardon, *Local Economic Development in Chicago 1983–1987: The Reform Efforts of Mayor Harold Washington* (PhD diss., Cornell University, 1990), 151–78; and Robert Brehm, "The City and the Neighborhoods," 253–59.

7. Later Developments in Chicago

1. There was significant resistance by labor, often against the more conservative international union leadership, to plant closings and the decline of private investment in manufacturing. There were heroic efforts in Youngstown, Ohio, by steelworkers who had been part of a union campaign based in Chicago. There were many attempts at worker management, particularly in small- and medium-sized firms. Important accounts include Staughton Lynd, *The Fight against Shutdowns: Youngstown's Steel Mill Closings* (San Pedro, CA: Singlejack Books, 1982); and William Foote Whyte, *Worker Participation and Ownership: Cooperative Strategies for Strengthening*

Local Economies (Ithaca, NY: ILR Press, 1983). Schemes involving the use of pension funds were popular, as in Jeremy Rifkin and Randy Barber, *The North Will Rise Again: Pensions, Politics and Power in the 1980s* (Boston: Beacon, 1978). A dramatic proposal for Detroit got some notice; see Dan Luria and Jack Russell, *Rational Reindustrialization: An Economic Development Agenda for Detroit* (Detroit: Wedgetripper, 1981). There was ample reinforcement from the side of state and local politics—one example was William Schweke, ed., *Plant Closings: Issues, Politics and Legislation* (Washington, DC: Conference on Alternative State and Local Policies, 1980).

2. Aaron S. Gurwitz and G. Thomas Kingsley, *The Cleveland Metropolitan Economy: An Initial Assessment* (Santa Monica, CA: Rand Corporation, 1982).

3. Joel Rast, *Remaking Chicago: The Political Origins of Urban Industrial Change* (DeKalb: Northern Illinois University Press, 1999).

4. Robert Mier, interview by the author, June 10, 1987.

5. Ibid.

6. Ibid.

7. Robert Mier, *Social Justice and Local Development Policy* (Newbury Park, CA: Sage, 1993), 196.

8. Xolela Mangcu, "Harold Washington and the Cultural Transformation of Local Government in Chicago, 1983–1987" (PhD diss., Cornell University, 1997).

9. Ibid., 139–40.

10. Ibid., 141.

11. Ibid., 158–60.

12. Ibid., 160–61; Mark Hornung, "Despite Woes, Mayor Firm on Affirmative Action," *Crain's Business Review,* March 23, 1987.

13. Marc Weiss and John Metzger, "Planning for Chicago: The Changing Politics of Metropolitan Growth and Neighborhood Development," 123–52 in *Atop the Urban Hierarchy,* ed. Robert Beauregard (Totowa, NJ: Rowman & Littlefield, 1989), 146.

14. Mangcu, "Harold Washington," 164.

15. One of the great sources of information on the conference is Michael Kammen, *The Populist Persuasion: An American History* (Ithaca, NY: Cornell University Press, 1995).

16. Mier provides this job history in his 1994 article, "Some Observations on Race in Planning," *Journal of the American Planning Association* 60 (Spring 1994): 235–40.

17. Merrill Goozner and Stanley Ziemba, "Big Gifts to Daley Reflect City's Divisions," *Chicago Tribune,* July 20, 1989.

18. Bill Granger and Lori Granger, *Lords of the Last Machine: The Story of Politics in Chicago* (New York: Random House, 1987), 209–10.

19. John McCarron, "'Reform' Takes Costly Toll… Chicago on Hold: Politics of Poverty," *Chicago Tribune,* August 28, 1988.

20. Ibid.

21. Ibid.

22. John McCarron, "Blue-Collar Dream Skews City Policy," *Chicago Tribune,* August 31, 1988.

23. Michael Miner, "'Politics of Poverty': Why Did John McCarron Do That?" *Chicago Reader,* September 16, 1988.

24. Wim Wiewel and Philip W. Nyden, "Introduction," in *Challenging Uneven Development: An Urban Agenda for the 1990s,* ed. Philip W. Nyden and Wim Wiewel (New Brunswick, NJ: Rutgers University Press, 1991), 9.

25. Philip W. Nyden et al., *Building Community: Social Science in Action* (Thousand Oaks, CA: Pine Forge, 1997), 20; Maureen Hellwig, interview by the author, May 25, 2000.

26. Mark J. Miller, "Project Assessment," in *Beyond Conventional Wisdom: An Assessment of the Community News Project* (Chicago: Community News Project of the Community Media Workshop, n.d.).

27. Rast, *Remaking Chicago,* 141.

28. Ibid., 150.

29. Editorial, *Chicago Sun-Times,* September 13, 1993.

30. Editorial, *Chicago Sun-Times,* October 13, 1993.

31. Patrick T. Reardon, "Daley Pushes Mixed-Income Housing with $228 Million Pledge," *Chicago Tribune,* October 12, 1993.

32. Kevin Jackson, interview by the author, May 25, 2000.

33. Ibid.

34. Ibid.

35. Thom Clark, interview by the author, 1999.

36. Jackson, interview.

37. Leon Pitt, "Affordable Housing Plan to Continue, Daley Says," *Chicago Sun-Times,* December 18, 1997.

38. Doug Gills and Wanda White, "Community Involvement in Chicago's Empowerment Zone," in *Empowerment in Chicago: Grassroots Participation in Economic Development and Poverty Alleviation,* ed. Cedric Herring et al. (Chicago: Great Cities Institute, University of Illinois at Chicago, 1998), 28–29.

39. Ibid., 43.

40. Ibid., 50.

41. Ibid., 64.

42. Ibid., 65.

43. Ibid.

44. Barbara Ferman and William Grimshaw, "The Politics of Housing Policy," in *Research in Urban Policy,* vol. 4, ed. Kenneth Wong (Greenwich, CT: JAI Press, 1992), 121.

45. Ibid., 121.

46. Ibid., 122–23.

47. Ibid., 124.

48. David C. Ranney, Patricia A. Wright, and Tingwei Zhang, *Citizens, Local Government and the Development of Chicago's Near South Side* (Geneva: UNRISD, 1977), 36–37.

49. Gills's characterization was as follows: "Daley views all neighborhood groups who strive for . . . empowerment . . . with suspicion. While he has stated that he supports access to neighborhood based organizations rhetorically, such access has been frustrated in actuality." Douglas C. Gills, "Community Development and the Downtown Growth Coalition: The Origin of PRAG," *PRAGmatics* 2 (January 1999): 4–7.

50. Judy Meima, quoted in Ranney, Wright, and Zhang, *Citizens, Local Government,* 46.

51. Dan Immergluck, "Building Power, Losing Power: The Rise and Fall of a Prominent Community Economic Development Coalition," *Economic Development Quarterly* 19 (2005): 211–24.

52. Dorothy Shipps, "The Politics of Urban School Reform: Legitimacy, Urban Growth and School Improvement in Chicago," with Joseph Kahne and Mark Smylie, *Educational Policy* 13 (September 1999): 518–45.

53. Jodi Wilgoren, "Daley Walks, Not Runs, toward Chicago Election," *New York Times,* February 25, 2003.

54. Dick Simpson et al., "Chicago's Uncertain Future since September 11, 2001," *Urban Affairs Review* 38 (September 2002): 129–30.

55. David Moberg, "Daley Coasting to Fourth Term," *Boston Globe,* February 23, 2003.

56. Alysia Tate, "Daley Woos Minorities with Rich Rewards," *Chicago Reporter,* February 1999.

57. Gary Rivlin, *Fire on the Prairie: Chicago's Harold Washington and the Politics of Race* (New York: Henry Holt, 1992), 198.

58. Ibid., 199.

59. Ibid., 197.

60. Melvin G. Holli and Paul M. Green, *Bashing Chicago Traditions: Harold Washington's Last Campaign* (Grand Rapids, MI: Eerdmans, 1989), 168.

61. Mier, "Some Observations on Race," 235.

62. Mier quoted Hollander in his interview: Robert Mier, videotaped interview, in *Harold Washington and the Neighborhoods: A Videotape,* produced by Wim Wiewel (Chicago: Center for Urban Economic Development, University of Illinois at Chicago, 1992).

63. Mier, "Some Observations on Race," 239.

8. Race, Class, and the Administrative Struggle

1. L. Herson Jr., "The Lost World of Municipal Government," *American Political Science Review* 57 (1957): 330–45.

2. John Mollenkopf laid out the idea of the "community option" in urban policy in *The Contested City* (Princeton, NJ: Princeton University Press, 1983), to which I owe a debt for this and other works, including an article cowritten with Jordan Yin and Jessica Pitt, "The Community Option in Urban Policy," *Urban Affairs Review* 32 (March 1997): 435–58. On the actual—and partial—revival of central cities in the 1990s, see Robert Fishman, "The Fifth Migration," *Journal of the American Planning Association* 71 (Autumn 2005): 357–66.

3. Jason Hackworth, *The Neoliberal City* (Ithaca, NY: Cornell University Press, 2007), 2.

4. Friedrich Hayek, *The Road to Serfdom* (Chicago: University of Chicago Press, 1944).

5. A hopeful analysis was that of Andrew Shonfield, *Modern Capitalism* (New York: Oxford University Press, 1965).

6. Samuel Bowles, "The Post-Keynesian Capital-Labor Stalemate," *Socialist Review* 65 (September–October 1982): 45–72.

7. Hackworth, *Neoliberal City,* 9–10.

8. N. Brenner and Nik Theodore, "Cities and the Geographies of 'Actually Existing Neoliberalism,'" *Antipode* 34 (2002): 349–79; J. Peck and A. Tickell, "Neoliberalizing Space," *Antipode* 34 (2002): 380–404.

9. Derek Shearer, "How the Progressives Won in Santa Monica," *Social Policy* 12 (Winter 1982): 7–14; Abdul Alkalimat and Doug Gills, *Harold Washington and the Crisis of Black Power in Chicago* (Chicago: Twentieth Century Books, 1989).

10. Mier made much of this concept in Robert Mier and Richard D. Bingham, "Metaphors of Economic Development," in *Theories of Local Economic Development: Perspectives from across the Disciplines,* ed. Richard D. Bingham and Robert Mier (Newbury Park, CA: Sage Publications, 1993), ch. 14, 284–304.

11. Stephen Coyle, interview by Stephen McGovern, May 12, 1992.

12. On linked development, see Larry Bennett, "The Dilemmas of Building a Progressive Urban Coalition: The Linked Development Debate in Chicago," *Journal of Urban Affairs* 9 (1987): 263–76.

13. See Todd Swanstrom, *The Crisis of Growth Politics: Cleveland, Kucinich and the Challenge of Urban Populism* (Philadelphia: Temple University Press, 1985) on the cooptation of Cleveland populists.

14. Joel Rast, *Remaking Chicago* (DeKalb: Northern Illinois University Press, 1999), 171; David C. Perry, "Remaking Chicago: the Political Origins of Urban Industrial Change," *Journal of the American Planning Association* 66 (Summer 2000): 323–24.

15. The standard source on linkage is Dennis Keating, "Linking Downtown Development to Broader Community Goals: An Analysis of Linkage Policy in Three Cities," *Journal of the American Planning Association* 52 (Spring 1986): 133–41; but supplement this with Boston Redevelopment Authority, *Survey of Linkage Programs in Other U.S. Cities with Comparisons to Boston* (Boston: Boston Redevelopment Authority, 2000). According to Keating, linkage has spread to a few other places: "In addition to Boston and San Francisco, other major cities that adopted it were Seattle, Sacramento, and San Diego. Smaller 'progressive' cities were Berkeley, Cambridge, Santa Monica." Personal communication, October 5, 2009.

16. Lewis Lapham, "Tentacles of Rage: The Republican Propaganda Mill; A Brief History," *Harper's Magazine,* September 2004, 31–41.

17. Outcomes in other places were less dramatic or noteworthy. "Progressivism," as I have defined it in terms of redistribution and participation, declined over time. In Berkeley, where the policy innovation was spectacular in the 1970s and 1980s, the voter base became more upper-middle class over time. BCA, adapting, softened its "progressive" stance. Hartford retreated from the hopes of an earlier progressivism, undermined by continued decline in its jobs base. Cleveland, still divided by race and class, maintained a progressive voice and the developing role of the Cleveland Housing Network.

18. I am indebted to Judy Branfman and other Boston people for emphasizing this point, though there were echoes in Chicago as well. Branfman, personal communication, November 30, 2009.

19. I heard this from a Flynn staffer. It was said with respect, but I suspect the sentiment was generally held.

20. Marie Kennedy and Chris Tilly, with Mauricio Gaston, "Transformative Populism and the Development of Community of Color," in *Dilemmas of Activism,* ed. Joseph Kling and Prudence Posner, 302–24 (Philadelphia: Temple University Press, 1990).

21. Ann Forsyth, *ReForming Suburbia: The Planned Communities of Irvine, Columbia and the Woodlands* (Berkeley: University of California Press, 2005), 242–52. On social and economic mix in new communities more generally, see Shirley Weiss et al., *New Communities U.S.A.* (Lexington, MA: Lexington Books, 1976).

22. Robert Mier, *Social Justice and Local Development Policy* (Newbury Park, CA: Sage, 1993), 88.

23. Stephen Coyle, interview by the author, October 27, 2009.

24. Swinney's work, which is extensive, is best seen on the website of the Center for Labor and Community Research. See Dan Swinney, "Building the Bridge to the High Road: Expanding Participation and Democracy in the Economy to Build Sustainable Communities," Center for Labor & Community Research, 2000, http://www.clcr.org/publications/pdf/building_a_bridge.pdf. For the Giloth and Moe argument, see Robert Giloth and Kari Moe, "Jobs, Equity and the Mayoral Administration of Harold Washington in Chicago (1983–87)," *Policy Studies Journal* 27 (1999): 129–46.

25. U.S. Bureau of the Census, *1980 Census of Population and Housing,* Boston, MA, Standard Metropolitan Statistical Areas PHC80–2-98, (Washington, DC: Bureau of the Census, 1983), table H-1; *1990 Census of Population and Housing,* Summary Social, Economic and Housing Characteristics: Massachusetts: 1990CPH-1–23, (Washington, DC: Bureau of the Census, 1992), table 15.

26. Coyle, interview by the author, October 27, 2009.

27. Peter Dreier, personal communication, September 11, 2000.

28. Giloth and Moe, "Jobs, Equity."

29. The employment numbers are in chapter 1, table 1.2.

30. The data are from 1990 Census table P077, Summary File 3; and 2000 Census table P49, Summary File 3. The data on educational attainment by race are from 1990 Census Table P058, Summary File 3; and 2000 Census Tables P148A through P148I, Summary File 3.

31. Chuck Turner, interview by the author, October 1, 2004.

32. Hackworth, *Neoliberal City,* 200. Hackworth cited a comment in Peter Marcuse and Ronald van Kempen, eds. *Globalizing Cities: A New Spatial Order?* (Oxford and Malden, MA: Blackwell, 2000), 272.

❧ INDEX

ACORN (Association of Community Organizations for Reform Now), 46, 47, 75

activists: activities and issues for, 2, 3, 49–50, 79–80, 82, 174; in Chicago and its city hall, 110, 122; in economic development, role of, 42; in Flynn administration, 61–62, 64; links with academia, 38–39

Addams, Jane, tradition of, 100, 101

Agnos, Art, 32, 34

Alexander, Stephen, 135, 137

Alinsky, Saul, 100–102

Alschuler, John, 20, 26, 27

Ansara, Michael, 45, 46–47, 74–75, 76

Arroyo, Felix, 95

Atkins, Thomas, 53–54

Bach, Eve, 14, 17, 18–19

Banfield, Edward, 96–97

Baron, Hal, 107, 115

Bates, Tom, 18

BCA. *See* Berkeley Citizen Action

Beer, Samuel, 14

Berkeley, California, as progressive city, 14, 17–19, 184

Berkeley Citizen Action (BCA), 17–19

Bick, Barbara, 24

Bilandic, Michael, 100, 114

Bishop, Elbert, 40

black(s)

in Boston, 41–42, 52

in Chicago: leadership in neighborhood development, 108, 110; and 1983 campaign, 114, 116–17; and political culture, 97–98, 99–100; Washington supporters, 121

mayors, 168

See also Chicago, black population in; race and class; racism and race relations

Bledsoe, Alex, 63, 70–71

Boston: affordable housing plans and production, 2, 42–43, 48–52, 60–61, 66, 67, 87–89, 213n74; busing controversy, 52–55; community development in, 36–43; demographic changes, 94–95, 195–97; economic development and strategies, 41–42, 90–93; general situation in 1983, 59–60; multiethnic groups in, 50; neighborhood movement, growth and importance of, 43–47, 61; progressive reforms, 185; public facilities department, 87–88. *See also* CDCs; Flynn, Raymond; racism and race relations; Roxbury

Boston Globe: on Chicago under Daley, 166–67; and Flynn, 57, 71; political reporting by, 55, 56, 82

Boston Linkage Action Coalition, 75–76

Boston Redevelopment Authority (BRA), 62, 67; and city-owned land, 68; Planning and Zoning Advisory Councils (PZACs), 71, 73, 78; reports of, 65, 91; and Roxbury, 69, 80; successes, 71–73, 76, 194

Bowen, Barbara, 44, 45, 46

Boyle, Jeff, 165

Branfman, Judy, 83, 84, 213n60

Bratt, Rachel, 42

Brazier, Arthur, 102, 104

Brehm, Robert, 124

Brophy, Paul, 68

Brown, Willie, 34

Burlington, Vermont, as progressive city, 5, 29–30, 184

Burlington Community Land Trust (BCLT), 30

Butler, Cecil, 107, 108

Byrne, Jane, 100, 110, 114, 117

Cabral, Andrea, 95

Campen, James, 86